Aztec City-State Capitals

ANCIENT CITIES OF THE NEW WORLD

D1592765

UNIVERSITY PRESS OF FLORIDA

Florida A&M University, Tallahassee
Florida Atlantic University, Boca Raton
Florida Gulf Coast University, Ft. Myers
Florida International University, Miami
Florida State University, Tallahassee
New College of Florida, Sarasota
University of Central Florida, Orlando
University of Florida, Gainesville
University of North Florida, Jacksonville
University of South Florida, Tampa
University of West Florida, Pensacola

ANCIENT CITIES OF THE NEW WORLD

Edited by Michael E. Smith, Arizona State University; Marilyn A. Masson, University at Albany, SUNY; John W. Janusek, Vanderbilt University

Ancient Cities of the New World is devoted to the study of the ancient urban sites of Mesoamerica and South America. This series is designed to present theories, models, and approaches that shed light on the region's diverse, ancient urban patterns and polity organization. Major, overarching topics to be explored in the series are urban form (size, architecture, and layout) and urban lifestyles (ethnicity, gender, households, neighborhoods, and craft activities). Books include important works focused on a single key ancient city or analyzing a collection of cities and towns within their regional contexts. The series features cross-disciplinary works in archaeology, art history, and ethnohistory written for a broad scholarly audience.

Aztec City-State Capitals

Michael E. Smith

Foreword by Marilyn A. Masson and John W. Janusek

University Press of Florida
Gainesville/Tallahassee/Tampa/Boca Raton
Pensacola/Orlando/Miami/Jacksonville/Ft. Myers/Sarasota

Library of Congress Cataloging-in-Publication Data
Smith, Michael Ernest, 1953–
Aztec city-state capitals/Michael E. Smith; foreword by Michael E. Smith,
Marilyn A. Masson, and John W. Janusek.
p. cm.—Ancient cities of the new world)
Includes bibliographical references and index.
ISBN 978-0-8130-3245-0 (alk. paper)
1. Aztecs—Urban residence. 2. Aztec architecture. 3. Aztecs—Antiquities.
4. City planning—Mexico—History. 5. City-states—Mexico—History.
6. Mexico—Antiquities. I. Title.
F1219.76.U74S56   2008
972.00973'2—dc22

The University Press of Florida is the scholarly publishing agency for the
State University System of Florida, comprising Florida A&M University,
Florida Atlantic University, Florida Gulf Coast University, Florida Interna-
tional University, Florida State University, New College of Florida, Univer-
sity of Central Florida, University of Florida, University of North Florida,
University of South Florida, and University of West Florida.

University Press of Florida
15 Northwest 15th Street
Gainesville, FL 32611-2079
http://www.upf.com

Contents

Figures

Tables

Foreword

The book series Ancient Cities of the New World is designed to facilitate the analysis of urbanism among civilizations of the Americas. This series promotes books that provide accessible synopses of urban patterns in places where publication has not kept up with fieldwork. While the study of any past urban center can claim to be about ancient cities or urbanism, this book series includes studies that employ specific theories, models, and approaches drawn from the scholarly literature on such topics. As the criteria for urbanism are often debated in the study of New World complex societies, the books in this series contribute significant information about cross-cultural expressions of urban form, function, meaning, and social life. These works may highlight single urban centers or they may analyze cities from a regional perspective. Clear and authoritative, they are critical resources for students, members of the interested public, and scholars in fields such as anthropology, history, political science, and urban planning.

As the inaugural volume for the series, Michael E. Smith's *Aztec City-State Capitals* adopts a comparative, regional approach to the study of urbanism in the Postclassic central Mexican highlands. It provides a wealth of information about Aztec cities that has never before been compiled and analyzed. The book will serve as a valuable reference for students and scholars who wish to learn about Aztec centers beyond the widely published but unique imperial capital of Tenochtitlan. Smith draws on multiple theoretical approaches and outlines four dimensions by which urban organization can be studied: urban form, urban life, urban meaning, and urban function. Evidence for formal planning at some Aztec political epicenters is reflected in repetitive arrays of architectural features of historical and symbolic significance. This author also documents variation in the complexity of cities' urban functions, explores urban-rural similarities and differences, and compares the organization of Aztec capitals with cities beyond central Mexico. The city-state capitals documented in this book potentially share key similarities with central places in other regions of Mesoamerica. This work is important to anyone interested in past Mesoamerican cities and ancient urbanism globally. Michael E. Smith is a coeditor of the Ancient Cities of the New World series.

Marilyn A. Masson and John W. Janusek
Series Editors

Preface

Most of the Aztec cities described in this book are very poorly known to anyone except a few specialists. Archaeological fieldwork is only reported in obscure technical reports, and in some cases the excavations were never published at all. I began gathering reports and data on these sites many years ago with the idea that it might be useful to compile and publish the information at some point. It was not until I was conducting research on Postclassic Mesoamerica from a world-systems perspective in the late 1990s that I began to take a systematic look at the archaeological and historical accounts of Aztec cities outside Tenochtitlan. In preparing for a conference on the Postclassic Mesoamerican world system (Smith and Berdan 2003), I looked for evidence that growing commercialization had an effect on urbanization in central Mexico. In other areas of the world, the expansion of precapitalist markets and commercial exchange stimulated the growth of cities and urban commercial features such as marketplaces, shops, warehouses, and the like (for example, Abungu 1998; Leong 1990; Morrison 1997). Although the Postclassic commercialization of Mesoamerica was deep and widespread (Smith and Berdan 2003), I could find little clear evidence that this process had much of an effect on Aztec city-state capitals (although it did affect the imperial capital Tenochtitlan).

What I discovered, however, was that the forms and processes of Aztec urbanization were intimately linked to the political dynamics of the *altepetl*, or city-state. A body of research on non-Western urban built environments revealed some of the forces that structured the physical forms of ancient cities. The models and concepts of Kevin Lynch, Amos Rapoport, Jerry Moore, Richard Blanton, Adam T. Smith, and other scholars helped explain many of the architectural and spatial features of Aztec city-state capitals, and they stimulated me to write this book.

Aztec City-State Capitals has a dual purpose. First, it is a descriptive account of the poorly known archaeological data on Aztec cities outside of the imperial capital Tenochtitlan. I want to thank Joyce Marcus for encouraging me to assemble these data and to start writing this book. The other purpose of this book is to present an argument for the political nature of Aztec urbanism. In contrast to many prior authors, who interpret ancient cities as expressions of the cosmologies and religious beliefs of their inhabitants, I interpret Aztec cities as the deliberate material expressions of the political and ideological actions of kings and nobles. In this book I use the term "ideology" as it is used in all of the social sciences except archaeology: Ideology consists of "ideas and beliefs that help legitimate the interests of a dominant social power in the face of opposing interests" (Eagleton 1991: 28–30). For some reason most archaeologists ignore this definition and use the term as a synonym for religious ideas, an indefensible choice if archaeology aspires to be a comparative social and historical science.

I would like to thank a number of colleagues for useful discussions of urbanism over the years; many of the ideas and perspectives on urbanism presented in this book grew out of these conversations. First, my professors, George Cowgill, David Grove, and Lawrence Crissman, started me thinking about urbanism in a systematic way as a student. My views continued to develop through interaction with colleagues such as Richard Blanton, Ray Bromley, Arlen and Diane Chase, George Cowgill, Mogens Herman Hansen, Cynthia Heath-Smith, Kenneth Hirth, Marilyn Masson, Jerry Moore, Thomas Morton, Ben Nelson, William Sanders, Monica Smith, and Barbara Stark.

I offer sincere thanks to the following colleagues who read and commented on drafts of one or more chapters: Anthony Aveni, John Chance, Marco Janssen, Guilhem Olivier, and Barbara Stark. Frances Berdan, George Cowgill, and José Luis de Rojas read and commented on all eight chapters, and I am very grateful. These colleagues saved me from a number of errors, and their observations helped improve the book in many ways. Three reviewers for the University Press of Florida—Stacie King, Marilyn Masson, and Edward Sisson—read the completed manuscript carefully and offered numerous constructive comments, critiques, and suggestions; I thank these helpful colleagues.

The following colleagues kindly responded to various queries on things Aztec while I was writing the book: Juan José Batalla Rosado, Frances Berdan, Elizabeth Boone, Edward Calnek, Michel Graulich, Leonardo López Luján, Rikke Marie Olsen, Carlos Santamarina, and Emily Umberger.

Early versions of some of the ideas in this book were presented at two conferences. The Mesoamerican urbanism conference, sponsored by Pennsylvania State University and the Instituto Nacional de Antropología e Historia, was held at Pennsylvania State University in September 2004. I particularly appreciate the logistical and intellectual efforts of Robert Cobean and William Sanders. My paper for that conference contained the genesis of chapters 4 and 5 of this book. The meeting of the Sociedad Española de Estudios Mayas on the founding of Mesoamerican cities was held in Pamplona, Spain, in

September 2005. I acknowledge the efforts of Andrés Ciudad Ruiz and María Josefa Iglesias Ponce de León in Pamplona. Chapter 3 of this book is a modified version of the paper I presented in Pamplona. I thank the organizers and participants at these conferences for providing stimulating events that not only helped me develop some of the ideas of this book but also moved the comparative study of ancient urbanism forward in constructive directions.

During the preparation of this book, Juliana Novic helped with database work and other tasks, Tiffany Souppa measured the areas of structures, and Amber Nichols copyedited the text of the penultimate draft. Cynthia Heath-Smith's contributions are too numerous to list, and I dedicate the book to her.

1

City and Society in Aztec Central Mexico

Public buildings are physical testimonies of the use of power. (Moore 1996: 2)

Aztec cities—built in central Mexico between the twelfth and fifteenth centuries A.D.—were political capitals, designed and built by kings to show off and reinforce their power, their wealth, and their legitimacy. Cities certainly had religious and economic significance, but these pale in comparison with their political roles within Aztec society. Although the idea of cities as the material expressions of the grandeur of ancient kings calls to mind the great ruins of the ancient world—Babylon, Persepolis, Angkor, Teotihuacan, or Tikal—most Aztec cities were modest in size and scale. Only Tenochtitlan, the imperial capital, stands out as a large metropolis. That city, however, was completely atypical of Aztec urban settlements. The small sizes of other Aztec cities was a direct consequence of the form of political organization found in Late Postclassic central Mexico—the city-state, or *altepetl* in Nahuatl, the Aztec language.

This book is about Aztec cities and their relationship to rulership and other social dynamics within the altepetl. As in other city-state cultures around the world (Hansen 2000a), it is impossible to fully separate Aztec urbanism and cities on the one hand from kings and political dynamics on the other. Capital cities were the central focus of the state, and the state was the political or administrative expression of the capital. My argument for a political interpretation of urbanism goes against some common ideas about Aztec cities and about ancient cities in general. For example, there is a scholarly tradition that emphasizes the religious and cosmological aspects of ancient cities (Malville and Gurjal 2000; Wheatley 1971), and when this notion is applied to the Aztecs (for example, D. Carrasco 1999b) the resulting interpretations suggest that religion was the primary force generating and shaping Aztec urbanism. I show below (in this chapter and in chapter 5) that such a notion does not accord with the data. Religion is important for understanding Aztec cities (chapters 3, 4, 5), but it played a smaller role than kingship and political dynamics. Ideas certainly played a major role in shaping the design and operation of Aztec cities, but in contrast to the emphasis on cosmology or world view (also known as "cosmovision") expressed by most authors, I prefer to stress political ideology as a source of ideas influential in Aztec urbanism (Eagleton 1991; Hicks 1996).

The political interpretation of cities also goes against one of the dominant traditions of urban scholarship in the ancient world. Most archaeologists define cities and urbanism in terms of population size and density. When this approach is applied to the Aztecs, Tenochtitlan is the only settlement that can be classified as a city, leaving the other capitals of the altepetl in a category of noncity, or nonurban place. I argue below that this viewpoint—the demographic definition of urbanism—is far too limiting and that an alternative functional definition of urbanism makes more sense in helping us to understand Aztec society. Because these settlements were the residences of kings and the seats of government, they exercised considerable influence over their hinterlands. This kind of influence—whether administrative, economic, or religious—is known as an urban function, and settlements where urban functions are concentrated can be classified as urban settlements. Aztec altepetl capitals were fully urban settlements and they can be described using the term "city."[1]

Tenochtitlan, with its overwhelming size and importance, has long overshadowed other Aztec cities. When the conqueror Hernando Cortés and his soldiers entered Tenochtitlan in A.D. 1519, the Aztec imperial capital was the largest city that had ever existed in the New World. Although not as large as Paris or some Chinese cities at the time, it was far larger than anything the conquerors had seen back home in Spain. Beyond its size, Tenochtitlan was impressive for the monumentality of its towering pyramids, for the tens of thousands of people in the streets and markets every day, and for the opulence created by a powerful expanding empire. The inhabitants of Tenochtitlan, the Mexica people, had built their city from scratch on an island, and the many canals reminded the Spaniards of Venice. The early Spaniards were overwhelmed by Tenochtitlan, and the first written accounts of Aztec society—by Cortés himself and some of his soldiers—reflect a sense of awe toward the city.

Soon after the fall of Tenochtitlan to the Spaniards in 1521, scholarship began on Aztec society. Missionary friars from Spain learned Nahuatl and began asking questions about ancient customs and beliefs. Most of this early research focused on Aztec religion. The friars believed that an understanding of native beliefs and rituals would help them convert people to Christianity. Today the accounts of Friars Bernardino de Sahagún (1950–82) and Diego Durán (1971) remain the richest descriptions of Aztec religion. But chroniclers such as Sahagún and Durán, and numerous others, were also curious about other aspects of Aztec history and society, and the content of their books reflects this wider interest.

One of the topics discussed by sixteenth-century Spanish and native chroniclers was Aztec cities. Just as Cortés and the conquerors were impressed by Tenochtitlan, so too were the friars fascinated by the capital city. In fact, early writers devoted so much attention to Tenochtitlan that they almost forgot to describe other Aztec cities. With the exception of some descriptions of Texcoco written by Fernando de Alva Ixtlilxochitl (1975–77), a descendent of the Texcoco dynasty, no other Aztec city received more than a brief or cursory description by early writers.

This early colonial focus on the imperial capital, at the expense of the several hundred other Aztec cities, would have pleased the ancient Mexica kings who built and ruled Tenochtitlan. Most Aztec cities had a basic plan that makes them easy to identify in comparison with earlier Mesoamerican cities. But Tenochtitlan was different. Its builders were powerful kings who ruled an expanding empire, and one of their goals was to make Tenochtitlan into a unique city, different from other Aztec settlements. They largely succeeded in this task, and as a result Tenochtitlan became the most atypical of Aztec cities.

Although Tenochtitlan has consistently received all the attention—starting with the early Spanish friars and continuing with modern scholars—other cities were far more important in the lives of the Aztec people. In spite of the expansion of the Aztec empire, central Mexico was a fragmented political landscape in which the altepetl was the primary administrative unit. Nearly all Aztec cities were altepetl capitals. For most people, their local altepetl capital was the place they paid their taxes, the setting of the market where they bought and sold their goods, the location of the temples where they worshipped, and the place they went to socialize. It was the political, economic, and religious focus of life for nobles and commoners alike. From the perspective of the several million Aztecs, altepetl capitals were far more important than the distant Tenochtitlan.

These biases in favor of Tenochtitlan—promoted by the imperial propaganda of the Mexica kings and furthered by the omissions in the descriptions of the chroniclers—play into the hands of scholars whose rigid definitions of cities as huge settlements would rule out the smaller capitals as true cities (Sanders and Webster 1988). If we rely upon the historical record alone, it is hard to counter this argument. Luckily, parts of many Aztec altepetl capitals survive archaeologically. The fieldwork at these urban sites, however, is not very widely known. Much of the research has only been published in technical reports in Mexico and the United States, and some projects have never been published at all. For example, Teopanzolco, a site mentioned frequently in this book, was excavated in the 1920s, but no reports were ever published. The architecture and a few artifacts are available for analysis today, however, and we can still learn from this and other early excavation projects.

The two primary goals of this book are to bring Aztec altepetl capitals to light and to present an argument for the importance of political dynamics in shaping their forms, growth, and operation. A subsidiary goal is to place Aztec urbanism within the wider context of processes of urbanization in the ancient and modern worlds.

WHAT IS A CITY?

My view of urbanism departs from many scholarly and popular treatments. In most theoretical approaches the focus is on the urban settlement itself. Urbanism is defined as an attribute of settlements; some settlements are urban, others are not. In the dominant view today, what I call the demographic definition of urbanism, cities are seen as big complex places with huge populations. If one accepts that definition, then Tenochtitlan was certainly a city, but most Aztec altepetl capitals were something less than fully urban. They were much smaller than Tenochtitlan, with less dense populations and lower levels of economic and social complexity.

In my perspective—the functional approach to urbanism—urbanism is an attribute of societies, not of individual settlements. The most important thing about urban centers is not how many residents they have or what they look like, but how they functioned within their regional contexts. Cities, modern and ancient, are the hubs for many activities and institutions that affect large parts of society, both rural and urban. Before turning to Aztec altepetl capitals, it will help to describe this theoretical perspective in more detail and contrast it with other perspectives on ancient urbanism.

The Demographic Definition of Urbanism

The demographic definition of urbanism emphasizes the size and density of urban populations. This is the most common approach to defining cities in the scholarly literature, from archaeology and history to sociology and modern urban studies. The demographic definition was stated most explicitly in a classic article by sociologist Louis Wirth: "For sociological purposes a city may be defined as a relatively large, dense, and permanent settlement of socially heterogeneous individuals" (Wirth 1938: 8). This definition was introduced explicitly into Mesoamerican archaeology by William Sanders and Barbara Price (1968: 46). Over the years, Sanders has continued to promote and refine the demographic definition of Mesoamerican cities (for example, Webster and Sanders 2001).

The demographic definition of urbanism has two primary advantages for the study of ancient cities. First, it draws clear attention to large, densely populated cities as special places within an urban society. Aztec Tenochtitlan, and Classic period Teotihuacan a millennium earlier, were quite different from other Mesoamerican settlements, and Wirth's definition helps us understand just what is unique and interesting about these ancient metropoli. Second, the demographic definition closely matches our modern, Western, folk definition of cities. We all know that cities are bigger, denser, and more socially complex places than villages or small towns, and Wirth's definition sounds right to modern ears.

Against these advantages are some serious drawbacks to the demographic definition of urbanism. First, it assumes that all cities, ancient and modern, were basically the same. If an ancient culture—such as the Classic Maya—lacked large, dense settlements, then it lacked cities and was not an urban culture (this is the viewpoint of Sanders, in the works cited above). This approach is too limiting for most anthropologists, who are trained to explore and analyze differences among cultures. Why must Mayan cities resemble modern cities? Cities in tropical areas, for example, were (and are) very different from cities in nontropical regions. The second drawback of the demographic approach is that it only allows a single type of urban settlement within a given society. Yet most urban societies, in the past and present, have more than one kind of city.

A fundamental argument of this book is that Aztec altepetl capitals were fully urban settlements, but of a very different form and organization from Tenochtitlan. The demographic definition celebrates Tenochtitlan as a "real city" but relegates the settlements covered in this work to a lesser status. Although Wirth's definition certainly highlights an important aspect of Aztec cities, there is more to urbanism than big, dense, complex settlements.

The Functional Approach Taken in This Book

In the functional approach cities are defined not by their intrinsic attributes but by their roles in society.[2] In complex societies, settlements are typically specialized or differentiated from one another. Activities and institutions that affect people over a broad area—beyond the place where they are centered—are called urban functions. A settlement that is the location of one or more urban functions is considered urban. Cities are large urban settlements with many urban functions, and towns are smaller urban settlements with fewer urban functions. The functional approach was pioneered in the 1960s in the field of economic geography, where the focus was on retail marketing functions. Settlements with retail market functions are called central places, and many regions contain a hierarchy of central places. Central place theory is a body of concepts that treat settlement size and location with respect to economic functions (Berry 1967).

Although a number of archaeologists applied central place theory to the analysis of ancient settlements (for example, Smith 1979), this approach was too limited for widespread use. Central place theory assumes the existence of a regional market system, an institution lacking in many ancient econo-mies (Smith 2004). Ethnologist Richard Fox (1977) broadened the functional perspective on urbanism to include political and religious functions in addi-tion to economic functions, and Joyce Marcus (1983) applied this expanded functional definition to ancient Mesoamerican cities. From the functional perspective, Classic Maya capitals were definitely urban settlements because they were the setting for administrative and religious activities or functions that affected a broader hinterland. Proponents of the demographic approach criticized this approach, arguing that most Maya centers did not have a large enough population to be considered true cities (Webster and Sanders 2001).[3] One of the goals of this book is to provide an extended case study of the func-tional approach to ancient urbanism.

The major disadvantage of the functional definition of urbanism is that it is not clear just how many urban functions are required for a settlement to be considered urban. Do the urban functions have to affect a large hinterland, or just the immediate vicinity? Do they have to affect thousands of people, or just a few? The major advantage of this approach is that it is sensitive to variation in urban forms and processes. A single urban society can have different types of cities—political capitals, trade centers, and the like—or different sizes of urban settlements, either cities or towns (Skinner 1977). Furthermore, all societies do not have to have the same types of cities. Maya and Inka cities were primarily ceremonial and administrative in nature, for example, whereas Swahili cities and medieval European towns were oriented most strongly toward mercantile trade.

Discussion

Although the demographic definition of urbanism contributes some insights, overall the functional perspective is more useful for the analysis of Aztec al-

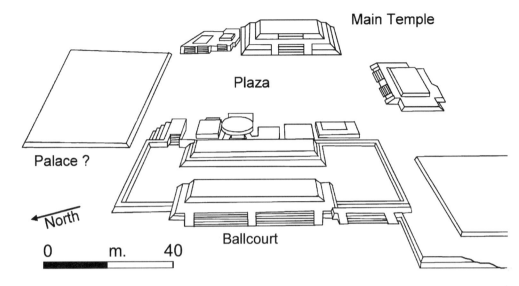

Figure 1.1. Coatetelco, a city in Morelos. (From Smith 2003a: fig. 8.2.)

tepetl capitals. It is the broadest and most flexible definition of urbanism, and it is also the most easily applied definition for many Aztec urban settlements. A drawing of the central district (the urban "epicenter") of the Aztec city of Coatetelco (fig. 1.1) illustrates this situation. Most of the site of Coatetelco lies buried today under a modern village of the same name (see chapter 2), and the total size of the ancient city is not known. There are no surviving historical documents on this site. Therefore, the demographic definition of city, which requires data on population size and density, cannot be applied to Coatetelco.

The functional perspective, on the other hand, allows us to make inferences about the urban attributes of Coatetelco without knowing the total population. The religious buildings point clearly to an important religious function for this settlement (fig. 1.1). Only a small number of Aztec settlements had ballcourts and temples like this. The presence of a likely palace similarly indicates an administrative function for Coatetelco, and the orderly and planned layout of buildings around a plaza suggest the hand of a powerful ruler. It is likely that people in a broad hinterland were subject to a leader based at Coatetelco, and they probably attended ballgames and ceremonies in its plaza on a regular basis. This complex of buildings clearly indicates administrative and religious functions and allows us to classify Coatetelco as an urban settlement.

THE FOUR DIMENSIONS OF MESOAMERICAN URBANISM

Aztec cities were part of an ancient Mesoamerican urban tradition, and they share many characteristics with other Mesoamerican cities. In this section I review aspects of the Mesoamerican urban tradition, organizing my discussion around four themes or dimensions of urbanism: urban form, urban life, urban function, and urban meaning. These are aspects of the urbanization process, and any comprehensive analysis of an ancient city or group of cities needs to consider all four dimensions. The remaining chapters in the book will fill in the details of these four dimensions for Aztec altepetl capitals.[4]

Urban Form

The dimension of urban form includes the topics of city size (area, population, and population density), housing, public architecture, layout, and planning. These topics constitute the physical description of an urban settlement, and form is the most direct and accessible urban theme for archaeological analysis. Aspects of urban form (population size and density) compose two of the four components of Wirth's (1938) definition of the city; aspects of urban life (permanence and social heterogeneity) are the other two components.

Attributes of urban form are some of the distinctive traits shared by the cities of ancient Mesoamerica. In the realm of public architecture, most Mesoamerican cities have palaces, ballcourts, and several types of temple pyramids. Three principles of spatial organization are found in most Mesoamerican urban centers: (1) public buildings are typically arranged around formal open plazas, (2) most public architecture is clustered in a central area often called the "urban epicenter," and (3) the urban epicenter shows planning, whereas surrounding residential zones typically are unplanned or irregular in orientation and layout (fig. 1.1). Aztec altepetl capitals clearly conform to these basic Mesoamerican patterns. Chapters 4, 5, and 6 discuss urban form in Aztec altepetl capitals.

Urban Life

The dimension of urban life includes topics such as social diversity within urban centers (ethnicity, social class, occupation, gender), social organization (households and neighborhoods), and the economic, religious, and public lives of urban residents. Much archaeological research on the nonmonumental areas of Mesoamerican cities, especially excavations of residences, has been directed at this theme (for example, Healan 1989; Hirth 2000). As noted above, social diversity is the third aspect of Wirth's definition of the city.

There appears to have been considerable variation among Mesoamerican cities in the parameters that affected the nature of urban life. Some cities had high population densities and others were more dispersed; some cities had numerous craft specialists, whereas others had few; and some cities had a great diversity of housing styles and sizes, suggesting complex patterns of social inequality, while others had two major types of housing, suggesting a simple class hierarchy. Urban life was diverse in ancient Mesoamerican cities, a theme addressed in chapter 6.

Urban Functions

As noted above, urban functions are activities and institutions in an urban center that affect people in a larger hinterland beyond the settlement itself (Fox 1977; Trigger 1972). The most common functions of urban centers in ancient Mesoamerica were in the realms of administration, religion, and economics (Marcus 1983). The relative importance of these different functions in particular cases is sometimes a topic of debate. Regional economic functions, such as craft production and exchange within the hinterland of an urban center, have been studied at a number of Mesoamerican cities. Regional administrative functions generally involved rulership and relations of tribute and subordination, topics that have been studied on the basis of newly deciphered Mayan written inscriptions (Martin and Grube 2000). Religious urban functions on a regional scale are less commonly studied by archaeologists, although these were important to most Mesoamerican cities.

Another component of the functional approach concerns the roles of cities beyond the regional level. Some cities—most notably Tenochtitlan—functioned as imperial capitals, a role that clearly contributed to their size and grandeur. Other macroregional urban functions include commercial exchange at ports and gateway cities, and the religious role of some cities as major shrines or pilgrimage destinations. The urban functions of Aztec cities are explored more fully in chapter 7.

Urban Meaning

One of the thorniest topics in the study of ancient cities is urban meaning. Many writers have a strong desire to see esoteric religious meanings in nearly all ancient buildings and cities, and this desire resonates with a body of scholarly and popular literature that promotes a universal model of ancient cities as sacred places (Malville and Gurjal 2000; Rykwert 1988; Wheatley 1971). Such a view does not stand up to archaeological data or to comparative anthropological understanding of the organization of human societies. In order to address the topic of urban meaning from a rigorous and realistic founda-tion, I employ Amos Rapoport's (1988, 1990a) model of multiple levels of architectural communication. Rapoport divides the topic of "the meaning of the built environment" into three levels: high-level, middle-level, and low-level meanings.

Rapoport's high-level meaning concerns the explicit symbolism of build-ings and cities within a religious or cultural tradition. This is perhaps the most common use of the phrase "urban meaning." High-level meanings are culturally specific and difficult or impossible to reconstruct in the absence of written texts. They also tend to be esoteric, understood by only a small minority within any urban culture. In Mesoamerica high-level meaning is most successfully addressed for Late Postclassic buildings with ethnohistoric documentation, such as the Templo Mayor of Tenochtitlan or circular tem-ples (see chapter 4). Although cosmological symbolism on the level of entire urban settlements is well documented for ancient urban traditions in China, India, and Cambodia (Mannikka 1996; Steinhardt 1990; Wheatley 1971), its presence in other urban traditions—where explicit written evidence is lack-ing—is problematic (Kemp 2000). For many Mesoamerican cities, discussion of cosmological meaning (for example, Pugh 2001; Stanton and Freidel 2005) must be regarded as speculative at best (Smith 2003b, 2005b). To use the example of Coatetelco, we have no direct evidence for the high-level meaning of any of the urban buildings or the town plan.

In Rapoport's scheme middle-level meaning concerns the transmission of messages about identity, status, and power. I use the concept of "architectural communication" in this book to address issues of middle-level meaning of Aztec buildings and cities (see below). Rapoport's low-level meaning con-cerns the influence of the built environment on the thought and behavior of individuals. I discuss this realm below under the concept of "townscape interaction."

THEORETICAL APPROACH

In this book I apply a number of theoretical models to the data on Aztec cities in order to further our understanding of Aztec urbanism and society. I avoid high-level social theory, particularly approaches that are part of the postmodern or postprocessual domain.[5] My overall theoretical approach—political economy—is materialist in orientation (Roseberry 1988; Smith 2004), and it requires a strong empirical foundation of archaeological and historical data. As a consequence I do not find it useful to spend much time in speculation over topics about which we have little information (such as the cosmological meaning of city plans). My approach allows a rich and realistic reconstruction of Aztec urbanism without having to rely upon guesswork. Instead of using highly abstract social theory, my analyses in this book make use of several lower-level theoretical concepts interpreted within a political economy framework. The most important of these are the functional approach to urbanism (described above), Aztec elite culture, architectural communication, and townscape interaction.

Aztec Elite Culture

"Aztec elite culture" refers to a variety of social practices undertaken by the Aztec nobility and to the material and ideological outcomes of those practices. Each Aztec altepetl had a royal family and other noble families who together owned most of the land and controlled the institutions of government. The number of nobles within any given altepetl was generally small, but interactions among noble families cut across altepetl lines. The most important of these forms of interaction were marriage alliances and common participation in state ceremonies. One of the end products of these interactions was the creation of a common elite culture that covered the entire area of central Mexico in the Aztec period.

This elite culture consisted of ideas (for example, myths and religious beliefs, calendrical knowledge, and political and social concepts), practices (for example, rituals and ceremonies and forms of social interaction), and their material expressions (for example, texts, portable art, and buildings). It was present among the nobles of every altepetl and at the same time existed in the interactions among the nobility of different altepetl. In some ways the concept of Aztec elite culture is similar to Mogens Hansen's (2000b) concept of "city-state culture." Hansen observed that city-states in many parts of the world and at different time periods tended to exist not as unitary polities but as groups of interacting polities that shared a common language and culture. This city-state culture bound groups of nearby city-states into systems of dynamic interaction.

The Aztec altepetl clearly participated in a distinctive Aztec city-state culture (M. E. Smith 2000; 2003a: 148–156), but Aztec elite culture was at the same time both more limited and broader in scope than city-state culture as discussed by Hansen. Aztec elite culture was one component of city-state culture, concerned more with elite matters and ideology and less with commonalities of language and other cultural expressions. It was broader in that it extended far beyond the Aztec heartland of central Mexico to embrace the entire area of the Triple Alliance (Aztec) empire. One of the practices that held the empire together was interaction among widely scattered elites (Berdan et al. 1996; Pohl 1994, 2003b; Smith 1986), and these patterns of economic and cultural interaction extended even beyond the bounds of the empire to embrace all of Mesoamerica (Smith and Berdan 2003). Richard Hingley (2005: chap. 4) provides an excellent analysis of similar processes in the Roman Empire, including the role of cities and urbanism in the network of Roman elite culture.

Aztec elite culture was not just a set of practices and traits that happened to characterize a group of people. It was an ideology in the sense of "ideas and beliefs that help legitimate the interests of a dominant social power in the face of opposing interests" (Eagleton 1991: 28–30). In other words, this elite culture had a strong political mission, which was to further the privileges and control enjoyed by the Aztec nobility (Brumfiel 1998; Hicks 1996). The process by which ideology is expressed in material terms, or transformed into tangible material expression, is known as "materialization" (DeMarrais, Castillo, and Earle 1996). Many aspects of Aztec cities can be viewed as materializations of Aztec elite culture. Cities were built by kings and nobles. Buildings and their arrangements sent ideological messages about power and identity. Aztec cities cannot be understood outside of the context of Aztec elite culture. One of the main processes involved in the materialization of ideology through urbanism was architectural communication.

Architectural Communication

Buildings send messages to a variety of audiences and at a variety of levels. I use the concept of "architectural communication" to analyze phenomena that pertain to Amos Rapoport's concept of middle-level meaning. Middle-level meanings are messages about identity, status, and power. The most common example of middle-level meaning in ancient states is the use of monumentality to express political power and control (Trigger 1990). Monumental buildings—those that are much larger than they need to be for utilitarian purposes—convey messages about the ability of the state to carry out large projects, to convert disorder to order, and to force individuals to conform to societal needs (Blanton 1989).

Another component of middle-level meaning is the explicit communication of messages through public art. Murals and smaller monuments—sculptures, stelae, altars, and so on—with or without written texts, typically convey specific messages about religion, politics, and appropriate behavior. In comparison to high-level meaning, middle-level meanings are far less culturally specific, and thus analogy and comparison are useful tools for understanding these meanings in the absence of written texts. At Coatetelco, the layout of the buildings, their size, and positioning all communicated middle-level messages about the power and identity of the rulers who built and ruled the city. As we will see, one of the most prominent of these messages concerned an adherence to the layout of the ancient city of Tollan (Tula).

Richard Blanton's (1994) notions of canonical and indexical communication are helpful here. Canonical communication is the use of architecture to convey adherence to a cultural norm or tradition. By erecting a particular kind of building, or in constructing a building in a particular style, the builder signals the participation of the building (as well as the builders and the users) in a larger cultural realm. Canonical communication sends messages of social, cultural, or class identity. In the case of Aztec cities, builders constructed a limited suite of standard buildings (temples, ballcourts, shrines, and palaces) because these were considered standard Aztec buildings, necessary for a settlement to be considered a proper Aztec city. Their presence sent messages about the participation of the city in the general system of Aztec culture and Aztec elite culture. These messages were in most cases directed internally, at urban residents or rural subjects of the king.

Indexical communication, on the other hand, is generally oriented toward the external world. It involves messages about power, wealth, and status. Monumentality—the construction of very large buildings to show off power—is a type of indexical communication. The largest Aztec temples, for example, were built by the most powerful political capitals. On the one hand the most powerful kings commanded more labor and resources to build larger buildings; on the other hand the construction and enlargement of monumental temples was a deliberate ideological claim about power and control, and the very act of building and enlarging such temples helped legitimize kings and contributed to their political power.

In examining the nature of architectural communication at Aztec cities, I am following a tradition of research by archaeologists (Blanton 1989, 1994; Earle 1997; Moore 1996; Smith 2003; Trigger 1990; Zanker 1998) and other social scientists (Doxiadis 1972; Lawrence and Low 1990; Lynch 1981; Rapoport 1990a; Scott 1998). Aztec cities were built and maintained as political and ideological statements by rulers. Whether or not these statements matched reality, the communication of social information through architecture and urban planning was an important part of the political dynamics of the altepetl.

Townscape Interaction

The term townscape was first introduced by British town planners to describe the visual qualities of urban buildings and open spaces. In the words of Cullen (1971: cover), townscape is "the art of giving visual coherence and organization to the jumble of buildings, streets and spaces that make up the urban environment." The concept was later modified and extended by scholars working in the British urban morphology tradition (for example, Lilley 2002; Whitehand 2001). In the words of geographer David Ley:

> Study of the town plan, its land-use units, and architectural forms together comprised an understanding of the townscape. From an essentially descriptive and classificatory project, work has now expanded to include the roles of the agents and institutions who have shaped the townscape, including property owners, developers, architects and planners. (Ley 2000: 843)

Most ancient townscapes had a strong political dimension. They were created (in the epicenter at least) by rulers and their builders in order to advance their political agendas of glory, power, legitimation, and control.

I use the concept "townscape interaction" to describe the processes of interaction between people and the built environment within cities. This is the realm of Rapoport's model of low-level meaning, or the influence of the built environment on the thought and behavior of individuals (Blanton 1994; Lawrence and Low 1990; Smith 2003). In the words of Winston Churchill, "We shape our buildings; thereafter, they shape us." Paul Zanker describes an approach similar to townscape interaction in his analysis of ancient Pompeii. He notes that "a townscape also represents the framework within which urban life takes place. It not only shapes the inhabitants but is shaped by them, for the buildings and spaces, having been constructed to embody certain messages and values, continue to communicate these same messages to succeeding generations" (Zanker 1998: 3).

Aspects of townscape interaction such as access to spaces, movement through the built environment, the visibility of features, and the behavioral effects of monumentality can be addressed with archaeological data (for example, Moore 1996; Rapoport 1990b). The low-level meaning of urban built environments in ancient Mesoamerica has received little attention to date, although promising starts have been made in the areas of access analysis (Hopkins 1987), line-of-sight visualization (Inomata 2001), and the visual characteristics of royal theatrical rituals among the Classic Maya (Inomata 2006).

I take a cue from innovative research on townscape interaction at Roman cities. William MacDonald (1986) uses the concept of "urban armature" for the system of roads, buildings, and spaces that formed the heart of Roman cities. These armatures were set up to guide traffic through the city and produce certain visual and aesthetic impacts upon visitors. They were not designed and built as single integrated projects, however. They were created over time through numerous separate construction episodes by different actors, all working within a common framework. Diane Favro (1996) takes this concept further to examine what the city of Rome would have looked like as one moved through specific streets and sections of the urban environment. Adam T. Smith (2000, 2003) examines the relationship between townscape interaction and other architectural processes on the one hand and political dynamics of early states on the other.

At Coatetelco an important aspect of townscape interaction or low-level meaning is the open nature of the central plaza. People could walk right into the plaza from several directions without hindrance. This is very different from the townscape of the imperial capital Tenochtitlan (where the central zone was surrounded by a wall that limited access) and many other cities of the ancient world. Townscape interaction will be addressed primarily in chapter 6.

AZTEC SOCIETY AND AZTEC CITIES

I use the term "Aztec" to refer to the several million people living in highland central Mexico during the Middle Postclassic (ca. A.D. 1100–1300) and Late Postclassic (ca. A.D. 1300–1520+) periods (M. E. Smith 2003a). Most of these people spoke the Nahuatl language, but there were significant numbers of speakers of other languages in this area, particularly languages of the Oto-Pamean group (for example, Otomi, Mazahua, and Matlatzinca). This definition of "Aztec" differs from that of many scholars, who restrict the term to the inhabitants of Tenochtitlan, or the people of the Valley of Mexico. Within the broad area of Aztec central Mexico, the Valley of Mexico (ca. 7,000 square km) and the valleys immediately surrounding the basin on the east, south, and west sides have the most evidence for city-states and city-state capitals. This is where most of the excavated sites are located, and this is the region where the historical dramas of the Aztec native histories were played out. In the landscape of modern Mexico, this area of Aztec city-state culture includes the Federal District (Mexico City), the entire states of Mexico, Morelos, and Tlaxcala, and parts of the states of Puebla and Hidalgo (fig. 1.2). Although some elements of Aztec city-state culture and urban form extend

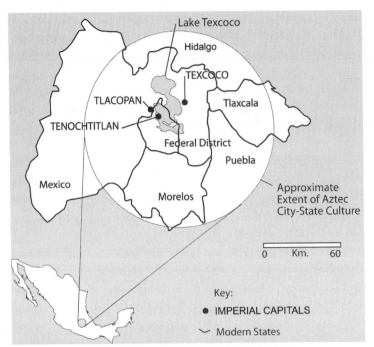

Figure 1.2. Map of the extent of Aztec city-state culture in relation to modern geographic boundaries.

farther than this into areas such as the Tehuacan Valley of Puebla, urbanism in such distant areas is not well understood and appears to diverge from the patterns of central Mexico. For this reason I omit discussion of these areas in most chapters.

The major justification for taking a wider spatial perspective on Aztec society than many authors is the high level of interaction and communication within the broader area of central Mexico. Economic exchange was extensive throughout this area and the archaeological record provides abundant evidence for widespread exchange of information and styles (Smith 2003e). Urban public architecture constitutes one of the major dimensions of stylistic similarity that united Aztec central Mexico into a single cultural zone. As we will see, basic architectural forms such as temple pyramids, palaces, and altars were similar—even standardized—throughout this area (fig. 1.2). On a higher level, principles of urban design and layout were also shared throughout Aztec central Mexico. Although each region of this broad area had its distinctive decorated ceramic styles, house forms, and other kinds of basic material culture, urbanism was a material realm that tied individual regions together. Although not all of the reasons for the high level of similarity in urban form in the Aztec realm are fully understood, one of the underlying social dynamics is clear: the relationship between urbanism and political organization.

As discussed more fully in chapter 3, the dominant political form throughout Aztec central Mexico was the altepetl or city-state. Ethnohistorical and archaeological data on Aztec city-states in the Valley of Mexico and Morelos are discussed by Hodge (1984, 1997) and Smith (2000). Small polities were not limited to the valley of Mexico and Morelos. In fact, the small polity was the major political form throughout the entire area of the Aztec empire and beyond (Berdan et al. 1996). Contributors to the book *The Postclassic Mesoamerican World* (Smith and Berdan 2003) identified causal interrelationships among a number of social processes that operated throughout all of Mesoamerica in the Middle and Late Postclassic periods: demographic expansion, agricultural intensification, the growth of commercial exchange, the development of new techniques of stylistic communication, the spread of common styles and iconographies, and a proliferation of small polities. Aztec city-state capitals were the spatial and material expressions of these small polities in central Mexico, and many aspects of their form and meaning derived directly from the actions and ideological claims of city-state kings.

SOURCES OF EVIDENCE

Information about Aztec city-state capitals comes from both historical texts and archaeological fieldwork. In this section I outline briefly the different types of evidence that are available. More concrete discussions are provided in the remaining chapters.

The Historical Record

Historical documents on Aztec society are typically divided into four categories.

Pictorial Codices

Pictorial codices are painted books produced by indigenous scribes. Only a few examples painted before the Spanish conquest still survive; most examples were painted in early colonial times, usually following ancient styles and principles. There are three types of pictorial codices: ritual almanacs (manuals for divination by priests and accounts of gods, rituals, myths, and the calendar), histories (accounts of the history of dynasties and peoples), and tribute records (lists of imperial tribute goods). There is a large body of scholarship on Aztec codices; among the studies most relevant to cities and urbanism are Boone (2000b) and Robertson (1959). A number of illustrations of cities and urban architecture from the codices are presented in this book (figs. 1.4, 2.14, 3.1, 3.2, 3.3, 4.2, 4.4, 4.6, 4.9, 4.10, 5.1, 5.5).

Reports of the Conquerors

Reports of the conquerors are written letters and accounts by Hernando Cortés and others that describe the initial encounter between the Spaniards and the Aztecs (for example, Díaz del Castillo 1963). These sources have some useful information on urbanism and architecture.

Accounts of the Chroniclers

Accounts of the chroniclers are written texts produced in the early colonial period that describe conditions and events before and after the Spanish conquest. Mendicant friars from Spain were among the best chroniclers of ancient times, particularly Bernardino de Sahagún (1950–82) and Diego Durán (1971, 1994). Many of the chroniclers have descriptions of cities and buildings. For city-state capitals, two of the most informative chroniclers were Fernando de Alva Ixtlilxochitl (1975–77), a descendant of the kings of Texcoco who wrote extensive accounts of the exploits of his royal ancestors, and Francisco de San Antón Muñon Chimalpahin (Chimalpahin Cuauhtlehuanitzin 1997).

Colonial Spanish Administrative Documents

Colonial period administrative documents were produced within the legal system of the Spanish empire. These documents—many written in Nahuatl—provide a wealth of detailed local information about conditions early in the colonial period, and much of the information also pertains to pre-Spanish times. Gibson (1964) synthesizes information from Spanish-language documents and Lockhart (1992) analyzes material from Nahuatl-language sources. For the study of Aztec city-states, administrative documents provide crucial information on the extent of administrative territories early in the colonial period. In many cases the size and structure of Spanish administrative units were defined on the basis of Aztec city-states, and most reconstructions of Aztec and Late Postclassic polities rely heavily on such documents (Berdan et al. 1996; Gerhard 1993; Hodge 1984).

An example of a colonial map used to reconstruct an Aztec polity is shown in figure 1.3. This is a map of the town of Coatepec in the Basin of Mexico

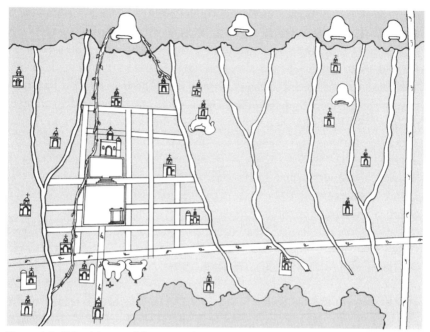

Figure 1.3. Colonial map of the town of Coatepec. Church and plaza indicate the location of the Aztec period city; smaller churches mark subject settlements. (From Hodge 1994.)

in the 1570s (Acuña 1984–88: vol. 6, p.150). Mary Hodge (1994) compared this and other maps and documents to archaeological settlement patterns to reconstruct the extent of the Aztec altepetl of Coatepec. The church and plaza in the middle of the town mark the location of the center of the Aztec and colonial cities. The small churches distributed across the map represent small settlements under the jurisdiction of Coatepec in both the colonial and Aztec periods. Although produced for Spanish authorities, this map follows Aztec convention in putting east at the top. The mountains east of Coatepec are shown along the top of the map, with rivers running west toward Lake Texcoco. Two irrigation canals are also shown. This map accompanies an administrative document (the *Relación Geográfica* for Coatepec) that contains other information about the preconquest city-state, including the date it was founded (ca. A.D. 1160), the names of many of its kings, and a diversity of political, economic, and religious observations. For more information on these maps, see Mundy (1996).

An important category that cuts across the various categories of historical document is "native history." The Aztecs, like other Mesoamerican peoples, had a clear sense of history and a tradition of preserving historical accounts. Most of these concern the histories of dynasties and peoples. History was transmitted orally, and historians used painted historical codices as mnemonic devices. Today we have access to Aztec native history in three forms. First, numerous historical codices have survived. These provide the bare outlines of events, typically dated in the Aztec year-count calendar (for example, Noguez 1978; Quiñones Keber 1995). Second, historical accounts were told to the chroniclers, who recorded the history in narrative fashion (for example, Durán 1994). Third, there are a few cases where pictorial codices have survived, along with explanations and commentaries from the early colonial period. The best example is a series of painted histories from Texcoco and the chronicles of Alva Ixtlilxochitl (see below).

Aztec native history must be interpreted carefully. The purpose of these documents and oral accounts was not to provide an accurate description of past events but to glorify kings, dynasties, and ethnic groups. Native history was an important component of Aztec elite culture. At several points kings burned ancient history books to start over with "correct" accounts of the past, and there is a large measure of bias in these histories. One problem is that as one moves back in time, the events grow less plausible and history grades into mythology. The degree to which we can trust Aztec native history for early periods (particularly for pre-Aztec events such as Tula and the Toltecs) is a topic of scholarly debate.

Archaeology

When Aztec city-state capitals are considered as archaeological sites, there is a clear dichotomy between sites with preserved monumental architecture but no residential remains, and sites with intact residential areas but little or no public architecture. Sites such as Tenochtitlan, Tlatelolco, Tenayuca, and Teopanzolco fit the first category. Today these are archaeological zones (an archaeological zone is a site protected and managed by the government and open to visitors) with large buildings located in the middle of modern cities that cover up their associated residential areas. Archaeological fieldwork at these sites proceeds by excavating large buildings using what has been called the "monumental archaeology" approach. This research provides important information on urban architecture, on urban layout and planning, and on political and religious institutions. Chapters 2 and 4 will detail much of the fieldwork from the monumental archaeology approach.

At other sites, residential areas have been preserved, and these have been analyzed with what can be called the "residential archaeology" approach. At these sites little or no monumental architecture survives. Fieldwork in the residential zones of cities like Chalco, Huexotla, Otumba, Xaltocan, and Yautepec illuminate urban social and economic patterns. House excavations provide information on domestic activities and on contrasts between nobles and commoners. Intensive surface collections of artifacts provide site-level spatial data on these and other issues. Craft production has been a major topic of interest for the residential archaeology approach. Chapters 6 and 7 present many of the findings of archaeological research at Aztec cities using the residential archaeology approach.[6]

Example: Archaeological and Documentary Perspectives on Twin-Temple Pyramids

The use of diverse types of historical and archaeological evidence to study Aztec altepetl capitals can be illustrated by the twin-temple pyramid, one of the most characteristic forms of Aztec urban architecture (fig. 1.4). These buildings consist of a single massive temple platform topped by two adjacent

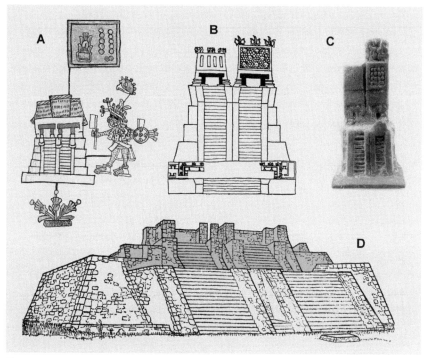

Figure 1.4. Representations of double-stair pyramids. A: Tlacopan, in the *Codex Telleriano-Remensis*, f. 40r (after Quiñones Keber 1995: 83); B: Texcoco, in the *Codex Ixtlilxochitl*, f. 112v (after Lesbre 1998: 16); C: ceramic model from the Museum der Kulturen Basel, Peter Horner (Baer 1996: 73); D: drawing of Teopanzolco pyramid (after López González 1966).

small temples, each with a separate stairway. The great majority of temple pyramids shown in the Aztec codices have a single temple and a single stairway, the typical layout of Mesoamerican temple pyramids (fig. 4.1). There are a few twin-temple pyramids in the codices, however. For example, the history section of the *Codex Telleriano-Remensis* (1995: 40r) depicts a ceremony at a twin-temple pyramid in the city of Tlacopan (fig. 1.4A; the name glyph is below the temple) in the year 12 Reed (A.D. 1491). The codex illustrates a double-stair pyramid topped by what looks like two rooms that share a common thatched roof.

The actual temple of Tlacopan has not survived, and we can ask if this image is an accurate depiction of structure. Since most pyramids shown in this codex have a single stairway, it is likely that the depiction of two stairways was deliberate. The purpose of this illustration, however, was not to show what the temple looked like but to illustrate a sacrificial ceremony that took place at the temple. My interpretation of this image is that the city of Tlacopan did indeed have a twin-temple pyramid, but that the particular form shown is not necessarily an accurate portrayal of that pyramid.

Another depiction of a double-stair pyramid, at Texcoco (fig. 1.4B), is found in the *Códice Ixtlilxochitl* (1996: fig. 112). More credibility can be given to the architectural details of this illustration because (1) its purpose was to show what the main temple of Texcoco looked like and (2) the image is corroborated by a textual description of the building by Juan de Pomar, author of the *Relación de Tezcoco*:

> The principal temple of these idols, Huitzilopochtli and Tlaloc, was built in the middle of the city [Texcoco], square and massive like a foundation of clay and stone and only the facings of masonry. Each side was 80 fathoms long [ca. 134 meters] and it was 27 fathoms high [ca. 45 meters]. It has 160 steps on the west side, that on which one ascended to it . . . [there were two stairways] both ending in a patio made at the highest point, where there were two large chambers, one larger than the other. In the larger one, on the south side, was the idol Huitzilopochtli; in the other, the smaller one, on the north side, was the idol Tlaloc. . . . To one side of it toward the door of the larger chamber of Huitzilopochtli there was a raised stone a yard in height with its top shaped like a trunk with a rounded top which they named *techcatl* and where they sacrificed the Indians. (Acuña 1984–88: 8:57–58; English translation from Thompson 1941: 16–17)

The two depictions of twin-temple pyramids from codices shown in figure 1.4 suggest that Texcoco and Tlacopan probably had pyramids of this form, although no archaeological traces of them have survived. Another source of evidence is small fired clay models of temple pyramids. As in the codices, most examples are single-stair pyramids, but several twin-temple pyramid models exist (fig. 1.4C); note the altar at the top of the right-hand stairway.

Also shown (fig. 1.4D) is a modern drawing of the twin-temple pyramid at Teopanzolco. This structure was excavated and reconstructed in a somewhat confusing fashion. Archaeologists uncovered evidence for two major stages of construction. The outer walls correspond to the second stage, which completely covered the first stage. The dark areas in fig. 1.4D are walls of the first stage, which include the bases of the walls of the two temples on top of the platform.

None of the different kinds of evidence for twin-temple pyramids alone— depictions in the codices, descriptions by the chroniclers, excavated architectural remains, or small clay temple models—provides an adequate understanding of their form or their distribution. Taken together, however, they provide insight into a major Aztec urban architectural form (these and other temples are discussed further in chapter 4). Thus we need to consider diverse types of evidence in order to understand Aztec cities and urban features.

HISTORICAL CONTEXT: TOLTECS AND AZTECS

The history of Aztec altepetl capitals begins with an earlier urban culture, the Toltecs of Tula. The Aztecs looked back to the Toltecs as their ancestors and drew explicitly on Tula and Toltec practices as sources of political and social legitimacy.

Tula, Tollan, and the Toltecs

Tula is a large urban archaeological site located in the state of Hidalgo, immediately north of the Basin of Mexico. Excavations at Tula in the 1940s and 1950s by Jorge Acosta revealed an impressive formal plaza flanked by several types of public architecture, including single-temple pyramids, ballcourts, altars, and an unusual structure with numerous column bases (fig. 1.5). Chronological research by Acosta and subsequent archaeologists indicates that this urban center dates to the Epiclassic (A.D. 700–900) and Early Postclassic (A.D. 900–1100) periods.

For the first half of Tula's existence, the city was focused around the central "El Corral" temple some distance from the plaza shown in figure 1.5. El Corral was a circular temple with a small attached altar decorated with skulls and crossed bones. At some point a new downtown area (fig. 1.5) was constructed and became the focus of Early Postclassic Tula. The city was burned or de-

Figure 1.5. Epicenter of Tula. Note the plaza layout, which was copied at Aztec urban centers. Photo from 1957, reproduced courtesy of the Companía Mexicana de Aerofoto.

stroyed, probably in the twelfth century, after which people using Aztec-style ceramics moved in and placed offerings at various places. In the Late Aztec period an Aztec altepetl named Tula was located near the ruins of ancient Tula. Archaeological fieldwork at Tula is reviewed by Mastache, Cobean, and Healan (2002); Healan (1989); and Cobean (1990).

The name Tula is derived from Tollan ("Where there are many reeds"), a Nahuatl term that designates a sacred ancient ancestral city. The inhabitants of Tollan were called Toltecs. Native historical accounts from all over Mesoamerica mention Tollan, and in ancient times the term was probably applied to a number of cities, including Tula, Teotihuacan, Cholula, Chichén Itzá, and others. It is clear that in the Aztec historical traditions some of the events associated with Tollan in fact pertain to the archaeological city of Tula. For example, the Aztec migration stories mention towns that the immigrants passed, and the towns that precede and follow Tollan are located near Tula.

In other respects, however, the Aztec descriptions of Tollan do not seem to match the actual ruins of Tula. Sahagún and other chroniclers describe Tollan as a wealthy and fantastic city with buildings constructed of precious stones. These sources assert that the Toltecs invented the calendar and all of the useful crafts of ancient Mesoamerica—clearly not the case. The key to understanding these exaggerated claims is the role that Tollan and the Toltecs played in Aztec ideology. To the Aztecs, the Toltecs were their ancestors who originated or provided all that was good in Aztec culture. Aztec kings gained legitimacy by showing (or asserting) direct descent from the Toltec kings. Aztec native historical accounts typically begin with the creation of the world, and then describe Tollan and the Toltecs, followed by accounts of Aztec origins.

The Aztecs clearly held Tollan and the Toltecs in great esteem. Given the ideological role of the Toltecs as great legitimizing ancestors and sources of Aztec identity (chapter 3), it is not surprising that the native histories exaggerate the accomplishments and grandeur of the Toltecs. What is surprising, however, is that many modern scholars take these biased accounts at face value, as if Aztec descriptions of Toltec kings and their exploits were simple factual narratives.[7] Whether or not one believes Aztec stories about the Toltecs, we are left with the fact that in Aztec times, Tollan and the Toltec past were potent ideological symbols, particularly to Aztec kings. We will see in chapters 3 and 5 that many Aztec kings participated in this Toltec ideology by designing their cities in imitation of the layout of Tula (fig. 1.5).

Aztec Chronology

There are two basic chronologies for Aztec civilization: archaeological and native historical. The archaeological chronology starts with Tula in the Early Postclassic period (A.D. 900–1100), followed by the Early Aztec period, also called Middle Postclassic (A.D. 1100–1300), and then the Late Aztec period, also called Late Postclassic (A.D. 1300–1520+). This sequence is outlined in table 1.1. In Morelos (the Mexican state immediately south of the Valley of Mexico), the Late Aztec period is further divided into two parts, called Late Aztec–A and Late Aztec–B (Hare and Smith 1996; Smith and Doershuk 1991). The archaeological chronology has reasonable support in stratigraphy, seriation, and radiocarbon dates, but it will remain rough and imprecise until the division of the Late Aztec period can be accomplished in areas outside of Morelos. Most Aztec cities were founded in the Early Aztec period and then continued in use until the Spanish conquest.

The native historical chronology, as mentioned above, begins with mythological events involving gods and creation episodes. These accounts then describe Tollan and the Toltecs. After the fall of Tula, the next story is the migration of the Aztec peoples from their northern homeland—Aztlan or Chicomoztoc (chapter 3). This leads to the founding of cities and dynasties, the expansion of the Tepanec empire, and finally the formation and expan-

Table 1.1. Aztec Chronology Chart

Date, AD	Archaeological Period		Event	Year
1500	Late Aztec B		Spanish Conquest	1519
1400	Late Aztec A		Triple Alliance Empire Formed	1428
			Tepanic Empire Formed	1370
1300	Early Aztec	*AZTEC CITY-STATE CULTURE*	Tenochtitlan Founded	1325
			(growth of city-states)	
1200			Arrival of Aztlan Migrants	1200
			Fall of Tula	1175
1100	Early Postclassic			
1000			(Tula and Toltec culture)	

sion of the Triple Alliance empire (table 1.1). The most complete analysis of Aztec native history is found in the books of Nigel Davies (1973, 1980, 1987); see also Boone (1994) and Nicholson (1971a). A more detailed look at the native historical story of the Aztec period is found in the descriptions of Aztec cities in the following chapter.

2

The Roster of Aztec Cities

Although there were several hundred Aztec city-state capitals in central Mexico at the time of the Spanish conquest, we have useful information about only a handful. These cases comprise my sample for this book. In this chapter I briefly describe this group of cities. My emphasis is on the examples with the most archaeological remains. Some major capitals with few archaeological remains (Azcapotzalco and Tlacopan) are also included, as well as a few towns that were not city-state capitals (Cuexcomate and Cihuatecpan, for example) and several examples of a special-purpose site, the hilltop ceremonial precinct.

The descriptions follow a common format. Each starts with the political status of the city, followed by a discussion of the archaeological site today and an outline of fieldwork projects at the site. I use the term "archaeological zone" for a government-run archaeological site that is open to the public; most of these sites fit in that category. I next describe some of the noteworthy urban features at the site. Many of these buildings, site plans, and other features are discussed more fully in chapters 4 and 5. The descriptions close with a list of the major publications on the site. Site descriptions are accompanied by the city's name glyph, if known.[1] The names and spellings of cities reflect the most common modern usage.

The presentation of cities follows a general chronological and spatial order, starting with the earliest Aztec cities and ending up with the imperial island capitals, Tenochtitlan and Tlatelolco. By ordering the chapter this way, I provide an outline of Aztec political history along the way. The cities described here are listed in table 2.1, and their locations are shown in figure 2.1.[2]

Table 2.1. Summary of Information on Aztec Cities

City	Data Monumental Archaeology	Residential Archaeology	Documentary	Area (ha.) Site	Epicenter	Population Size	Density[1]
Early Aztec capitals							
Tenayuca	x	x	x				
Teopanzolco	x				1.9		
Major Late Aztec capitals							
Azcapotzalco			x				
Tlacopan			x				
Texcoco	x		x	450		24,100	54
Other Cities in the Basin of Mexico							
Huexotla	x	x		300		17,100	57
Ixtapaluca	x	x		90	15.0	1,400	16
Otumba		x		220		10,700	49
Xaltocan		x		26			
Chiconautla	x	x					
Mexicaltzinco	x	x					
Cities in Morelos							
Palacio de Cortés	x						
Coatetelco	x	x			1.1		
Coatlan		x		15	1.0	800	53
Cuentepec					1.2		
Yautepec	x	x		209		15,100	72
Cities in Other Valleys							
Calixtlahuaca	x	x		100			
Cholula		x	x				
Zultepec	x				8.0		
Non-urban settlements							
Santa Cecelia Acatitlan	x						
Cihuatecpan		x		106		1,100	10
Cuexcomate		x		15	1.2	800	53
Cerro Tlaloc	x		x				
Malinalco	x		x				
Tepozteco	x						
The imperial capital							
Tenochtitlan	x	x	x	1,350	16.9	212,500	157
Tlatelolco	x		x				

Source: The area and population data are taken from Smith (2005).
Note:. 1. Density measures people per hectare.

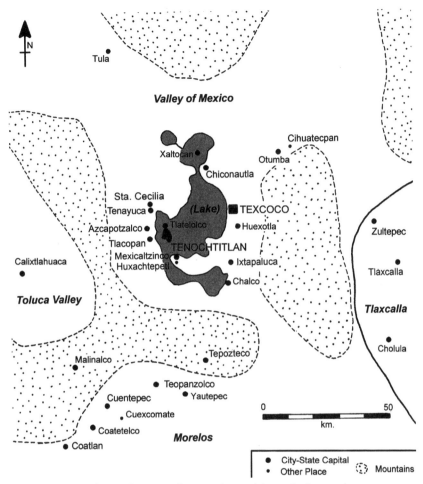

Figure 2.1. Map of central Mexico showing Aztec cities and other settlements.

EARLY AZTEC CAPITALS

TENAYUCA

According to native historical accounts, Tenayuca ("Place full of walls") was founded by Xolotl, a semilegendary ruler who may have lived in the thirteenth century, after the fall of Tula. If Xolotl was a real person, he could be considered the first Aztec king, and regardless of his historicity, Tenayuca can be considered the first Aztec city. Many later kings traced their ancestry to Xolotl, whose dynasty is often referred to as the "Chichimec dynasty." When one such descendent, King Tezozomoc of Azcapotzalco, began a process of imperial expansion in the mid-fourteenth century, Quinatzin (another descendent of Xolotl) moved the dynastic seat from Tenayuca to the eastern shore of Lake Texcoco. The Chichimec line became known as the Acolhua dynasty, and the Acolhua kings ruled Texcoco for several centuries. Tenayuca maintained a great symbolic importance within central Mexico as an ancient dynastic seat. The large size of the surviving main pyramid is a fitting monument to the political prominence of Tenayuca as one of the first capital cities in the Early Aztec period.

The Archaeological Site

Located in the northern part of Mexico City, the entire archaeological zone of Tenayuca fits into a modern city square block. Most of the site area is taken up by a large twin-temple pyramid (fig. 2.2), with a few small shrines nearby. There is a small museum at the site. The archaeological zone sits in the midst of a busy commercial and residential neighborhood, with a park on one side. The size of the Aztec city is not known, but some excavations several blocks

Figure 2.2. Final stage of the twin-temple pyramid in Tenayuca. Only the front stairway has been restored. Photograph by the author.

from the pyramid turned up some Aztec houses that were probably part of the ancient city.

The Tenayuca pyramid is surrounded by a wall of sculpted stone serpents. Bernal Díaz del Castillo visited the structure during the conquest of Mexico, calling Tenayuca a "town of serpents." When archaeologists became interested in Aztec sites in the 1920s (after the Mexican Revolution), Tenayuca was chosen as the setting for a major interdisciplinary fieldwork project directed by Ignacio Marquina. Tunnels were excavated into the tall mound of rubble, revealing a series of six stages of rebuilding and expansion (fig. 2.3). The latest ceramic sherds in the fill of the earliest stage platform were of the Coyotlatelco type from the Epiclassic period (A.D. 700–900). Although the pyramid could have been started long before the Aztec period, it is more likely that it was built by the earliest Aztec inhabitants immediately after they founded the city (before they had generated enough of their own broken pottery to be incorporated into the fill). Artifacts from the subsequent stages of construction suggest that most of the enlargements were in the Early Aztec period, with the final addition made in the Late Aztec period. Most of the pyramid from the final and largest stage had deteriorated, and the excavators decided to restore only the front stairways (fig. 2.2).

Urban Features

Although the twin-temple pyramid is just about all that survives at Tenayuca, this is one of the best-excavated and best-reported excavations of a major Aztec structure. The six stages of construction show a continual process of rebuilding and rededication. This sequence shows that Xolotl and the other early kings of the Chichimec dynasty adopted the ancient Mesoamerican practice of periodic enlargement and expansion of the central religious structures of a city. These were sacred locations charged with supernatural powers, and by expanding the temple kings could demonstrate their adherence to ancient practices while also showing off their unique accomplishments.

Four low stone platforms or shrines surround the central pyramid at Tenayuca. Three of these, on the two sides of the final stage temple, are shown on the plan (fig. 2.3). The fourth altar, attached to the front of the pyramid, is an unusual feature that is decorated—in both sculpture and painting—with human skulls and crossed bones. This is the earliest Aztec example of a *tzitzimime* platform, a shrine used in some way for curing and divination. This and other similar altars are discussed in chapter 4.

Tenayuca marks the initial appearance of the twin-temple plan—two temples, each with its own stairway, on a single pyramid platform—in central

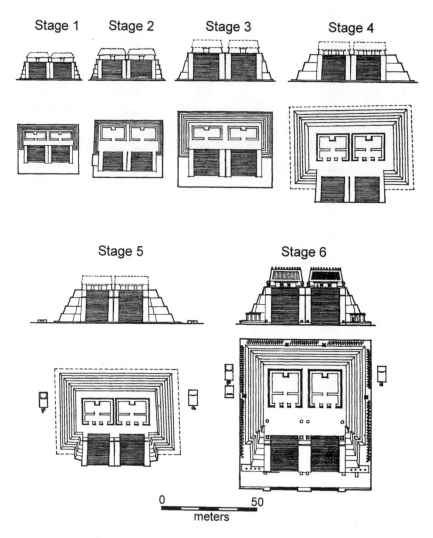

Figure 2.3. Construction stages for the twin-temple pyramid in Tenayuca. (After Marquina 1964: 169.)

Mexico. The historical antecedents of this form are not known, but its later use is amply documented in the central temples of Tenochtitlan and Tlate-lolco.

Illustrations: figs. 2.2, 2.3, 4.6
References: Acosta 1965; Anonymous 1935; Davies 1980; Marquina 1964

TEOPANZOLCO / CUAUHNAHUAC

Teopanzolco is the name of another archaeological zone that, like Tenayuca, fits into a square block in a modern city. Its main temple is smaller and the city block area is larger than at Tenayuca. As a result, the entire epicenter of the site is preserved in the middle of a residential district of modern Cuernavaca (fig. 2.4). This site was almost certainly the urban epicenter of the Early Aztec city of Cuauhnahuac (whose toponym, "Beside the trees," is shown here). Cuauhnahuac was one of the more powerful Early Aztec city-states, a peer and trading partner of Tenayuca. When king Tezozomoc of Azcapotzalco began his program of imperial expansion in the late fourteenth

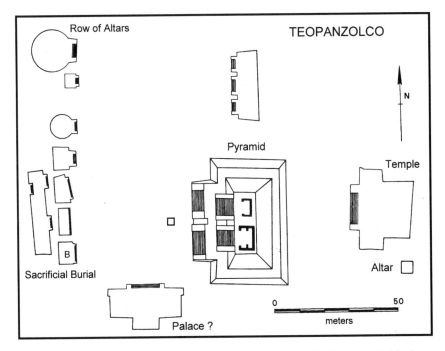

Figure 2.4. Epicenter of the Teopanzolco archaeological zone. This was probably the Early Aztec city of Cuauhnahuac. (From Smith 2003a: 40.)

century, Cuauhnahuac was a victim and the city became a tributary subject
of the Tepanec empire.

At about this time, the temple and other buildings in the Teopanzolco archaeological site were abandoned, most likely as a result of the Tepanec conquest. By the turn of the next century (A.D. 1500) Cuauhnahuac was again a
powerful regional state. Although subject to the Triple Alliance empire, the
king of Cuauhnahuac ruled over some 20 city-states in western Morelos.
The city center, however, was located in what is now downtown Cuernavaca,
about a kilometer from Teopanzolco. Cuauhnahuac was conquered again—
by Spaniards—in 1521. The conqueror Hernando Cortés built himself a large
residence on top of the palace of the king of Cuauhnahuac; that archaeological site (the Palacio de Cortés site) is discussed separately below.

The Archaeological Site

Teopanzolco shares many features with Tenayuca. Both were powerful capitals in the Early Aztec period, and both were dominated by a large twin-temple pyramid. They were the first Aztec sites to be excavated after the Mexican Revolution, resulting in the establishment of square-block archaeological
zones in the middle of modern cities. The discovery of the Teopanzolco pyramid has a more exotic story, however. In 1911 the troops of revolutionary
general Emiliano Zapata were shelling the federal troops in downtown Cuernavaca during the revolution. One of their cannons was set on top of a tall
mound, and the vibrations of the firing shook loose dirt and stones to reveal
the ancient walls of the Aztec temple. That mound, which turned out to be
the pyramid of Teopanzolco, was then excavated and restored by Alfonso
Caso and José Reygadas Vertiz in the 1920s.

The 1920s excavations were never published, although later writers described aspects of the fieldwork. In the 1970s Jorge Angulo returned to Teopanzolco to excavate and restore several of the other buildings. One important find was a sacrificial offering deposited in one of the shrines facing the
main temple (see below). In the 1980s I analyzed ceramics from Angulo's excavations and confirmed the Early Aztec dating of the site, which has yielded
no Late Aztec ceramics.

Urban Features

Like Tenayuca, the twin-temple pyramid dominates Teopanzolco. Excavators only identified two architectural stages, but this was neither as careful
nor as thorough an excavation as Tenayuca. It is possible that the remains
of smaller, earlier stages still lie within the pyramid. Also like Tenayuca, the
Teopanzolco temple is accompanied by a number of low platforms (fig 2.4).

These shrines, crucial architectural traits at all Aztec cities (chapter 4), play a major role in the urban layout of Teopanzolco. The eight platforms, of varying sizes and shapes, are aligned opposite the pyramid to form the western edge of the central plaza, and one small shrine is situated in front of the pyramid. The southernmost altar in the north-south row contained a chamber with the sacrificial burial mentioned above. More than one-third of the 92 skulls were accompanied by the top cervical vertebrae, an indication that the skulls originated through decapitation (as opposed to normal processes of decay). Associated offerings included a number of ceramic vessels and other objects.

Teopanzolco has one of the most complete urban epicenters of any Aztec site. The heavy line outlining the map in figure 2.4 is a modern wall that delimits the government archaeological zone today. I examined the surrounding neighborhoods in the 1980s, prior to construction activity that had filled in the area by 2000. Although there were traces of Aztec houses and residential debris, I could find no indications of additional public architecture outside of the single square block shown on the map. This suggests that the mapped architecture represents a complete, or nearly complete, picture of the Teopanzolco urban epicenter in the Early Aztec period. The significance of this epicenter layout is explored more fully in chapters 3 and 5.

Illustrations: figs. 1.4, 2.4, 4.5
References: Angulo Villaseñor 1976; González Miranda and Salas Cuesta 2001; Marquina 1964; Smith 2008: ch.2

MAJOR LATE AZTEC CAPITALS

AZCAPOTZALCO

After the heyday of Early Aztec city-states such as Tenayuca and Teopanzolco/Cuauhnahuac, two cities came to dominate central Mexico: Azcapotzalco and Texcoco. In the mid-fourteenth century, these were the capitals of small competing expansionist empires. The Tepanecs of Azcapotzalco ("On the ant heap") began their road to imperial success in 1347 with the conquest of the Early Aztec power Culhuacan. In 1371 Tezozomoc came to power in Azcapotzalco and continued the program of expansion by conquest begun by his predecessors. He soon gained the upper hand in central Mexico and created an empire rivaled only by the later Triple Alliance empire. Soon after his death in 1427, the so-called Tepanec empire was defeated in the "Tepanec war" by an alliance of polities led by Tenochtitlan and Texcoco. Azcapotzalco was demoted and the nearby Tepanec city of Tlacopan promoted to the status of capital as the third member (with Tenochtitlan and Texcoco) of the Triple Alliance.

Although Azcapotzalco was the most powerful city in central Mexico for half a century or more, very little is known about the empire or its capital. One reason is that the urban expansion of Mexico City has covered most of the city, and only a few scattered archaeological remains have been located. A second reason is that after their rise to power, the Mexica kings of Tenochtitlan systematically wrote Azcapotzalco and the Tepanec empire out of the history books.

The Archaeological Site and Urban Features

Virtually nothing is known about the archaeological site of Azcapotzalco, which lies buried under Mexico City. A number of excavations have been carried out in Azcapotzalco, but they encountered primarily remains from earlier periods. As the most powerful king in central Mexico for nearly half a century, Tezozomoc probably had a large and sumptuous palace. His actions as emperor are depicted in several historical codices and described in native historical sources (Santamarina 2006). This information comes primarily from the historians of his enemy city, Texcoco, and not from his successor city, Tenochtitlan, whose kings suppressed information on powerful non-Mexica kings. A brief mention of a market area surrounded by a stout wall at Azcapotzalco does survive, however (Carta de Azcapotzalco 2000: 221).

Illustrations: none
References: Carrasco 1984; Davies 1980; Dibble 1980; Santamarina 2005

TLACOPAN

In the Tepanec war that followed the death of Tezozomoc, Azcapotzalco was defeated and Tlacopan took its place as the major capital of the Tepanec peoples. Tlacopan's role in the Triple Alliance was definitely one of a junior partner; tribute from joint conquests was divided, with one-fifth paid to Tlacopan and two-fifth each to Tenochtitlan and Texcoco. The city of Tlacopan ("On the *tlacoxochitl*," a type of flower), now known as Tacuba, is buried under the western portion of Mexico City and very little archaeological fieldwork has been done. In the early twentieth century Manuel Gamio located several ruined pyramids of rocks and adobe bricks at Tacuba. He related these to some large pyramids noted by the conquerors Hernando Cortés and Bernal Díaz del Castillo in Tlacopan. One of these structures survives today in a small archaeological zone known as El Conde (named for a Manuel Conde, whose house once sat on top of the structure) in the town of Naucalpan. This is a low platform, some 2,400 square meters in extent, that probably served as a nonroyal palace. It is one of the very few surviving structures from the Tepanec polity. Depictions in codices suggest that the central temple of Tlacopan, like those of Tenochtitlan and Texcoco, was a twin-temple pyramid (fig. 1.4).

Illustrations: (none)
References: Carrasco 1984; Davies 1980; Gamio 1909–13; García Chávez 2004

TEXCOCO

Texcoco (also spelled Tetzcoco) was the capital of the Acolhua empire and one of the three imperial capitals of the Triple Alliance empire. The Chichimec dynasty was moved from Tenayuca to Texcoco ("On the alabaster pot"), near the eastern shore of Lake Texcoco, by Xolotl's descendant Quinatzin. A later ruler of this dynasty, Nezahualcoyotl, was one of the most accomplished and celebrated of the Aztec kings. Nezahualcoyotl's descendant, the chronicler Fernando de Alva Ixtlilxochitl, recorded his life story soon after the Spanish conquest. Nezahualcoyotl and his son, Nezahualpilli, conquered many towns throughout central Mexico. Nezahualcoyotl was famed as a statesman, soldier, builder, poet, scholar, astronomer, and lawgiver. He built much of the city of Texcoco, including a large and luxurious royal palace compound whose ruins were described by Alva Ixtlilxochitl about 1600.

The Archaeological Site

The Aztec city of Texcoco today lies buried under the modern city of the same name. An archaeological zone known as Los Melones ("The melons")

Figure 2.5. Early structure in Texcoco at the archaeological zone of Los Melones.
These mostly unexcavated mounds are all that remain of the Acolhua imperial capital.
Photograph courtesy of Jeffrey R. Parsons.

in Texcoco protects the remains of several large structures (fig. 2.5), but these
have not been excavated in detail. Earlier structures of adobe brick, shown
in figure 2.5, were followed by later structures built of stone and rubble. A
ballcourt ring and several stone sculptures have been recovered from the
area of Los Melones.

Urban Features

Fernando de Alva Ixtlilxochitl, who saw the ruins of the palace of his ancestor
Nezahualcoyotl and studied the surviving pictorial histories from Texcoco,
is one of the best sources of information about the ancient city. The palace
had living quarters for the king and royal family, servants' quarters, a throne
room, chambers for judges and officials, halls for warriors, historians, poets,
and scientists, and storehouses for weapons and tribute. He also listed gardens, temples, a ballcourt, a zoo, and a market, suggesting that part of his
description pertained not just to the royal palace but also to the entire urban
epicenter.

Nezahualcoyotl is said to have engineered a modification of the central
pyramid of the city from a temple dedicated to the god Tezcatlipoca to a
double-temple pyramid dedicated to Tlaloc and Huitzilpochtli (to match the
temple of Tenochtitlan); he then constructed a new temple to Tezcatlipoca.

If historical sources are correct, the central temple of Texcoco was slightly larger than that of Tenochtitlan (see chapter 4).

It has been estimated that Aztec period Texcoco covered 4.5 square kilometers and had a population of 25,000.

Illustrations: figs. 1.4, 2.5
References: Alva Ixtlilxochitl 1975–77; Lesbre 1998; Noguera 1972; Offner 1983; Parsons 1971

OTHER CITIES IN THE BASIN OF MEXICO

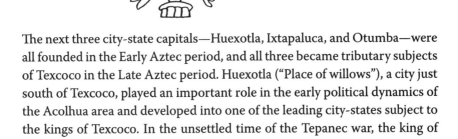

HUEXOTLA

The next three city-state capitals—Huexotla, Ixtapaluca, and Otumba—were all founded in the Early Aztec period, and all three became tributary subjects of Texcoco in the Late Aztec period. Huexotla ("Place of willows"), a city just south of Texcoco, played an important role in the early political dynamics of the Acolhua area and developed into one of the leading city-states subject to the kings of Texcoco. In the unsettled time of the Tepanec war, the king of Huexotla tried unsuccessfully to take over the Acolhua rulership from Texcoco.

The Archaeological Site

Huexotla is one of the few Aztec cities that have been the target of archaeological fieldwork from both the monumental and the residential approaches. Leopoldo Batres excavated and restored a number of structures in 1904, and additional work on the public architecture is described in a 1987 report. The reconstructed buildings today form the core of the official archaeological zone and include several rectangular platforms (fig. 2.6), a segment of a massive stone wall, and a circular temple located some distance to the south of the other structures (fig. 5.2)

In the 1970s Elizabeth Brumfiel carried out a program of intensive surface collections at Huexotla. By estimating the proportions of artifacts in different parts of the site, she was able to reconstruct aspects of domestic activities, including food preparation and craft production, and how they varied by urban sector and through time. One of her more interesting results is that,

Figure 2.6. Platform known as La Comunidad in Huexotla. Photograph by the author.

apart from textile production, almost no craft production was carried out at Huexotla. It appears that city-states in the center of the Basin of Mexico devoted most of their economic efforts to agriculture in order to feed growing urban populations, particularly in the imperial capitals.

Urban Features

Some of the excavated structures at Huexotla are unusual for Aztec sites. What appears to be the major temple is a modest single-stair pyramid facing west called La Estancia. Just behind this (to the east) is a large platform with an enigmatic series of rectangular rooms and passages (fig. 2.6). This building, today called La Comunidad, may have been the royal palace of Huexotla. Across the Río San Bernardino, south of these structures, is a complex of structures known as Santa María Grande, and even farther to the south is a fairly standard circular temple associated with a number of small shrines.

One of the most impressive urban features at Huexotla is a massive stone wall segment that runs north-south some 100 meters west of the main temples (fig. 5.2). Most scholars assume that this is the remnant of a wall that once encircled the entire epicenter of the city, much like the wall surrounding the Sacred Precinct at Tenochtitlan. No other traces of this wall survive, however, which makes me hesitant to accept this interpretation.

Illustrations: figs. 2.6, 4.3, 5.2
References: Batres 1904; Brumfiel 1980; García García 1987

IXTAPALUCA / ACOZAC

Ixtapaluca (also spelled Iztapalocan) was another polity within the Acolhua realm, subject to the kings of Texcoco. Iztapalocan means "On the hill of stone slabs." No ancient town glyph survives (Ixtapaluca is not listed in the *Codex Mendoza*), but scholars invented the glyph shown here in the 1970s so that the modern town would have an indigenous-looking toponym. Ixtapaluca had a king at the turn of the fifteenth century, but self-rule was ended in 1418, when the town was conquered by Tezozomoc of Azcapotzalco. After the Tepanec war, control of Ixtapaluca passed to Texcoco, and at the time of the Spanish conquest Ixtapaluca was ruled by nobles subject to the Acolhua king; there was no local king. Not much more is known of the city from documentary sources. This is one of the few Aztec city-state capitals that is relatively well known archaeologically, however.

The Archaeological Site

For an Aztec city-state capital in the Basin of Mexico, Ixtapaluca was in quite good shape until the late twentieth century. In the 1960s H. B. Nicholson and David Grove conducted test excavations at the main ballcourt in the urban epicenter, and Richard Blanton mapped numerous house foundations from residential districts at the site, which was known as Ixtapaluca Viejo (fig. 6.2). In the 1970s builders selected the area (supposedly without recognizing it as an archaeological site) for a large residential subdivision called the Acozac Sports and Residential Complex. When bulldozers cut a large mound (the likely royal palace) in half, archaeologists were called in. Eduardo Contreras excavated and restored several temples and altars in addition to the surviving portion of the palace. The largest mound, probably the remains of the principal temple of the city, was not excavated or restored (fig. 2.7). This structure gives a good idea of the look of an Aztec temple mound that has been cleared

Figure 2.7. Unreconstructed main pyramid in Ixtapaluca. This site is also known as Acozac. Photograph by the author.

of vegetation but not excavated except at the base. The archaeological zone, known as Acozac ("In the yellow water"), survives today. In the 1980s additional fieldwork was undertaken at the site by Jürgen Brüggemann.

Urban Features

Ixtapaluca is one of the few Aztec sites whose residences have been mapped (fig. 6.2), revealing an unplanned arrangement of houses spread out along two sloping ridges. The restored epicenter (the Acozac archaeological zone) has good examples of most of the major types of public architecture, including a single-stair pyramid, a ballcourt, part of a palace, and a series of small shrines. The arrangement of these buildings is unusual, however (see chapter 5), and the surviving buildings may represent only a portion of the urban epicenter.

Illustrations: figs. 2.7, 4.3, 4.5, 5.2
References: Blanton 1972; Brüggemann 1987; Contreras Sánchez 1976; Nicholson 2005

OTUMBA

Otumba was a city-state in the Teotihuacan Valley subject to Texcoco. The Aztec name for Otumba, Otompan, means "On the Otomi." The Otomi were the most numerous non-Nahuatl ethnic group in Aztec period central Mexico. A place called Otompan figures prominently in the Toltec period native history of central Mexico; one source claims that the Toltec empire was based on an alliance of Tollan (Tula), Culhuacan, and Otompan. Apart from questions about the reliability of native history for such early periods (see chapter 1), such passages may refer to an unspecified Otomi polity, not necessarily the town of Otumba.

The Archaeological Site

No monumental architecture survives at Otumba today. A large low hill in the center of the site probably marks the location of the urban epicenter, but public buildings have not survived as discrete individual mounds or structures, and none have been excavated. But what Otumba lacks in monumental architecture is more than made up for by the artifactual remains on the surface of the site today. Most of the Aztec city is located in cultivated fields, with only a small part covered by the modern town of Otumba. A program of systematic, intensive surface collections, combined with test excavations, was directed by Thomas Charlton, Deborah Nichols, and Cynthia Otis Charlton. Their most significant findings concern the organization of craft production at the site. Otumba has produced the most extensive, and best-documented, craft industries of any Aztec site.

Urban Features

The surface collections of the Otumba project provide evidence for a wide variety of craft industries, which have varied spatial distributions across the city (fig. 2.8). The major craft industry at Otumba was the production of tools from obsidian. Individual workshops (most likely attached to people's homes) specialized in the production of specific types of tools, with prismatic blade production most common in the city and biface production in rural workshops. Obsidian was also turned into several types of jewelry, including lip plugs, ear spools, beads, and pendants. Ceramic workshops produced

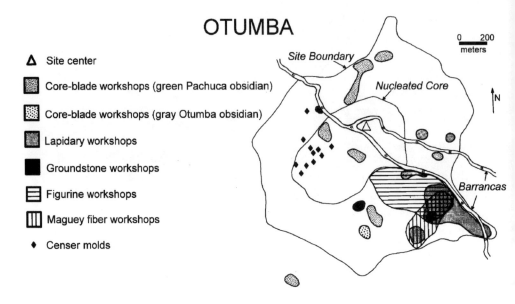

OTUMBA

Δ   Site center

Core-blade workshops (green Pachuca obsidian)

Core-blade workshops (gray Otumba obsidian)

Lapidary workshops

Groundstone workshops

Figurine workshops

Maguey fiber workshops

♦   Censer molds

Site Boundary

Nucleated Core

0   200
meters

↑N

Barrancas

Figure 2.8. Map of Otumba showing the spatial extent of the city and distribution of craft industries. (After Otis Charlton 1994: fig. 8.1; reproduced with permission.)

figurines, incense burners, and various other small objects. Cotton textiles were produced on a household basis throughout the city (as at all other Aztec sites), but textiles of the coarser maguey fiber were produced only in a few workshop areas. This rich evidence for craft production at Otumba is discussed further in chapter 7.

Illustrations: fig. 2.8
References: Charlton, Nichols, and Charlton 1991, 2000; Evans 2001b; Nichols, McLaughlin, and Benton 2000

XALTOCAN

Tenochtitlan and Tlatelolco were not the only Aztec cities located on islands. Xaltocan ("Place of the sand-spider") was an ancient town of Otomi speakers founded on an island in the northern, salty portion of the Basin of Mexico lake system. Its *tlatoani* (king) was deposed when the town was conquered by the Triple Alliance, and thereafter it was ruled by officials of the Acolhua state based in Texcoco. No public architecture survives, but test excavations and surface collections by Elizabeth Brumfiel contribute to our knowledge of economic and social patterns in Aztec cities. Starting with the founding of the town, the people of Xaltocan exploited lacustrine resources such as fish and waterfowl. In order to grow maize they built chinampa fields around the island, but for water they had to bring fresh water across the salty lake on a long aqueduct. As at other Aztec settlements, textile production was extensive, and in some periods obsidian tools were produced. Like Yautepec and Cuexcomate in Morelos (see below), Xaltocan yielded evidence of extensive commercial ties with other areas, and a decline in standards of living after conquest by the Triple Alliance empire.

Illustrations: none
References: Brumfiel 2005

CHICONAUTLA

Chiconautla was a city-state capital located near the edge of Lake Texcoco at the entrance to the Teotihuacan Valley. Its tlatoani was subject to the kings of Texcoco. Historical records suggested that it served as a point of transshipment for commerce between the imperial capitals and points to the east and northeast. In the 1930s George Vaillant excavated a modest palace at Chiconautla, but he never published his results. Christina Elson returned to Vaillant's notes and collections and has published a description of the palace structure (Elson 1999). It is likely that this was the residence of a middle- to high-ranking noble, but not the tlatoani.

Illustrations: none
References: Elson 1999

MEXICALTZINCO

Mexicaltzinco ("On the small place of the Mexica") was a small city located immediately south of Tenochtitlan across the southern causeway. Like Chiconautla, this city served as a transshipment point for commerce with Tenochtitlan. There were chinampas in Mexicaltzinco, and some of its residents made a living making salt. Chroniclers mention major temples in Mexicaltzinco (see chapter 4). Several structures have been excavated in salvage projects. A large house compound, with stone wall foundations and remains of adobe bricks, contained two sweat baths and a dock along a canal. The courtyard contained a rich deposit of several hundred ceramic vessels and other goods that may have been a termination offering for the structure. This is one of the few urban houses excavated at an Aztec site in the Basin of Mexico. Excavations in the modern churchyard uncovered a large circular altar and rectangular altar of some sort.

Illustrations: fig. 6.3
References: Ávila López 2006; Ávila López and Beutelspacher 1989; Blanton 1972: 156–159; Matos Moctezuma 1967

CITIES IN MORELOS

THE PALACIO DE CORTÉS SITE

We now move out of the Basin of Mexico to consider several Aztec cities in what is today the Mexican state of Morelos. After completing the conquest of Mexico, Hernando Cortés built himself a large, fortress-like residence in the city of Cuernavaca (the Spaniards' pronunciation of "Cuauhnahuac"). He chose as a location the site of the *tecpan* (palace) of the tlatoani of Cuauhnahuac. Cortés tore down the old structure and built his residence over the original foundations. In the 1970s the Palacio de Cortés was renovated and turned into a museum, the Museo Cuauhnahuac. During renovations, traces of the Late Aztec palace were encountered, and several Aztec period rooms, shrines, and other features were left intact for museum visitors to see.

Figure 2.9. The Palacio de Cortés site in modern Cuernavaca. The long stairs under the Spanish colonial building are from the Late Aztec palace of the king of Cuauhnahuac. Photograph by the author.

In front of the building the old steps of the Aztec tecpan can still be seen under the foundation of the Palacio de Cortés (fig. 2.9). This excavation was important for two reasons. First, it furnished stratigraphic evidence for the construction of the Late Aztec palace over an Early Aztec residential deposit related to the Teopanzolco site (see above). This is one of the few examples of a city whose epicenter was moved during Aztec times. Second, the features shown in figure 2.9 illustrate graphically the reason for the existence of so few Aztec urban epicenters today: Many were destroyed or covered over as the Spaniards built their new colonial society literally over the ruins of Aztec cities.

Illustrations: fig. 2.9
References: Angulo Villaseñor 1979; Smith 2008: ch.2

COATETELCO

Coatetelco ("Serpent on the mound") is an archaeological zone located in the modern town of the same name in the western part of Morelos (fig. 2.1). The preserved urban epicenter provides one of the best examples of a standard Aztec urban layout known as the Tula plaza plan (fig. 1.1), yet Coatetelco does not appear in documentary sources. It is in fact one of the few Aztec cities not mentioned as an altepetl capital in the historical record. One possibility for this situation is that Coatetelco was a city-state in the first part of the Late Aztec period but was conquered and stripped of its kingship before the Spanish conquest. If so, the most likely culprits are the Triple Alliance empire and the Cuauhnahuac conquest state. All of the city-states around Coatetelco were subject to the king of Cuauhnahuac, and the inhabitants of this town almost certainly also paid tribute to Cuauhnahuac.

The Archaeological Site

Raúl Arana excavated the urban epicenter of Coatetelco in the 1970s and restored most of the major structures. These include a modest single-stair pyramid (fig. 4.1), a ballcourt with numerous associated offerings (fig. 2.10), and a number of shrines and platforms, all grouped around a public plaza. Arana also excavated test pits that revealed occupation in both the Early and Late Aztec periods. I analyzed the ceramics from Arana's excavations and worked out the chronology of the site.

Urban Features

The ballcourt at Coatetelco is one of the few Aztec ballcourts to be excavated. Under the main stairway of the western platform Arana encountered a series of elite burials with hundreds of grave goods, including ceramic vessels, obsidian, greenstone beads, and bronze objects. Miniature plain jars and polished red cups for drinking pulque were the predominant kinds of ceramic vessel in these offerings. An enigmatic, carefully stacked pile of manos (basalt tools for grinding maize on a metate) was found adjacent to the ballcourt. Five small shrines were built on the plaza side of the ballcourt. A stone sculpture of Xipe Totec (the flayed-skin god) had been placed as an offering next to the circular shrine. Artifacts from Arana's test pits suggest that the social and economic conditions of the people of Coatetelco were similar to those at other settlements in western Morelos, such as Cuexcomate and Capilco (see below).

Figure 2.10. Ballcourt at Coatetelco. Photograph by the author.

Illustrations: figs. 1.1, 2.10, 3.5, 4.1
References: Angulo Villaseñor 1984; Arana Álvarez 1984; Smith 2008

COATLAN

Coatlan ("Where there are many snakes") was a city-state subject to the king of Cuauhnahuac, but unlike Coatetelco, Coatlan appears in the standard written sources such as the *Codex Mendoza* and various early colonial accounts. After the Spanish conquest, the town of Coatlan was moved across a river to be closer to colonial period roads. This left the ruins of the Aztec town, called Coatlan Viejo today, intact in what became the cultivated fields of the modern town. Roger Mason conducted a program of intensive surface collections at the site in the 1970s. His results were similar to Brumfiel's findings at Huexotla (see above) in that he found evidence for textile production in all parts of the site, but no other craft activities could be identified. None of the public architecture has been excavated, but the configuration of mounds appears to conform to the Tula plaza plan (see chapters 3 and 5). Coatlan Viejo was occupied in both the Early and Late Aztec periods.

Illustrations: fig. 3.5
References: Mason 1980a

CUENTEPEC

Cuentepec ("On the furrowed hill") was a city-state subject to the king of Cuauhnahuac; the inhabitants of Cuexcomate and Capilco (see below) may have been subject to the king of Cuentepec. Little is known of the political history of the polity, but the archaeological site survives today in a remote part of the state of Morelos. Osvaldo Sterpone and I made a sketch map of the epicenter in 1988 (see fig. 3.5), but no systematic fieldwork has been done at the site. The layout resembles that of Coatetelco, with a tall pyramid and a ballcourt flanking the public plaza. There is a palace structure on the south side of the plaza, similar in layout to the Cuexcomate palace but larger. After the Spanish conquest the settlement of Cuentepec was moved twice. First the city center was moved several kilometers to the south and a Christian chapel was built, and then the settlement was reestablished across a deep ravine in a location more accessible to roads.

Illustrations: fig. 3.5
References: Smith 1992

YAUTEPEC

Yautepec ("On the hill of the *yauhtli* flower") was a powerful city-state capital located in central Morelos. There were some 50 individual city-states within the area that is now Morelos, and most of them were subject to one of several powerful regional states, which were in turn subject to the Triple Alliance empire. Cuauhnahuac was the largest of the regional states, and city-states such as Coatlan and Cuentepec were subject to the king of Cuauhnahuac. Yautepec was another of the regional states, and five or six city-states in the Yautepec River Valley were subject to the king of Yautepec.

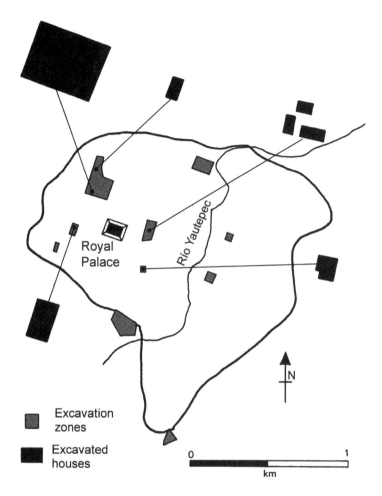

Figure 2.11. Map of Yautepec showing excavation areas and excavated houses. The houses are drawn at a common scale; the largest measures 23 by 18.5 meters.

The Archaeological Site

The site of Yautepec lies under the modern town of the same name. The central feature, protected in an archaeological zone today, is a large, low platform nearly 7,000 square meters in size. This structure, the palace of the kings of Yautepec, was partially excavated by Hortensia de Vega Nova. In the 1990s I directed a project of mapping and excavation in Yautepec. Through surface survey we identified the boundaries of the Aztec city under the modern town. We then conducted excavations in 14 places throughout Yautepec (fig. 2.11), revealing several commoner houses and an elite compound.

Urban Features

The royal palace is the only example of public architecture excavated at Yaute-pec, and it was only partially cleared. The main value of Yautepec for under-standing Aztec urbanism comes from the residential excavations. As one of the only Aztec urban centers with extensive household excavations, Yautepec provides information on urban life at a major Aztec city. Craft activities were widespread at Yautepec, but at much lower levels than at Otumba. Residen-tial patterns—from house architecture to population density to domestic activities as revealed by the artifacts—were remarkably similar to patterns at the smaller sites of Cuexcomate and Capilco. These data are discussed further in chapter 6.

Illustrations: figs. 2.11, 6.3
References: de Vega Nova and Mayer Guala 1991; Smith n.d.a; Smith et al. 1994; Smith, Heath-Smith, and Montiel 1999

CITIES IN OTHER VALLEYS

 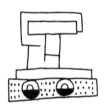

CALIXTLAHUACA

Calixtlahuaca ("Place of the plain of houses") is an archaeological zone just north of the modern city of Toluca, to the west of the Basin of Mexico. A second possible toponym—a circle with a turkey or other bird—is found on relief sculptures at the site and may relate to the original name of the site or its dynasty. Prior to Mexica conquest of the area in 1478, the city, a power-ful regional capital, was known as Matlatzinco ("Place of the Matlatzinca"). It was either subject to or allied with the Tepanec empire. After the Mexica conquest the city was stripped of its dynasty. The city of Tollocan (Toluca) was selected as the Triple Alliance provincial capital and Calixtlahuaca was demoted to a tribute-paying town under Tollocan. This region was multilin-gual in Aztec times, with numerous speakers of the Nahuatl, Matlatzinca, Otomi, and Mazahua languages. The Toluca Valley formed a buffer zone be-tween the Triple Alliance and the Tarascan empires, and the motivation for the Mexica conquest of the region was to stop Tarascan expansion.

The Archaeological Site

The archaeological site of Calixtlahuaca covers the sides and top of Cerro Tenismo, a small volcano (fig. 2.12). It was first excavated in the 1930s by José García Payón, who uncovered and restored a number of large buildings. The most notable structure is a circular pyramid (fig. 2.13) which contained a buried offering of a life-sized sculpture of a priest impersonating Ehecatl, the wind god. A stone sacrificial altar was excavated next to the stairs at the base of the temple. Other public structures at the site include a large royal palace

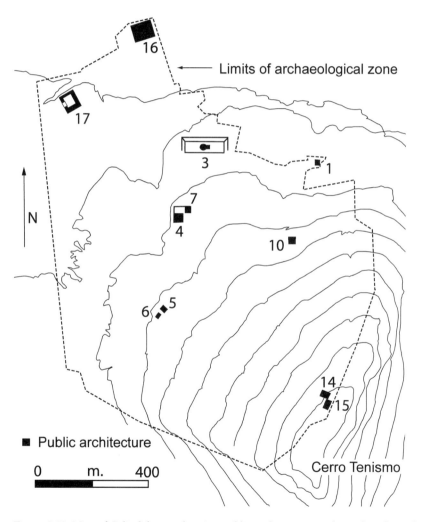

Figure 2.12. Map of Calixtlahuaca showing public architecture in the archaeological zone.

Figure 2.13. Circular temple in Calixtlahuaca. Photograph by the author.

and several small temples and altars. García Payón also excavated a series of burials with rich offerings, and a number of stone sculptures and reliefs in both the imperial Mexica style and a local style. In 2006 a crew from Arizona State University under my direction remapped Calixtlahuaca, and in 2007 we excavated a number of houses and terraces at the site.

Urban Features

Calixtlahuaca provides some of the best preserved examples of Aztec urban public architecture, including the circular temple, the palace, and several of the smaller temples. Although these buildings are not dated as securely as one would like, they most likely were built prior to the Mexica conquest of the site. This suggests that the widespread distribution of Aztec architectural forms and styles throughout central Mexico occurred long before the expansion of the Triple Alliance empire. Although the buildings at Calixtlahuaca closely resemble examples from the Basin of Mexico, their organization and layout differ greatly from other Aztec cities. Instead of being concentrated in an urban epicenter, these structures are scattered throughout the city, mostly on the hillside, with little clear indication of a central plan.

In contrast to the similarities between the site's public buildings and those at other Aztec sites, the houses uncovered in my recent excavations are quite distinctive. All were built on terraces constructed on the slopes of Cerro Tenismo. Several have finely made exterior stone pavements, and all houses—commoner and elite—had well-constructed wall foundations of cut stones. More care was put into residential stonework at Calixtlahuaca than at the other sites discussed in this book.

Illustrations: figs. 2.12, 2.13, 4.3, 4.9, 8.1
References: García Payón 1979, 1981; Smith et al. 2007; Smith et al. 2003

CHOLULA

Cholula ("Place of gushing water") is located east of the Basin of Mexico, near the city of Puebla. Unlike most Aztec cities, Cholula was an ancient urban center with a significant pre-Aztec occupation. Its Classic period pyramid was the largest pyramid ever built in ancient Mesoamerica. Today a large Christian church sits atop this "Great Pyramid," which looks like a mountain. Indeed, the Aztec name of that pyramid, which was in ruins at the time, was Tlachihualtepetl, or "Manmade Mountain."

During the Aztec period, Cholula was renowned in at least three ways. First, it was an ancient holy center, home of one of the major cults of Quetzal-coatl. Spanish conquerors reported hundreds of temples in Cholula, which was a major pilgrimage destination in Aztec times. Second, Cholula was a revered seat of legitimate Toltec-derived political authority. Indeed, it is sometimes called "Tollan-Chololan" in the sources, and one of Cholula's several place glyphs (see above) includes the reeds that designate Tollan. Kings from many parts of central Mexico came to Cholula to have their authority validated, typically by having their nose pierced ceremonially by a priest of Quetzalcoatl. Cholula's third claim to fame was its role as an important economic center. Its markets and merchants were known over large areas, and its elaborately painted polychrome pottery was the finest in all of Late Postclassic Mesoamerica. According to Spanish conquerors, Motecuhzoma would only use Cholula polychrome serving dishes for his meals. In the Late Aztec period, Cholula was one of a group of allied city-states that success-fully resisted conquest by the Triple Alliance; others include Tlaxcala and Huexotzinco.

The Archaeological Site

The Great Pyramid of Cholula, and much of the ceremonial architecture excavated near the pyramid, date to the Classic and Early Postclassic periods.
By Aztec times the Great Pyramid was in ruins, although the immediate area
was the setting for some temples and burials. One Postclassic feature, called
the "Altar de craneos," was one of the earliest examples of a tzitzimime platform to be excavated (chapter 4). Excavations in other parts of the modern
city of Cholula have uncovered residential structures and other features from
Aztec times, but little survives of the urban center of the Aztec period city. It
has been estimated that the Aztec city covered up to eight square kilometers
and had a total population of 30,000 to 50,000.

Urban Features

The lack of archaeological data on Aztec period Cholula is made up for by
the existence of a remarkable map of its urban epicenter. Cholula is the only
Aztec city outside of Tenochtitlan whose urban layout is depicted in codices. The *Historia Tolteca-Chichimeca,* a pictorial codex that describes Postclassic political and social dynamics in the Puebla/Tlaxcala area, contains a
two-page color map of Cholula's epicenter (fig. 2.14). Several historical codices from Cuauhtinchan, a town south of Cholula (the so-called *Mapas de
Cuauhtinchan*), also depict the major temples and palaces of Cholula. The
elaborate map in the *Historia Tolteca-Chichimeca* shows the main plaza of
Cholula as it looked at the time of Spanish conquest (my interpretation of
this map is based upon Lind n.d.). Following Aztec conventions, east is to
the top in this map. The plaza was dominated by the ornate Temple of Quetzalcoatl on the left (north) side. South of this are two facing buildings that
served as offices or temples of the two head priests of the Quetzalcoatl cult.
In the southwest (lower right) corner is a large building labeled a *calmecac,*
or school, which faces a semicircular courtyard. In front of the calmecac is a
circular altar labeled the *iztaczollin,* or "white quail."

The image in the upper right of the plaza, a hill sign with a frog on top,
is the glyph for Tlachihualtepetl (the Great Pyramid), suggesting that this
ruined building was still venerated as a sacred place within the Aztec period
urban center. In the middle of the west (bottom) side of the map is a long
council hall with the six nobles who formed the governing council of the
Cholula altepetl. The short sides of the plaza are composed of a series of
rectangles with temples, people, and name glyphs. These appear to represent
the original Nahua social groups who settled Cholula in the twelfth or thirteenth century. The east (top) edge of the plaza is formed by six palaces of

Figure 2.14. Colonial period map of the epicenter of Cholula from the *Historia Tolteca-Chichimeca*. (After Kirchhoff, Odena Güemes, and Reyes García 1976: 26v–27r.)

nobles. One of the *Mapas de Cuauhtinchan* shows a large walled enclosure just north of the Cholula plaza where the Quetzalcoatl priests performed the ceremonial piercing of the nose to legitimize visiting kings.

Illustrations: fig. 2.14
References: Lind n.d.; McCafferty 1996; Noguera 1937; Reyes García 1977

ZULTEPEC

Zultepec ("On the hill of quail") is an archaeological site located in the Mexican state of Tlaxcala, north of Cholula. Zultepec was part of the large and complex city-state of Tlaxcalla, an ally of Cholula in the successful resistance of conquest by the Triple Alliance. Nothing is known of the political status or dynamics of ancient Zultepec. Part of the urban epicenter of Zultepec was excavated by Enrique Martínez Vargas and Ana María Jarquín Pacheco, revealing a circular temple, a large residential compound (perhaps a palace), and several altars and shrines. The most spectacular find was an offering of human skulls—belonging to Spaniards and their Indian allies captured during the Spanish conquest—each with a large perforation on the sides for hanging on the poles of a skull rack, or *tzompantli*.

The architecture at Zultepec is important for the same reason as the Calixtlahuaca architecture: It shows that typical Aztec forms and styles had a broad distribution within central Mexico, including cities in the enemy state of Tlaxcala.

Illustration: fig 5.1
References: Martínez Vargas 1993, 2003; Martínez Vargas and Jarquín Pacheco 1998

SMALL TOWNS

Small towns are important for our understanding of Aztec city-state capitals in two ways. First, some of these, such as Santa Cecelia Acatitlan and Cuexcomate, furnish good examples of architectural forms common in Aztec cities. Second, such settlements provide part of the regional context for Aztec city-state capitals and help highlight the urban characteristics of Aztec cities (this theme is explored further in chapter 7). This section describes three residential settlements that were not city-state capitals (Santa Cecelia Acatitlan, Cihuatecpan, and Cuexcomate); four mountaintop shrines (Cerro Tlaloc, Huixachtecatl, Malinalco, and Tepozteco) are then described in the next section.

SANTA CECILIA ACATITLAN

A small twin-temple pyramid is located at Santa Cecilia Acatitlan, just two kilometers north of Tenayuca. As one of only five such temples known today (the others are in Tenayuca, Teopanzolco, Tenochtitlan, and Tlatelolco), this is an important architectural feature. The structure was first excavated by José Reygadas Vértiz in the 1920s (fig. 2.15). Later, Eduardo Pareyon conducted more excavations in the 1960s and restored the two temples at different architectural stages (fig. 2.16). The southern temple, on the right, was rebuilt all the way up to the roof. The temple had deteriorated completely (fig. 2.15), and Pareyon made a fanciful reconstruction based upon images in the codices. The northern temple, in contrast, was excavated more fully and restored to an earlier construction stage. Visitors to the site today are

Figure 2.15. Excavations of the twin-temple pyramid at Santa Cecilia Acatitlan during the 1920s. Photograph courtesy of the Getty Research Institute.

Figure 2.16. Restored twin-temple pyramid at Santa Cecilia Acatitlan in 2005. This reconstruction shows two construction stages: (*left*) the earlier and smaller stage of the north temple, and (*right*) the later, larger stage of the south temple. Photograph by the author.

sometimes confused and interpret this structure as a single-temple pyramid with a small platform attached on the north side instead of a twin-temple pyramid reconstructed to two different stages. The outline of the foundation of the later stage north temple can be seen clearly in figure 2.16, however. Several low platforms survive in front of the temple. Unfortunately, neither excavation was adequately published.

Illustrations: figs. 2.15, 2.16
References: Pareyon Moreno 1972; Reygadas Vértiz 1928

CIHUATECPAN

Cihuatecpan ("Woman palace") was a large village or town that was probably part of the Otumba city-state (see above). Excavations by Susan Evans provide evidence for the nature of Aztec houses and domestic activities in this area. Because so few Aztec urban houses have been excavated, particularly in the Basin of Mexico, the Cihuatecpan structures help illuminate patterns of Aztec urban life. In contrast to the small, one-room houses at sites such as

Yautepec and Cuexcomate in Morelos, many of the Cihuatecpan houses are larger, with multiple rooms. Houses like this are also known from maps in early colonial documents from Tenochtitlan/Mexico City, suggesting that the multiple-room house was the norm in Aztec cities in the Basin of Mexico. Among the structures excavated by Evans is a small tecpan, or palace. Although Evans calls Cihuatecpan a village settlement, the palace suggests at least low-level urban functions, and the settlement may be classified as a small town.

Illustrations: fig. 6.3
References: Evans 1988, 2001a

CUEXCOMATE

Cuexcomate ("Granary") is a small Aztec period town site I excavated in the 1980s. It was located approximately equidistant from three city-state capitals—Miacatlan, Acatlipa, and Cuentepec—all of which were subjects of the king of Cuauhnahuac. There is no record of this town in documentary sources. The site takes its name from a series of circular stone foundation walls that resemble the bases of traditional granaries—*cuezcomatl* in Nahuatl—still used in some rural villages in this area.

The Archaeological Site

Cuexcomate was selected for excavation because the foundations of houses were visible on the surface. Along with Ixtapaluca it is one of the few Aztec settlements whose residential zone has been mapped (see fig. 6.1). The site consists of approximately 150 houses spread out along a sloping ridge on either side of a small urban epicenter with two elite compounds (one in each of the Late Aztec–A and Late Aztec–B periods) and a small temple. The hillsides surrounding the site were covered with agricultural terraces.

Urban Features

Cuexcomate is an interesting case for contrasting definitions of urbanism. From the demographic perspective, a settlement of 800 people can hardly be called a city or an urban settlement. From the functional perspective, on the other hand, Cuexcomate has several features that suggest a limited range of regional administrative and religious functions. The site has an elite compound and a small temple, and its epicenter conforms to the Tula plaza plan found at Morelos altepetl capitals such as Teopanzolco and Coatetelco. These features suggest regional urban functions on a small scale. Cuexcomate is located in an agricultural zone far from any city-state capitals. This suggests that at the level of the city-state, the site and area functioned in a rural capacity. The houses I excavated at Cuexcomate are similar to those I later dug at Yautepec (small, one-room adobe structures), smaller and simpler than urban houses in the Basin of Mexico.

Illustrations: figs. 6.1, 6.4, 7.3
References: Smith 1992, 1993, 1994

ISOLATED TEMPLES AND RITUAL COMPOUNDS

CERRO TLALOC

The archaeological site of Cerro Tlaloc consists of a large rectangular enclosure built on the summit of Mount Tlaloc, one of the high volcanoes forming the eastern edge of the Basin of Mexico. The enclosure, roughly built of large stones carried up the mountain, measures about 50 by 60 meters. It was entered by a 150-meter-long causeway, and the interior contained rooms, walls, and other features. The chronicler Diego Durán described rituals dedicated to the Aztec rain god Tlaloc at this structure. Only limited archaeological testing has been done at Mount Tlaloc, but archaeologists have located fragments of the stone idol and many broken censers and "Tlaloc jars" (ceramic water jars decorated with images of the rain god). The enclosure may have been aligned to point to Tenochtitlan.

Illustrations: none
References: Aveni, Calnek, and Hartung 1988; Nicholson 2003a; Townsend 1992; Wicke and Horcasitas 1957

HUIXACHTEPETL
(CERRO DE LA ESTRELLA)

Huixachtepetl ("On the hill of the thorn bushes") is a mountain within the altepetl of Mexicaltzinco, close to Tenochtitlan. Known today as Cerro de la

Estrella, this hill had great symbolic importance to the Aztecs. It was here that the initial stages of the elaborate calendric renewal rite called the New Fire Ceremony took place (Elson and Smith 2001; Furst 1992). The toponym shows the temple on top of a hill, with a fire drill signaling the new fire at its base. This temple was first built in the Epiclassic period (A.D. 700–900), then rebuilt several times in the Aztec period.

Illustrations: fig. 4.2E
References: Arana Álvarez and Chacón 2006; Pérez Negrete 2002

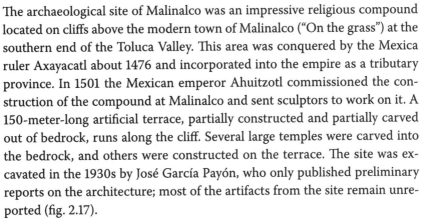

MALINALCO

The archaeological site of Malinalco was an impressive religious compound located on cliffs above the modern town of Malinalco ("On the grass") at the southern end of the Toluca Valley. This area was conquered by the Mexica ruler Axayacatl about 1476 and incorporated into the empire as a tributary province. In 1501 the Mexican emperor Ahuitzotl commissioned the construction of the compound at Malinalco and sent sculptors to work on it. A 150-meter-long artificial terrace, partially constructed and partially carved out of bedrock, runs along the cliff. Several large temples were carved into the bedrock, and others were constructed on the terrace. The site was excavated in the 1930s by José García Payón, who only published preliminary reports on the architecture; most of the artifacts from the site remain unreported (fig. 2.17).

Two impressive circular rock-cut temples dominate Malinalco. The entrance to the so-called Eagle Warrior Temple was guarded by sculptures of jaguars, and it contains massive sculptures of eagles and a jaguar on the interior. This cave-like building has been much discussed in the literature. A single-temple pyramid is the largest constructed building at the site, which also contains a small, circular temple and some low altars. An elaborately carved wood vertical drum (*huehuetl*) was found at Malinalco. This object, one of the finest examples of Aztec woodcarving known today, has images of dancing jaguars and eagles.

The symbolism and uses of the Malinalco compound have been much debated. There is clearly symbolism of warfare and the associated solar cult at the site. The dominant interpretation of the main rock-cut temple is that it

MALINALCO

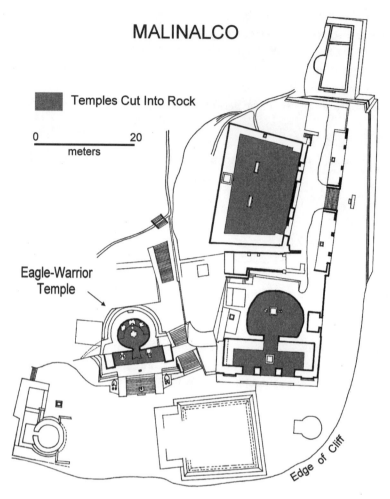

Figure 2.17. Map of the hilltop ceremonial precinct in Malinalco. (Smith 2003a: 166.)

served as a ritual precinct for elite Aztec eagle warriors, a view supported by the prominence of sculpted eagles and jaguars and a large mural of a warrior or deity procession painted in a nearby temple.

Illustration: fig. 2.17.
References: (García Payón 1947; Hernández Rivero 2004; Matos Moctezuma 1999; Noguez 2006; Townsend 1982).

TEPOZTECO

The Tepozteco site sits on top of cliffs overlooking the modern town of Tepoztlan ("Where there is much copper," site of an Aztec city of the same name). The major feature at the site is the so-called Temple of Tepozteco, a small single-temple pyramid whose excavated temple is in remarkably good shape (fig. 2.18). The inner walls are lined with carved inscriptions depicting

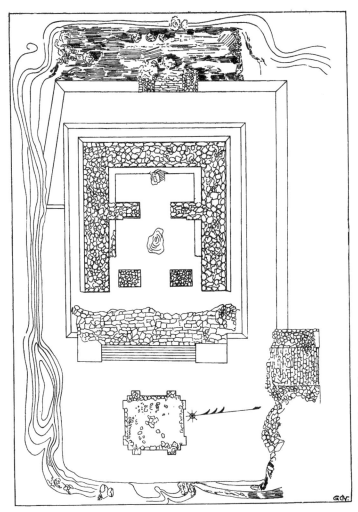

Figure 2.18. Plan of the Temple of Tepozteco in Tepoztlan. (After Ceballos Novelo 1928: 106.)

offerings and sacrifices related to the god of pulque (an alcoholic drink used by the Aztecs). A stone panel with the name glyph of the Mexica king Ahuitzotl (ruled 1486–1502) was recovered at this temple and is now on display at the National Museum of Anthropology in Mexico City. Many authors attribute construction of the temple to Ahuitzotl based on the carving, but in fact the temple was built in Early Aztec times (A.D. 1100–1350), long before Ahuitzotl was born. The Mexica king probably sponsored a rebuilding or rededication of the structure. Near the temple are some residential terraces with traces of domestic activities; these may be where priests of the temple lived. Ulysses S. Grant visited this temple in 1848 but was not impressed, stating that "it showed no particular marks of architectural taste, mechanical skill, or advanced civilization" (Grant 1999: 99).

Illustrations: fig. 2.18
References: Nicholson 1991; Seler 1993; Smith 2008

THE IMPERIAL CAPITAL

TENOCHTITLAN

If one can believe the propaganda-filled Mexica native histories, the island city of Tenochtitlan ("Place of the rock and cactus fruit") was founded in the year 2 House, or A.D. 1325. The presence of Early Aztec ceramics at the bases of many excavations suggests that there was settlement on the site before that date (see discussion in chapter 3). During the second half of their first century, the Mexica of Tenochtitlan were vassals of king Tezozomoc of Azcapotzalco. When the Triple Alliance defeated Azcapotzalco in the Tepanec war of 1428, Tenochtitlan became a powerful political capital. As the empire expanded steadily after that date, Tenochtitlan grew in power at the expense of Texcoco and Tlacopan, and by the time Cortés arrived in 1519 the Mexica island city was the preeminent urban center in Mesoamerica.

The amount of information available for Tenochtitlan, historical as well as archaeological, exceeds the quantity of data from all of the above Aztec cities combined. In this section I provide only a brief glimpse of Tenochtitlan, and for more information I refer the reader to some of the many useful books and articles published on the imperial capital.[3]

The Archaeological Site

The size and grandeur of Tenochtitlan greatly impressed two chroniclers of the Spanish conquest, Hernando Cortés and Bernal Díaz del Castillo. Díaz describes their first view of the city:

> These great towns and cues [temple pyramids] and buildings rising from the water, all made of stone, seemed like an enchanted vision from the tale of Amadis. Indeed, some of our soldiers asked whether it was not all a dream. (Díaz del Castillo 1963: 214)

A reconstruction painting of Tenochtitlan (fig. 2.19) gives an the idea of the city in 1519, although at the scale the buildings are depicted the city should be three times larger than shown in the painting. The conquerors tore down the largest pyramids and an influx of immigrants from Spain began the task of remaking Aztec Tenochtitlan into Spanish colonial Mexico City. Two major types of documentary evidence provide many details of urban form, urban life, and urban meaning in Tenochtitlan. First, the eyewitness accounts of the conquerors and the early colonial reports of the chroniclers focus on the central walled sacred precinct, its temples, and the ceremonies that took place there. Second, administrative documents illuminate many aspects of life in Tenochtitlan just before and after Spanish conquest, from the houses and

Figure 2.19. Detail from a painting of Tenochtitlan by Miguel Covarrubias in the Museo Nacional de Antropología e Historia, Mexico City. Based on the size of the buildings and sacred precinct, the city should be three times as large as painted here. Photograph by the author; reproduction authorized by the Instituto Nacional de Antropología e Historia.

fields of the farmers living along the city's edges to the wills and testaments of nobles and commoners. The presence of farmers living within the largest Mesoamerican city shows the importance of this trait as a basic feature of Mesoamerican cities.

The most spectacular and best known archaeological remains from Tenochtitlan were uncovered at the site of the main temple, the Templo Mayor, excavated starting in 1978. Scholars had long known the buried locations of the temple and its associated ceremonial buildings in the sacred precinct, but a chance discovery in 1978 revealed that the remains of the Templo Mayor were far better preserved than anyone had thought. An ongoing program of excavations and analysis has brought to light the architectural stages of the temple and a series of elaborate offerings rich in both economic and symbolic value (see chapter 5).

Long before the Templo Mayor excavations, a program of rescue excavation was initiated in Mexico City. The most extensive results have come from the expansion of the urban metro system. In one case a small circular temple was restored in the middle of the busy Pino Suárez metro station, where tens of thousands of commuters pass by daily. Unfortunately, the results of most of the rescue excavations are only available in limited-distribution technical reports.

Urban Features

The references listed below provide detailed discussions of the architecture, layout, and other urban features of Tenochtitlan. Many of the urban features of the imperial capital resembled the city-state capitals reviewed above. Tenochtitlan adopted many urban features from earlier city-state capitals (for example, twin-temple pyramids), leading to numerous similarities in architecture, urban layout, and other features. In these cases, we can use the abundant documentary evidence from the capital to illuminate other Aztec cities. For example, descriptions of skull racks or circular temples from the capital are relevant to understanding these features at other Aztec cities. On the other hand, many of the urban characteristics of Tenochtitlan were utterly unique within the Aztec empire. To mention only a few examples, it was the only Aztec city with a large walled ceremonial precinct, the only city with an orthogonal layout, and the only city whose population size and density could rival the ancient Teotihuacan. Some of these unique features were byproducts of the urban growth that accompanied imperial expansion, and others were deliberately achieved through the actions of the Mexica kings, who endeavored to create a unique and different kind of city. The historical trajectories of these urban features are discussed in chapters 5 and 8.

Illustrations: figs. 2.19, 5.3, 6.3
References: Alcocer 1935; Boone 1987; Calnek 1976, 2003; Kellogg 1995; López Luján 1994; Matos Moctezuma 1979, 1988; Novic 2006; Rojas 1986

TLATELOLCO

Tlatelolco ("On the round earth mound") was a "twin city" to Tenochtitlan, located at the northern end of the same island. Native historical sources state that Tlatelolco was founded in A.D. 1358 by a group of Mexica. There are hints in the native historical sources that Tlatelolco may have been more prominent and powerful than Tenochtitlan early on, during the period of control by Azcapotzalco. Tlatelolco's marketplace was a major source of its wealth and power. The long-distance merchants known as *pochteca* were based in Tlatelolco, and its marketplace grew into the largest in all of Mesoamerica. For the Spanish conquerors, the size and complexity of this market was one of the most remarkable features of the Aztec capital. Cortés wrote that 60,000 people attended the market daily. After a dispute between the two kings, Axayacatl of Tenochtitlan fought and defeated Moquihuix of Tlatelolco in 1473, perhaps to better control the marketplace. As part of their rewriting of history to glorify themselves, the kings of Tenochtitlan tried to eliminate references to the early power and glory of Tlatelolco (just as they did with Azcapotzalco), making it difficult to reconstruct the city's early history.

The Archaeological Site

In the 1940s excavations in Tlatelolco, now part of Mexico City, uncovered a large portion of the urban epicenter. Apparently surrounded by a wall, like Tenochtitlan, the Tlatelolco precinct was also centered on a large twin-stair pyramid. Later excavations revealed a series of very rich offerings in front of a modest circular temple. In addition to numerous other temples Tlatelolco has a large number of low platforms or shrines. One small platform was associated with a buried offering of perforated skulls like those of Zultepec; this

Figure 2.20. Tlatelolco's Plaza of the Three Cultures, where Aztec, colonial, and modern architecture coexist. Photograph by Louise Burkhart; reproduced with permission.

may have supported a skull rack. Today the reconstructed epicenter is part of the Plaza of the Three Cultures, with Aztec buildings, a colonial Spanish church, and modern high-rise apartment buildings (fig. 2.20).

Urban Features

The architecture of the Tlatelolco epicenter is well preserved and provides a good sample of Aztec urban public architecture. Many features of this precinct resemble the sacred precinct of Tenochtitlan, particularly the large twin-temple pyramid. Tlatelolco served as both an independent urban center early in its history and a neighborhood of Tenochtitlan after conquest by Axayacatl and the growing together of the two island cities.

Illustrations: fig. 2.20, 4.5, 5.4
References: González Rul 1996, 1998; Guilliem Arroyo 1999; Klaus 1999

3

The Founding of Cities and Dynasties

The beginning, as every one knows, is of supreme importance in everything,
and particularly in the founding and building of a city.
(Plutarch 1936: 8.321 a-b)

According to the native historical sources, Aztec cities were founded when a migrating ethnic group settled down, when a king established a new realm, or both. Because migrations, ethnicity, and dynasties were major components of social identity—not only in Aztec Mexico but also in many ancient states—stories of their origins are typically filled with mythological elements of dubious historical validity. Royal lineages and ethnic groups told stories about their origins and historical development, and these myths played important roles in political and cultural dynamics at the time of the Spanish conquest and on into the colonial period.

In spite of the strong ideological component of Aztec native accounts of city and polity foundations, it is possible to gain an understanding of the basic processes involved, even if the specifics of individual city foundations may never be known with much certainty. The archaeological data on settlement continuity and urban form correspond well with key aspects of the native historical patterns. Although we will never be able to document the founding of any Aztec city with the level of detail known for some city-state cultures (such as classical Greece), we can describe the overall processes quite well.

One of the key concepts in the founding of cities is the formal act of foundation, an official act of an administrative or religious nature that establishes a city as a legitimate entity. Some cities grow slowly and never experience such an act of foundation, others have formal foundations marked by ceremonies, and still others claim falsely that a foundation took place in the distant past. It is useful to distinguish formal political foundations from formal religious foundations. The former acts, such as medieval town charters (Lilley 2002: 42–74), establish a city as a legitimate social entity within a wider administrative context. Religious foundations involve ceremonies and invoke the gods to provide a supernatural sanction to the city (for example, Oudijk 2002; Rykwert 1988). Both types of formal city foundation acts are attested in Aztec native histories, most commonly, however, for the city of Tenochtitlan.

AZTEC CONCEPTS OF CITIES AND URBANISM

The indigenous Aztec view of the nature of cities and towns is difficult to reconstruct because few historical sources treat this subject directly. Nevertheless, a variety of sources suggest that, to the Aztecs, the essential features of a city were the royal palace and the temple dedicated to the cult of the patron deity. When the Mexica stopped along their migration from Aztlan to establish a town at Coatepec, they did not yet have a tlatoani or an altepetl. The chronicler Hernando de Alvarado Tezozomoc described their first actions: "The Mexicans erected their temple, the house of Huitzilopochtli, and they laid down Huitzilopochtli's ball court and constructed his skull-rack" (Sullivan 1971: 317).

When a king founded an altepetl, on the other hand, his first action was to build his palace. In describing the actions of king Toteoci Teuhctli in founding an altepetl, Chimalpahin states:

He built himself a palace at the place called Chalchiuhtepec. He brought there each division of calpolli [a social group], his vassals the Acxoteca and he also soon established their market so the Acxoteca could engage in commerce there, and a jail where people were confined. (Schroeder 1991: 125)

One of the Nahuatl terms for city, *totecuacan*, means "place of our lords" (Carrasco 1999: 16), again suggesting the importance of kings and other nobles in the native conception of the city.

Chimalpahin's failure to mention a temple in the quotation above is surprising, since numerous sources point to the importance of temples in native conceptions of cities. For example, the glyph for the conquest of a city in the *Codex Mendoza* and other pictorial sources was a burning temple. Joyce Marcus describes basic similarities among native conceptions of cities among the Aztec, Maya, Mixtec, and Zapotec peoples:

What was most important to him [a typical Mesoamerican] was the fact that he belonged to a particular region controlled by a specific native ruler, to whom he owed allegiance and tribute and from whom he received protection and civic-ceremonial leadership. And unless the ruler's city or residence had a wall around it, the boundary between it and the countryside it dominated was far less striking to the Indian then than the archaeologists today. (Marcus 1983:208)

James Lockhart (1992: 19), in discussing Nahuatl-language administrative documents, downplays the importance of cities within the altepetl, claiming that "a dominant capital city was not really compatible with the principles of altepetl organization. The notion of a city separate from the altepetl did not enter into the vocabulary in the form of any distinct word." The use of a single toponym to designate both the capital city and the entire polity is in fact quite common in city-state cultures (Hansen 1997, 2000b), and thus Lockhart's discussion of vocabulary in a certain type of document cannot be used to argue that cities lacked importance in the organization of the altepetl. Lockhart goes on to suggest (1992: 19) that words for city and town are rare in the Nahuatl-language documents he has studied, but Pedro Carrasco (1999: 16–20) identifies several Nahuatl terms for city and town.[1]

In my view, the fact that cities were not prominent institutions in the colonial period documents studied by Lockhart and his students says little about the actual status of cities and urbanism in the preconquest period. In Lockhart's model the tlatoani was merely the head of the most influential *calpolli* (see chapter 6) in an altepetl. The "capital" of the altepetl, according to Lockhart, was not a city with features distinct from other settlements but a settlement where several calpolli heads, including the tlatoani, happened to live. The idea that capital cities were not differentiated from other settlements is clearly contradicted by the archaeological evidence, however. Aztec altepetl capitals have public architecture that is not found in other settlements. They were cities whose functional and demographic characteristics differed greatly from smaller settlements (this theme is explored more fully in chapter 7).

IDENTITY POLITICS: CHICHIMECS AND TOLTECS

The Aztecs traced their origins to two very different types of ancient peoples: Chichimecs and Toltecs. The Chichimecs were fierce warrior nomads from the north. Their cultural attributes were defined in opposition to the prevailing characteristics of the Aztec peoples in the Late Postclassic period. Chichimecs wore skins rather than clothing made from cloth, hunted wild game instead of planting maize, and lived in campsites rather than permanent towns. These Chichimecs moved into central Mexico from their northern homeland and settled down. Eventually they became Aztecs by adopting

Mesoamerican traits such as cloth, maize, and settled towns. This "rags-to-riches" story was a source of ethnic pride to the Aztecs.

For purposes of ethnic pride and social identity in the Late Postclassic period, the Chichimec story had two major themes:

- Our ancestors were nomadic hunters and fierce warriors.
- Our ancestors came from elsewhere and took possession of the land.

These themes were prominent in the native historical sources on the foundations of Aztec towns and dynasties.

In most cultural traits the Toltecs were the complete opposites of the Chichimecs. Not only did the Toltecs wear clothing made from textiles, but their royal garments were the finest textiles in ancient Mesoamerica and were imitated by later Aztec kings. The Toltecs made and wore the finest and most luxurious jewelry; in fact, they were said to have invented all of the arts and crafts of ancient Mesoamerica (and the calendar as well). The Toltec capital Tula was not just a large permanent city, it had buildings made of precious stones. The Toltec kings were gods or godlike beings who ruled an immense empire with great wisdom and skill. Needless to say, most of these statements are either mythical fabrications or great exaggerations.

In terms of ethnic and dynastic identity, Aztec stories about the Toltecs had the following major themes:

- The Toltecs were settled farmers who ate maize and lived in cities.
- Our ceremonies, myths, gods, and our entire civilization came from the Toltecs.
- The legitimacy of our kings is proven by their descent from the Toltec kings.
- Our cities are re-creations of Tula.

Again, these themes play important roles in the native historical chronicles of the founding of Aztec towns and dynasties in the Early Aztec period and were an important ideological component of Aztec elite culture. I begin with the Chichimec theme.

CHICHIMECS FROM THE NORTH

The Acolhua historical codex known as the *Mapa Quinatzin* (Douglas 2003) illustrates the contrast between Chichimecs and Toltecs (fig. 3.1; see box 1).

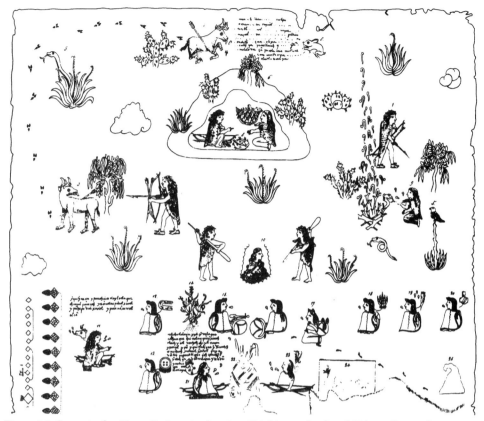

Figure 3.1. Scene in the *Mapa Quinatzin* showing Chichimecs (*top*) and Toltecs (*bottom*). Reproduction courtesy of Eduardo Douglas.

CHICHIMECS AND TOLTECS IN THE *MAPA QUINATZIN*

This image, the first of three panels that make up the *Mapa Quinatzin,* was painted in the early colonial period to illustrate the glorious heritage of the Acolhua dynasty of Texcoco. My discussion is based upon the analysis of Douglas (2003). The top half of the image shows Chichimecs: people who wear animal skins, have rough hair, live in caves, and use bows and arrows to hunt. Their desert homeland is signaled by plants such as the maguey and the nopal cactus. At the bottom are the Toltecs: people who wear cloth garments, have neat hair, grow maize, and live in cities (symbolized by the toponym for Culhuacan in the lower right). In this image, the "Toltecs" are the civilized people of the Aztec city-states, not the inhabitants of Tula.

Quinatzin (the great-grandson of the legendary Chichimec king Xolotl) is shown as an infant in the cave at the top. At lower left he is depicted in Chichimec garb as the king (sitting on the royal reed mat) in discussion with some Toltec lords. The various Toltecs with glyphs are leaders of six social groups that came together to form the six main districts of the city of Texcoco. Quinatzin was the first king of Texcoco, whose foundation was marked by the settlement of a group of Toltec migrants. For further discussion, see Douglas (2003) or Boone (2000b: 191–194).

Quinatzin, the king who moved the Acolhua capital from Tenayuca to Texcoco, begins life as a Chichimec in a cave at the top of the image and ends life as a Chichimec king ruling over Toltec nobles at the bottom of the image. This scene stresses the contrast between the Chichimec and Toltec ways of life and illustrates the process by which Chichimecs became Toltecs over time. It illustrates the first theme of the Chichimec stories, the claim that the ancestors were nomadic hunters and fierce warriors.

The second Chichimec theme, the idea that the ancestors came from elsewhere and took possession of the land, is also a common element in the native historical record. In numerous sources, altepetl were founded when migrating groups settled down. Since an altepetl could not exist without its capital city, the foundation of an altepetl must have included the foundation of its capital city. Some of the best historical information on the Aztec view of the altepetl comes from the native chronicler Chimalpahin. Susan Schroeder (1991), who has analyzed Chimalpahin's descriptions of the altepetl and other social and political institutions, notes, "In Chimalpahin's histories the establishment of an altepetl seems to be something that occurs when a migrating group becomes sedentary" (121). The most prevalent migration story in the sources, and the one with the most historiographic support, is the migration from Aztlan.

The Aztlan Migrations

One of the most widespread stories in the Aztec native historical sources describes the origins of the Aztec peoples in a place called Aztlan. There were numerous Nahuatl-speaking ethnic groups in central Mexico, and each group claimed to come from Aztlan. Sources such as the *Codex Boturini*, also called the *Tira de la Peregrinación* (1944), show eight groups setting out from Aztlan on their journey south. Such scenes typically show several groups from the Basin of Mexico (for example, the Tepaneca, Acolhua, Xochimilca, or Chalca) and several groups from the surrounding valleys (for example, the Matlatzinca, Tlahuica, Malinalca, or Huexotzinca), plus the Mexica as the final migrants. These Chichimec groups migrated south, stopping periodically for longer or shorter intervals. One of their stops was at the seven caves of Chicomoztoc. Some historical sources omit Aztlan and describe the migrations as starting at Chicomoztoc. The migrants passed the ruins of Tula, then went through the post-Tula dynastic seat of Culhuacan, and finally settled in their new territories, probably in the thirteenth century. Of the many ethnic groups to come from Aztlan, we know the details of the journey of only the Mexica of Tenochtitlan.

The Aztlan migration was the basic origin account of the Aztec peoples and thus a major source of ethnic pride. Although origin myths typically have little historical validity (Henige 1982), there are several reasons to accept the basic outlines of the Aztlan account as historically accurate. First, the Aztlan chronicle was quite widespread among the Aztec peoples of central Mexico. Second, the various versions—many only represented in very fragmentary form—show a high level of agreement (Smith 1984). Third, this account finds general support in the field of historical linguistics, which shows that the Nahuatl language originated far to the north of central Mexico and arrived in central Mexico quite late, during Classic to Early Postclassic times (Kaufman 2001). Fourth, archaeological settlement pattern data (reviewed below) suggest that the Early Postclassic to Early Aztec transition (in the twelfth century) was a time of settlement disruption and the arrival of migrants.

The Aztlan migrations form the background for Aztec urban history. In the native historical sources, most towns were founded by the newly arrived groups from Aztlan, although it is not clear whether towns were established immediately upon arrival (a form of foundation by colonization) or built after an interval of time. I review the Aztlan migrations in Smith (1984); for a more recent study of the documentary sources, see Castañeda de la Paz (2002).

Settlement Continuity

Although the archaeological remains of the Early Aztec period cannot be traced to a northern Mexican homeland, the archaeological record of settlement patterning supports the notion that a major group of migrants arrived in central Mexico at the start of the Aztec period. The key observation is the lack of continuity of occupation between time periods as calculated from the data of regional surveys. In a stable situation with little in-migration, most sites will continue to be occupied from one period to the next. When populations are growing but the proportion of continuously occupied sites is low, however, this indicates that most sites were established as new foundations, a common occurrence when migration is a significant process.

In both the Yautepec Valley (Smith 2006) and the Basin of Mexico (Parsons et al. 1983) the transitions between the Early Postclassic (Toltec) and Early Aztec periods have the lowest continuity of settlement of any time period (table 3.1). Both values are far below the average continuity for all periods. These low levels of settlement continuity at the start of the Early Aztec period contrast with much higher levels of continuity between the Early and Late Aztec periods. The higher levels suggest that once they were settled, the Nahuatl peoples had stable communities in a time of population growth.

Table 3.1. Settlement Continuity across Periods

Period	Number of Sites	Continuity with Following Period
Yautepec Valley		
Terminal Formative	50	50.0
Classic	253	24.5
Epiclassic	120	39.2
Early Postclassic	149	22.8*
Early Aztec	134	52.2
Late Aztec–A	172	76.7
Late Aztec–B	199	
Average		44.2
Basin of Mexico		
Terminal Formative	163	23.3
Early Classic	208	67.8
Late Classic	159	28.9
Epiclassic	120	38.3
Early Postclassic	421	11.6*
Early Aztec	162	87.7
Late Aztec	884	
Average		42.9

Note: "Continuity" is the percentage of sites that continue to be occupied in the following period. The Toltec to Early Aztec transition is marked with an asterisk.

The expansion of the numbers of sites between the Early and Late Aztec periods is striking (table 3.1). When site numbers are combined with site sizes to make population estimates, it becomes clear that this period witnessed one of the largest population surges in the entire pre-Columbian New World. The population of the Basin of Mexico grew from around 175,000 people in the Early Aztec period to nearly one million in the Late Aztec period (Sanders, Parsons, and Santley 1979: 184–195, 215), and similar patterns characterized other parts of central Mexico. The arrival of the Aztlan migrants contributed to the population growth, but much of the increase must have come from natural processes of demographic increase.

FOUNDATION RITUALS

The various groups of Aztlan migrants dispersed to distinct parts of the central Mexican landscape. From this point on the native historical sources focus heavily on the histories of kings and dynasties. There are few explicit references to the founding of individual cities apart from Tenochtitlan. The Aztlan stories tell how the people in a particular city-state or region settled down, and other historical accounts tell how individual dynasties and states

were founded. It is not unreasonable to infer that these two kinds of founda-
tional events—the arrival of peoples and the founding of dynasties—involved
the establishment of new towns that became the capitals of altepetl. As in the
case of the Greek poleis (city-state), it can be difficult to separate historical
descriptions of cities from descriptions of polities.

One of the most explicit images of the foundation of an Aztec town and
dynasty concerns the altepetl of Tepechpan, located in the Teotihuacan Valley. A scene in the codex known as the *Tira de Tepechpan* (Noguez 1978: pl.
2) illustrates the foundation and its associated rituals and symbolism (fig. 3.2;
see box 2).

Figure 3.2.
The founding
of Tepechpan
from the *Tira
de Tepechpan*
(Noguez 1978:
lám. 3.). Drawing
from Olko
(2005:402);
reproduced with
permission.

THE FOUNDING OF TEPECHPAN

As redrawn in figure 3.2, the codex known as the *Tira de Tepechpan* shows the
founding of the Tepechpan dynasty (and town) in the year 11 Rabbit, or A.D.
1334. This image reveals many of the common features of foundation events
in the native historical sources. The year count runs continuously along the
bottom of the image, from left to right, with a line connecting the event to
the appropriate year. The founding king of Tepechpan, Icxicuauhtli, is seated

continued

continued

on a throne (a reed seat) on top of a glyph that means stone; this sign is one of the toponyms for Tepechpan, which means "On the stone foundation." We know he was the king because of the reed mat and his royal crown or diadem. His wife, Tozquetzin, is shown above him. Behind the king is a cave with a monster mouth, a symbol for the caves of Chicomoztoc through which the Aztlan migrants passed. Behind the cave are a maguey plant and two types of cactus, symbols of the arid northern desert where the Chichimec ancestors came from.

In front of Tozquetzin is an altar with three decapitated and sacrificed animals: a butterfly, a bird, and a snake. This scene symbolizes the offerings made as part of the rituals of foundation. Behind the altar is the toponym for Culhuacan, an important stop along the migration from Aztlan and a symbol of Toltec heritage. Under the altar are five couples; the men have name glyphs. The speech scrolls indicate that these couples are talking with Icxicuauhtli. They probably represent the leading nobles in the Tepechpan city-state at the time of its founding. They serve as witnesses to the foundation sacrifices, and their presence suggests that the rule of Icxicuauhtli was legitimate and accepted by the leading families in the realm. Icxicuauhtli may be dividing the land of Tepechpan among these noble families. Stephanie Wood (1998a) has discussed the role of women in Aztec town foundations; arguing for the importance of couples in the historical codices, she notes that "countless Mesoamerican manuscripts feature men and women sitting together on landscapes, as apparent indicators of lineage, community, territory, and possibly shared rulership" (248). For further discussion of the *Tira de Tepechpan*, see Noguez (1978) and Diel (2005).

This image of the founding of Tepechpan depicts the formal political foundation of the dynasty, accompanied by ceremonies of foundation. It is reasonable to infer that these events also signaled the formal foundation of the city of Tepechpan.

Types of Foundation Rituals

The *Tira de Tepechpan* illustrates two kinds of foundation rituals: sacrifices of animals and consultation with leading nobles. These and other foundation rituals were widely practiced in ancient Mesoamerica. Michel Oudijk (2002) discusses foundation ceremonies as depicted in Aztec, Mixtec, and Zapotec sources to mark the formal taking of possession of new land. The close link between cities and states suggests that these rituals also related to the founding of new towns and cities. I have modified Oudijk's scheme slightly to describe four major types of formal foundation rituals; these are also discussed in García-Zambrano (1994) and Boone (2000a). López Austin (1994: 217–218) discusses other religious aspects of the foundations of settlements.

Shoot Arrows to the Four Directions

When the Chichimec prince Xolotl arrived in the Basin of Mexico to establish his capital at Tenayuca, he shot arrows to the four cardinal directions to signal possession of the land. As a Chichimec, he carried a bow and arrows (see also García-Zambrano 1994).

Perform Sacrifices and Other Key Ceremonies

Susan Schroeder (1991: 122) points out that in the writings of Chimalpahin, "also essential to the formation of the altepetl was each founding group's possession of a deity." One of the first acts upon founding an altepetl and its capital city was to build a shrine and make offerings to the patron god, as in the Tepechpan codex. Conch trumpets and other musical instruments were used to mark the foundation events. Mixtec codices, on the other hand, emphasize the starting of a new fire with a fire drill as the key foundation ceremony (Boone 2000a). Although there are some cases of drilling a new fire to found towns in the Aztec sources, the new fire ceremony in central Mexico was used more commonly to commemorate the completion of a 52-year calendrical cycle (Elson and Smith 2001). The Aztlan migrants carried sacred bundles on their migration (Olivier 1995), and foundation ceremonies may have involved some kind of offering related to those bundles.

Measure and Demarcate the Boundaries of the City-State

Once a dynasty and town were founded, the king sent nobles off to measure the boundaries of the polity. These survey crews walked the boundaries in a counterclockwise direction and made a list of specific boundary markers, which could be natural features such as hilltops or streams or constructed features such as piles of stones.

Several examples of setting the boundaries of city-states are provided in the codex known as the *Historia Tolteca-Chichimeca* (Kirchhoff, Güemes, and Reyes García 1976). The founding of Cuauhtinchan, a city located south of Cholula, is illustrated in figure 3.3. The town's glyph is in the center. A trail of footprints shows the arrival of its Chichimec founders—with bow and arrows—from the north (like most Aztec maps, east is at the top). A date of 8

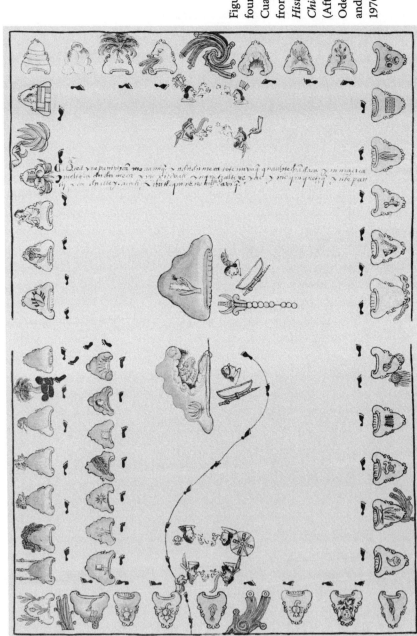

Figure 3.3. The founding of Cuauhtinchan from the *Historia Tolteca-Chichimeca.* (After Kirchhoff, Odena Güemes, and Reyes García 1976: 36r.)

Reed is given for the foundation event; Kirchhoff, Güemes, and Reyes García (1976: 18) assign a date of A.D. 1174 to this event, although this is far from a firm conclusion. The glyphs around the periphery are the polity's boundary markers. The boundaries are being measured by a survey crew of four individuals, shown consulting with one another at the left and right of the map. Two of these individuals are the high priests of Cholula, evidence of this city's important politico-religious role in regional politics. The footprints around the periphery show the course of the survey crew as they walked along the boundaries.

The delineation of territorial boundaries is common in early colonial documents. For example, in talking about the foundation of the altepetl, Chimalpahin stated that "then they established the altepetl of Amequemecan in that year and they set all the boundaries as to how they were and ruled" (Schroeder 1991: 127). As I show below, however, it is likely that this practice was a colonial period invention projected back into the pre-Hispanic past to justify territorial boundaries in the colonial period.

Divide City-State Land among Nobles

Most land in Aztec city-states was owned or controlled by nobles (Lockhart 1992). Once a dynasty and town were founded, the king had to divide up the land among the leading lords; this may be what is depicted in the Tepechpan foundation scene (fig. 3.2) and in the depiction of the foundation of Tenochtitlan in the *Codex Mendoza* (Berdan and Anawalt 1992: f. 1r). In some cases, kings who were engaged in territorial expansion sent nobles out to take possession of new lands. For example, Tezozomoc of Azcapotzalco, ruler of the Tepanec empire (see chapter 2), "installed his sons, of which he had many, as lords of the colonies [towns] that he founded" (Carta de Azcapotzalco 2000: 219).

These foundation rituals can be considered formal religious foundation acts for Aztec cities. Whether such acts really happened is uncertain, but it is clear that this kind of formal foundation act was ideologically important to the Aztecs, or at least to Aztec elite culture, at the time of Spanish conquest.

Tenochtitlan

There is far more historical information on the founding of Tenochtitlan than for any other Aztec city, and I will not repeat the details here (see Carrasco 1999a; Davies 1973; Heyden 1989; Sullivan 1971). The basic story is that the Mexica people established Tenochtitlan on an uninhabited small island in the swamp of Lake Texcoco. Their ancestors had fled into the swamp to escape a pursuing army from Culhuacan. The Mexica patron god, Huitzilopochtli, had promised them a homeland to build a city. While in the swamp the Mexica saw a sign from their god—an eagle sitting on a cactus holding a snake in its beak—and knew that they had found their homeland. They immediately built a temple to Huitzilopochtli, and soon a busy town was established. Several years later another group of Mexica founded Tlatelolco in the northern portion of the island. Heyden (1989) describes the story of the founding of Tenochtitlan, which included many supernatural components.

In Aztec historical accounts such as the *Codex Mendoza*, it is claimed that Tenochtitlan was founded in the year 2 House, or A.D. 1325. As noted in chapter 2, archaeological excavations at the Mexico City Cathedral and other locations has uncovered deposits of Early Aztec ceramics (A.D. 1100–1350) under the Late Aztec ruins of Tenochtitlan (Vega Sosa 1979). The Early Aztec material suggests that the island was occupied prior to 1325, in contrast to the accounts in Mexica native history. This implies that either the Mexica arrived on the island before 1325, or that some other group lived there before the Mexica arrived in 1325.[2] These Early Aztec deposits were heavily disturbed by later occupation, and no architecture from that period has survived.

Three types of foundation can be identified for the city of Tenochtitlan. The first is the initial settlement of the island. Although this event does not survive in native historical accounts, the Early Aztec ceramics mentioned above provide archaeological evidence for it. The second foundation is the story described in official Mexica history with the eagle and the cactus, which presumably took place in A.D. 1325. This was the formal religious foundation of the city, sanctioned by the god Huitzilopochtli and accompanied by the construction of a temple. The third foundation of Tenochtitlan was a formal political foundation as signaled by the establishment of the first legitimate (that is, Toltec-derived) Mexica dynasty with the accession of King Acamapichtli in A.D. 1372.

THE TOLTEC HERITAGE

If the Chichimec theme produced pride in the barbarian and warlike aspects of the ancestors, the Toltec theme stressed their civilized and cultured nature. The *Mapa Quinatzin* (fig. 3.1) illustrates many of the attributes of Toltecs as portrayed in the Aztec historical accounts: clothing made of woven cloth, neat hair, cultivation of maize, and life in cities. These traits comprise the first of the major Toltec themes in Aztec historical sources. One interpretation of this scene is that the act of settling down and founding cities marked the transition from Chichimec to Toltec. The other Toltec themes listed above are concerned less with the Toltecs as civilized peoples than with the Toltecs as the exalted ancestors who lived in the great ancient city of Tollan.

Toltec Greatness

Aztec nobles looked back at the Toltecs and saw a culture and a people far more advanced and civilized than any other culture, before or after. The city of Tula, or Tollan, was described as a wonderful place where everyone was wise and good and buildings were constructed of gold and jewels. This is the second major Toltec theme in the Aztec histories: Tula and the Toltecs were the originators of many key aspects of Aztec culture. It is clear that Tula and the Toltecs had strong ideological meanings to Aztec nobles, although we now know that most of the things the Aztecs claimed about the Toltecs were either wrong or greatly exaggerated. It would be absurd today to consider the Toltecs as the inventors of the calendar and the various Mesoamerican arts and crafts, since we know that these traits originated several millennia before the Toltecs. In fact, it strains credibility to think that the Aztecs themselves would have been so naïve as to believe this.[3] Instead, it makes more sense to view Aztec descriptions about the Toltecs as ideological claims, not as literal descriptions.

The third Toltec theme is the belief that the legitimacy of Aztec kings depended upon their descent from the ancient Toltec kings of Tula. Aztec rulers traced their genealogies back to the Toltecs, and legitimate descent could pass through either the male or female line (Gillespie 1989). For example, the Mexica of Tenochtitlan transformed themselves from a simple ethnic group to an altepetl when Acamapichtli, son of a Mexica noble and a princess from the Toltec dynasty at Culhuacan, took office in 1372.

For present purposes, however, it does not matter whether the Aztecs had an accurate view of Toltec accomplishments. The important points are that (1) the Aztecs venerated and celebrated all things Toltec and (2) they expended considerable effort pursuing these views of the Toltecs. This is clearest in the layout of urban epicenters.

Tollan Reborn in Aztec City Plans

There is no doubt that the Aztecs were familiar with the ruins of the city of Tula (figs. 1.5, 3.4). Sahagún states that the Mexica excavated for Toltec relics there (Sahagún 1950–82, bk.10:165). Someone in Aztec times built a small platform or shrine in front of the largest pyramid, Temple C. This feature is not shown on maps of the Toltec period city of Tula (fig. 3.4), but it is barely

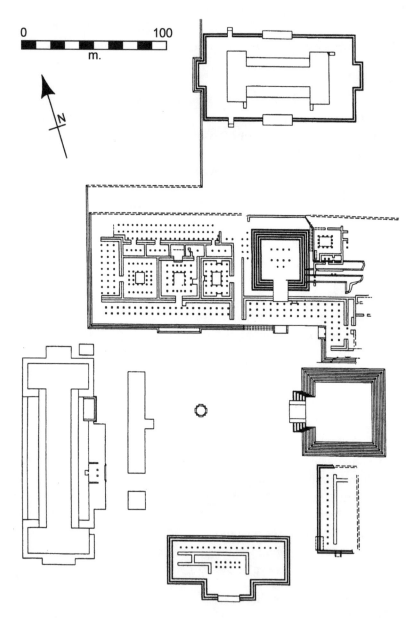

Figure 3.4. Map of the epicenter of Tula. (After Mastache, Cobean, and Healan 2002: 92.)

visible on the air photo of the site (fig. 1.5) as a low mound of rubble to the north (left) of the stairway. As discussed in chapter 4, such shrines were a fundamental component of Aztec urban planning, and if Aztec builders were going to add an architectural feature to Tula, the small platform seems a logical choice.

Additional evidence that Aztec kings were familiar with the ruins of Tula comes from the plans of several urban epicenters in Morelos (fig. 3.5). The layouts of these four altepetl capitals share the following traits with Tula:

- Buildings are arranged formally around a plaza.
- The plaza is approximately a square in shape.
- The largest temple is located on the east side of the plaza, and its stairway and entrance face the plaza.

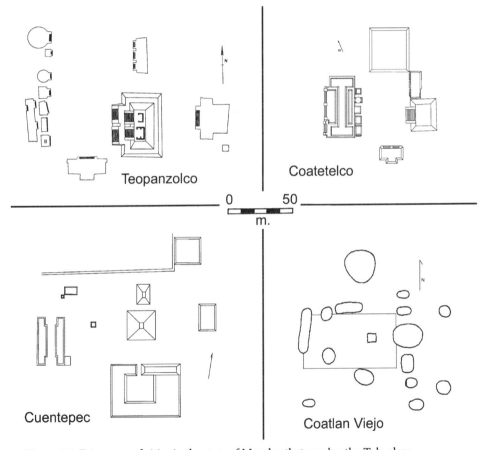

Figure 3.5. Epicenters of cities in the state of Morelos that employ the Tula plaza plan. (Sources: Teopanzolco and Coatetelco, by the author; Cuentepec, by Osvaldo Sterpone and the author; Coatlan Viejo, after Mason 1980b: 53.)

Other resemblances with Tula are shared by some but not all of the four Aztec cities. Like Tula, Coatetelco and Cuentepec both have ballcourts—oriented north-south—located on the west side of the plaza; and Coatetelco and Teopanzolco both have T-shaped buildings on the south side of the plaza. These Aztec epicenters are all smaller than Tula's epicenter, but the resemblance is clear. The layout of Coatetelco is particularly striking in comparison to Tula. Although some of the planning principles evident in figures 3.4 and 3.5 were widely shared in Mesoamerica (for example, a rectangular plaza formally defined by the largest temples), the specific layout of these cities is distinctive and does not resemble other Mesoamerican urban centers. The most logical explanation for this similarity is that the Aztec cities were laid out in imitation of Tula. I call this layout of epicenter buildings the Tula plaza plan.

It is easy to suggest why the builders of Aztec capital cities wanted to imitate the layout of Tula. Aztec kings legitimized their rule through references to their Toltec royal ancestors, and the urban layouts were a materialization of that ideological claim, supporting it with strong visual evidence. The Aztec city plans were probably established with a formal political foundation act. It is difficult, however, to suggest how this imitation came about. Did Toltec nobles or architects fleeing the destruction of Tula take up residence in the new Aztec towns? Did Aztec kings or builders travel to the ruins of Tula to study the city plan? Or perhaps the Tula city plan was preserved in painted codices that were consulted by Aztec kings or architects. The presence of Early Aztec period offerings in the middle of the central plaza at Tula suggests some sort of Aztec activity at the Toltec ruins during the period when the rulers of Teopanzolco and other Morelos cities were laying out their buildings in imitation of Tula.

One interesting aspect of this phenomenon is that the Toltec plan is found in all of the preserved Aztec epicenters in Morelos, but it is not obvious at Aztec cities in the Basin of Mexico. While cities in the latter region exhibit some of the elements of Tula's layout (see chapter 5), they show much less resemblance than the Morelos cities. Even Cuexcomate (Smith 1992), a small town in Morelos that was not the capital of an altepetl, has a modest epicenter laid out like the examples in figure 3.5 (see fig. 6.1). Were the Morelos cities founded earlier than their counterparts in the Basin of Mexico, giving them a closer historical connection to Tula? Teopanzolco was an Early Aztec city, but the public architecture at most Aztec cities (in both Morelos and the Basin of Mexico) cannot be dated precisely with current evidence. Or perhaps the Morelos city-states were less powerful and their kings felt a greater need to make public ideological statements about adherence to a Toltec ideal.

In any case, it seems clear that a number of Aztec cities in Morelos were laid out in imitation of Tula, providing visible evidence, to both Aztecs and modern observers, for the importance of the Toltec concept in the founding of Aztec cities. This is the fourth Toltec theme for the Aztecs. The construction of cities in the image of Tula can be viewed from the perspective of social memory (Fentress and Wickham 1992). Susan Alcock (2002) shows how some ancient societies memorialized earlier societies through the construction of monuments and the architectural modification of the landscape. She uses the concept of "memory theater" to refer to architectural spaces designed to invoke and celebrate specific memories of the past. Just as the Romans modified Athens and other Greek cities to evoke Classical Greek culture, so did the Aztecs design their cities to evoke the greatness of the Toltec past.

ORGANIZATION OF THE ALTEPETL

The features of the altepetl founded in the Early Aztec period can be reconstructed using historical sources from the time of the Spanish conquest. In this section I review the basic administrative structure of the altepetl and the role of territoriality in Aztec society.

Administrative Organization

An altepetl consisted of a legitimate king—the tlatoani—and a population of nobles and commoners subject to the king. In physical terms the altepetl was made up of a capital city, a series of smaller settlements (towns, villages, and isolated farmsteads), and the farmland worked by the polity's population. The following discussion is based upon Smith (2000), Hodge (1984), and Lockhart (1992); fuller discussion and documentation can be found in those sources. A council of high nobles chose the tlatoani from among the male members of the royal lineage. Kings had to be successful warriors, and they were expected to lead their forces into battle. The legitimacy of their lineage—its descent from the Toltec kings—was a major concern of Aztec kings. At some point these rulers (or their scribes) modified the ancient format of pictorial dynastic histories to devise a new format to keep track of the deeds and events of their dynasty. The new histories, called today continuous year-count annals (Boone 2000b), were maintained in every altepetl; the *Tira de Tepechpan* is a good example.

Kings were assisted by high-ranking nobles who filled a variety of administrative and religious positions (the individuals talking with the king of Tepechpan in fig. 3.2 are probably such nobles). Although documentation is not extensive, we know of the existence of tax collectors, treasurers, judges, military officers, teachers, priests, and miscellaneous royal advisors. Among the important nobles were the heads of smaller administrative units called *calpolli*. A calpolli consisted of a group of people, mainly commoners, who lived near one another and typically shared a profession or other economic and social traits. Although the noble calpolli heads were the final authority, the day-to-day running of calpolli activities was in the hands of a council. A calpolli could correspond to a farming town (such as the settlement of Cuexcomate; see chapter 6) or a neighborhood in a city. In addition to their common economic activities, the members of calpolli were also bound together by worship of a patron deity and their common position as subjects of the calpolli head.

A typical altepetl in the Basin of Mexico had a population of 10,000 to 15,000 and covered an area of 70 to 100 square km, while in Morelos most altepetl had 5,000 to 10,000 people in an area of 50 to 80 square km (M. E. Smith 2000). Relations among altepetl were both friendly and antagonistic, often simultaneously. Nobles had numerous forms of interaction across altepetl lines, including marriages, alliances, and common participation in key ceremonies. Royal marriage alliances were key components of Aztec diplomacy. Commerce crossed altepetl lines, providing linkages among both commoners and nobles. Altepetl often warred with one another, and a successful conquest led to a relationship of subjugation between the two polities and the payment of tribute from the loser to the winner. The subjugated polity typically retained its king, however, and it remained a functioning administrative unit even while subject to another altepetl.

For the study of urbanism, a key aspect of altepetl organization is that all of the major institutions—administrative, religious, and economic—were concentrated in the capital city. Because of basic similarities in the nature and organization of the various Aztec altepetl, Aztec cities had a basic level of similarity. Each had to have a royal palace, residences for high nobles as well as commoners, state temples and other religious buildings, and places to base economic institutions such as markets and craft production.

Territory and the Altepetl

My discussion above deliberately avoids the definition of altepetl given in one of the most authoritative discussions of the altepetl, chapter 2 of James

Lockhart's book, *The Nahuas After the Conquest* (Lockhart 1992). He defines the altepetl as "an organization of people holding sway over a given territory" (14). This definition falls into a common trap that has caught many scholars of the Aztecs and other ancient states: the assumption that ancient peoples had concepts of political territoriality similar to modern nation-states. In the modern world polities are defined in terms of their land or territory. Nation-states have clearly marked borders that are defended against incursions by other nation-states. The members or citizens of a nation-state consist in large part of those people who live within the state's borders; some citizens may live outside of the borders, and non-citizens may live within the borders. But regardless of the complexities involved, there are clear borders that are physically marked, officially recognized, and actively defended.

An alternative conception of polity definition, called "capital-centric" by Berman (2005), emphasizes people, not territory. As I suggest above, an altepetl consisted of all of the people subject to a king, wherever they happened to live. In many cases the members of an altepetl lived in a single continuous territory. In some cases, however, the subjects of neighboring kings lived interspersed with one another to such a degree that it is impossible to draw discrete territorial boundaries between the polities. The best known example concerns the altepetl of Tepechpan, Acolman, and Teotihuacan in the Teotihuacan Valley (this is the Aztec altepetl of Teotihuacan, not the Classic period metropolis). This situation was first pointed out by Charles Gibson (1964:44–47); see figure 3.6. It is simply not possible to draw any kind of rational territorial boundaries around the subject villages of these three altepetl.[4] This distribution of settlements, however, makes perfect sense from the alternative, people-focused perspective. Rik Hoekstra (1990) shows how the people-focused perspective of pre-Hispanic central Mexico was transformed under Spanish rule into the European territory-based viewpoint of the organization of native communities (see also Chance 1996: 134–135).

This perspective, in which polities are defined not by territory and boundaries but by relations of personal subjugation or allegiance, may have been widespread in ancient Mesoamerica. Several recent analyses of Classic Maya city-states take this position (for example, Grube 2000). Houston (2006: 205) suggests that "the Maya community at the polity level had a strong characteristic of a centripetal organization focused on the rulership rather than of a corporate group with clear boundaries."[5]

This notion does not imply that land or territory were unimportant in the Aztec conception of the altepetl. Susan Schroeder points out the complex relationship between land and altepetl in the writings of Chimalpahin, perhaps

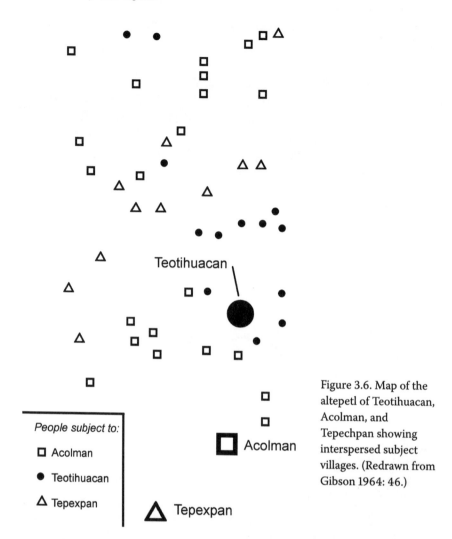

Figure 3.6. Map of the altepetl of Teotihuacan, Acolman, and Tepechpan showing interspersed subject villages. (Redrawn from Gibson 1964: 46.)

our best guide to native conceptions of the nature of the altepetl. On the one hand, "land is crucial to the altepetl" (Schroeder 1991: 126). "But if an altepetl has territory with known limits, it is not the same thing as a given territory. For various reasons, an altepetl can cease to exist when its group leaves the area" (127–128).

The alternative model clearly goes against the emphasis on defining a polity's boundaries as discussed above with rituals of foundation. How can these two opposing views of the nature of the altepetl be reconciled? I offer two plausible scenarios, but this remains an open question in need of additional research. First, perhaps polities were initially defined in terms of territory and boundaries as described in native historical sources, but then the borders became less important as populations grew and political dynamics changed. If so, then both perspectives are valid, one for the foundation of altepetl and the other for the situation at the time of Spanish conquest. This proposal, however, goes against the widely attested cross-cultural association between territoriality on the one hand and population level and resource quantities on the other (Dyson-Hudson and Smith 1978; Sack 1986). Comparative data, in other words, suggest that territoriality should have been much stronger in Aztec polities at the time of the Spanish conquest (with higher populations and extensive landscape modification for intensive agriculture) than at the time of their foundation, casting doubt on this first scenario.

My second suggestion, a more likely scenario, is that the emphasis on territory and borders may have been a colonial period invention that did not accurately describe the situation before the Spanish conquest. Although scenes such as the Cuauhtinchan foundation (fig. 3.3) were meant as depictions of events several centuries before the Spanish conquest, these documents were in fact produced in the colonial period, painted in order to submit them to Spanish courts as part of the legal process by which indigenous towns secured title to their traditional lands (Wood 1998b). By arguing that their community's borders had been established many centuries earlier, by a process understandable to the Spanish legal system, colonial period Nahuas strengthened their legal position within Spanish courts (Diel 2005; García-Zambrano 1994).

This observation suggests that the concept of delineating territorial boundaries may owe more to the requirements of the Spanish legal system than to a role as a valid ancient ritual of foundation. In the words of Lori Boornazian Diel (2005: 184):

> In the pre-Hispanic era, pictorial histories functioned as tools of persuasion, arguing for a community's rights, autonomy, and prestige. The painted histories served a similar function following the Spanish conquest, with artists modifying their histories to meet the needs of the changing colonial system.

4

Public Architecture and the Urban Townscape

These three pueblos [Mexicaltzingo, Coyoacan, and Huitzilopochco] in pagan times had many temples, and very high towers, that were white-washed, that from afar glimmered like silver in the sun, and they ornamented the towns greatly. (Torquemada 1975–83: 2:150–151; author's translation)

Although the architecture of these cities may have been less impressive to the chronicler Juan de Torquemada than the buildings of Tenochtitlan were to Bernal Díaz del Castillo (see chapter 2), Torquemada nevertheless suggests that typical Aztec cities could have large and attractive stone buildings. Unfortunately he is one of the few chroniclers to look beyond the imperial capitals of Tenochtitlan and Texcoco and mention, much less describe, their public architecture. The archaeological zones reviewed in chapter 2 should lay to rest any thoughts that the lack of such descriptions in the written records points to a lack of imposing buildings at Aztec cities outside of Tenochtitlan.

In this chapter I review the different types of public buildings found in Aztec cities. I use the term "public architecture" to refer to buildings that were not simple domestic dwellings. These buildings were "public" in two ways: They were highly visible structures that could easily be seen by the public and their uses and social significance related to a public social or civic realm above that of the individual household. All known examples of Aztec public architecture were built at least partially of stone, typically with facades of well-finished cut stones enclosing rubble-filled cores. I also describe large stone sculptures that served as sacrificial altars.

I classify Aztec buildings in six general categories: double-temple pyramids, single-temple pyramids, circular temples, ballcourts, shrines, and palaces.[1] Some of these can be further subdivided by form and use. The occurrence of these six types at the Aztec cities is shown in table 4.1. Some of these types, such as double-temple pyramids and ballcourts, were highly standardized in form and size, whereas others, such as single-temple pyramids, altars, and palaces, showed far more variation.

Table 4.1. Occurrence of Public Architecture

City	Pyramid, Double-Temple	Pyramid, Single-Temple	Circular Temple	Ball-court	Shrine	Palace
Early Aztec capitals						
Tenayuca	x				x	
Teopanzolco	x	x			x	
Major Late Aztec capitals						
Azcapotzalco						
Tlacopan	d					x
Texcoco	d			d		d
Other Cities in the Basin of Mexico						
Huexotla		x	x		x	x
Ixtapaluca		x	x	x	x	x
Otumba						
Xaltocan						
Chiconautla						x
Mexicaltzinco					x	
Cities in Morelos						
Palacio de Cortés					x	x
Coatetelco		x		x	x	
Coatlan		x				
Cuentepec		x		x	x	x
Yautepec						x
Cities in other valleys						
Calixtlahuaca		x	x		x	x
Cholula		d			x	
Zultepec		x	x		x	
Non-urban settlements						
Santa Cecelia Acatitlan	x					
Cihuatecpan						x
Cuexcomate					x	x
Cerro Tlaloc					x	
Malinalco		x			x	
Tepozteco		x			x	
The imperial capital						
Tenochtitlan	x	x	x	x	x	d
Tlatelolco	x	x	x		x	
Number of cities represented:	7	13	6	5	17	12

Key: x = archaeological evidence; d = documentary evidence.

A useful concept in the discussion of urban public architecture is "townscape" (see chapter 1). This theme is explored in greater detail in chapter 5, but this chapter suggests some of the contributions of the various types of building to Aztec townscapes.

CONSTRUCTION MATERIALS AND METHODS

Most Aztec public buildings consisted of stone platforms or rooms built on top of stone platforms. These platforms were built in a standard manner. Outer sloping walls were constructed using finished stone blocks, often cemented into place with lime mortar. As the walls went up, the interior space was filled with rocks, earth, and trash. The trash is important for archaeologists, since potsherds from these contexts (called "fill") can provide information for estimating a building's date of construction.[2] When the platform reached the desired height, its top was finished off with a floor of shaped stone blocks, and then rooms or other features were built if needed. Stairways were built on one side of the platform to reach the top.

Completed walls and floors were often covered with a lime stucco or plaster. This plaster was durable and served to protect the building from wear and the elements, sometimes for many centuries. Many plaster floors and walls were resurfaced periodically. Walls and floors were often painted a solid color, most typically red; sometimes walls were painted with complex scenes and geometric designs with sacred symbolism. López Luján, Torres, and Montúfar (2004) provide an extensive discussion of construction materials for the Templo Mayor of Tenochtitlan, and much of their information probably applies to other cities as well.

Aztec builders, like those of other Mesoamerican cultures, periodically enlarged and rebuilt their temples, called *teocalli* in Nahuatl. A new platform, larger in area and height, was simply constructed over the shell of the older platform. For temples the rooms on top were usually torn down during these episodes of rebuilding, and archaeologists often find traces of temple wall foundations on top of the earlier stages of pyramids. Figure 2.3 shows six consecutive stages of construction for the double-temple pyramid of Tenayuca, documented by tunneling into the structure. Excavators at Teopanzolco (fig. 1.4) and Santa Cecilia Acatitlan (fig. 2.16) left parts of both early and late stage platforms visible when they restored the buildings for public view.

Mesoamerican kings and their architects had reasons for rebuilding their temples and other buildings. First, enlargements were sometimes carried out to coincide with important calendric intervals. For example, many Maya temples were rebuilt to celebrate the ending of a *katun*, a 20-year period with important religious and political significance (Jones 1991; Schele and Freidel 1990: 325). Although it has been proposed that Aztec rulers may have rebuilt temples for the New Fire Ceremony, which celebrated completion of a 52-year calendric cycle, there is little clear documentary or archaeological data to support the notion. A second reason for rebuilding a larger and more impressive temple periodically was to emphasize the power and glory of the ruler. Without having to build a huge building from scratch, a king could take credit for a large, new temple. Third, by keeping the location of the new temple in the same place as an older building, rulers were maintaining traditions of sacred spaces.

SINGLE-TEMPLE PYRAMIDS

(figs. 1.1, 2.7, 2.18, 4.1, 4.2A–F, 4.10, 5.1, 5.7A, 7.3)
> This great city [Tenochtitlan] contains many mosques, or houses for idols, very beautiful edifices situated in its different parishes or wards. The principal ones are served by priests of their cult who live all the time in these temples. For these priests they provide very good lodgings set apart from the shrines in which they keep their idols. (Zorita 1963: 159)

The single-temple pyramid (fig. 4.1) was an ancient Mesoamerican form widely adopted by Aztec rulers and builders. In Mesoamerica, pyramids were massive solid structures, usually rectangular in plan, with sloping sides and a flattened top that served as a base for one or more small temples. Most Mesoamerican pyramids had a single stairway to the top, but some had two or four stairways. Some pyramids covered royal tombs, but most did not. All Aztec cities, except the most powerful capitals, used the single-temple pyramid as their major temple, and most or all Aztec cities had additional, smaller, single-temple pyramids in addition to their main temple. Depictions of Aztec temples in the codices (fig. 4.2) are overwhelmingly of the single-temple form, which can be considered the standard Aztec temple form.

The stairway is almost always flanked by sloping surfaces (typically referred to by the Spanish term *alfarda*), and these all exhibit a change in their slope near the top. This feature can be seen in the Stage 1 stairway of the double-temple Teopanzolco pyramid (fig. 1.4D), and it is also apparent and in pictorial images of both single- and double-temple pyramids (fig. 1.4A–B, 4.2D–F). Although the functional significance (if any) of this feature is unknown, it is a good stylistic marker that distinguishes Aztec pyramids from other Mesoamerican temples (Robertson 1974; Umberger and Klein 1993).

Figure 4.1. Single-temple pyramids. A: Coatetelco; B: Calixtlahuaca. Photographs by the author.

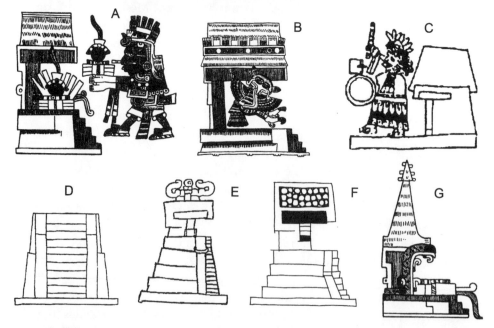

Figure 4.2. Temple images in the Aztec codices. A–F: single-temple pyramids; G: circular temple. (A, G: *Códice Borgia*, 14; B: *Códice Borgia*, 18; C, D: *Codex Borbonicus*, 36; E: *Codex Telleriano-Remensis*, 42r; F: *Codex Mendoza*, f. 19r.)

The fact that nearly all Aztec pyramids as well as representations of pyramids in the codices exhibit the change in alfarda slope suggests that this feature had great significance to Aztec architects and scribes.

In choosing the single-temple pyramid as the dominant form of temple, Aztec kings were following ancient Mesoamerican patterns of architecture and planning. In the language of architectural communication, this practice is an example of canonical communication (chapter 1). Their implementation of this idea, however, was highly variable. Single-temple pyramids were far from standardized in their size, form, and orientation, having much more variety than double-temple pyramids. In terms of their political and social roles, two kinds of single-temple pyramids can be identified: the central temples of city-state capitals and other temples, called here "secondary urban temples." The largest surviving examples, unreconstructed pyramids at sites such as Ixtapaluca (fig. 2.7) and Cuentepec (chapter 2), fall into the first group. Most of these structures were located facing west on the east side of their city's central formal public plaza (see chapter 5); thus their stairway was approached from the plaza. Although known examples are much smaller than most of the double-temple pyramids (see below), these pyramids dominated their townscape visually and symbolically. As the tallest building in the city, located adjacent to an open plaza, these structures stood out to visitors approaching the city and loomed over visitors in the plaza. Some examples were quite small, however (fig. 4.1), with a lower level of visual domination.

Ethnohistoric records suggest that every Aztec city-state had one or more patron deity whose image, in stone or wood, was housed in a central temple attended by professional priests (Acuña 1984–88). Commonly mentioned forms of offering at the temples include the burning of copal incense, offerings of paper and birds, music and dance, bloodletting or autosacrifice by priests, and human sacrifice. A city's patron god or gods were venerated at the ceremony of Tepilhuitl, one of the 18 monthly public ceremonies. Although we know the names of some of the patron gods, there are few specific associations between a named deity and a specific temple (outside of the Templo Mayor of Tenochtitlan). Most such cases were specialized temples, not the main temples of city-state patron deities. For example, the cultic association of the small single-temple pyramid at Tepozteco with the gods of the beverage pulque is known from carved reliefs at the temple (see chapter 2).

Single-temple pyramids that served as secondary urban temples were smaller in size. Structure 4 at Calixtlahuaca (fig. 4.1B) is a good example of this type of temple. Unfortunately, we know next to nothing about the uses or symbolism of such temples. The written records of individual cities rarely

Table 4.2. Types of Temples in a Ritual Cycle in the *Códice Borgia*

Temple	Patron Deity	Association	Page
Temple of jade	Tonatiuh	Heat	49
Temple of flint knives	Itzlacocliuhqui and Tonallehque	Cold	50
Temple of jade	Cinteotl	Maize	51
Temple of death	Mictlantecuhtli	Death	52
House of gold and flowers	Tonatiuh		49
House and jade and maize	Tepeyollotl and Chalchiuhlicue		51
House of bones and death	Mictlantecuhtli and Tecpatl		52

Source: The images are in the *Códice Borgia* (1993: 49–52), and the interpretations are from Anders, Jansen, and Reyes García (1993: 261–277).

mention secondary temples, and the few examples known archaeologically were either excavated hastily or else poorly written up (for example, there is only minimal documentation for the excavations of the temples shown in figure 4.1). Just as there is considerable variation in the sizes of single-temple pyramids, so too do they show significant variety in their orientations and locations within cities.

Temples served as houses for stone or wood images of a deity, and the platform in front of the temple, at the top of the stairs, was the setting for various public ritual activities. In figure 4.2A, for example, the deity Xiuhtecuhtli—one of the nine gods who served as "lords of the night"—or a priest serving as an *ixiptla*, or deity impersonator,[3] brings an offering of burning rubber to a temple that already has such an offering burning. Figure 4.2C shows the goddess Cihuacoatl in front of a small temple; she was probably the patron of this temple, and the image most likely portrays the deity's sculpture, which stood inside the chamber. The most widely attested public ceremony to occur at the tops of pyramid stairs is human sacrifice. A stone altar was set up in front of the temple for the purpose; these ceremonies are discussed below. Temple interiors were the settings for various private ceremonies by priests, but little information survives about these activities.

In the ritual codices there are temples dedicated to a wide variety of deities. For example, table 4.2 lists the temples illustrated in a four-page passage in the *Códice Borgia* that describes "the four directions and the center." This passage presents diverse aspects of divination and cosmology in relation to the 260-day ritual calendar (Anders, Jansen, and Reyes García 1993: 261). There are objects, deities and scenes arranged in groups of four, including four main temples associated with heat, cold, maize, and death. The same four temples are depicted in the *Codex Féjerváry-Mayer* (Anders, Jansen, and Pérez Jiménez 1994: figs. 33, 34).

Most representations of single-temple pyramids in the codices are quite standardized, with only a few standing out as different in form and decoration. This could suggest that temples dedicated to the various deities were similar in form (which is what the archaeological evidence suggests). Alternatively, it could be due to standardization in depiction by Aztec scribes who simplified their task by painting temples of diverse form in a similar manner. Temples in Mixtec codices are also standardized (Garza Tarazona de González 1978).

DOUBLE-TEMPLE PYRAMIDS

(figs. 1.4, 2.2, 2.3, 2.4, 2.15, 2.16, 5.3)
> In idolatrous times it was named teocalli. It is high, just an artificial mountain
> with levels, with steps. Some have one hundred steps, etc. And on its summit
> there stood two small houses, or just one; there the image of the demon, the
> devil, was guarded. (Sahagún 1950–82: bk. 11, p. 269)

The double-temple pyramid is the most distinctive type of Aztec building, a form rarely used by other Mesoamerican cultures.[4] Double-temple pyramids were the largest Aztec structures and were only erected at the most powerful political capitals (this is an example of indexical communication, as discussed in chapter 1). Seven examples are known (table 4.1). Three of these—the main pyramids at Tenochtitlan, Tlatelolco, and Tenayuca—are the largest surviving Aztec buildings. Each was rebuilt and enlarged numerous times (fig. 2.3) by successive kings. The term "teocalli" was used for both single- and double-temple pyramids.

The earliest double-temple pyramid, built in the Early Aztec period at Tenayuca, may have been designed and/or built by the semilegendary king Xolotl. We do not know the motivation or origin of this innovation, nor the symbolic associations of the twin temples, each with its own stairway. My own guess is that the two temples may have symbolized the two sources of Xolotl's legitimacy and identity, the Chichimec and the Toltec (see chapter 3), although it would be speculation to suggest the specific deities worshipped in these temples. The final stage of this pyramid is the largest surviving Aztec temple. The main pyramid at Teopanzolco, also built in Early Aztec times, was quite a bit smaller than the Tenayuca building. As noted in chapter 2, Teopanzolco was the site of the powerful Early Aztec capital Cuauhnahuac, and it is possible that this structure was built in imitation of the Tenayuca temple.

The tradition of building double-temple pyramids at powerful capitals continued in the Late Aztec period. The Templo Mayor of Tenochtitlan has more documentary evidence than any other Aztec building, and it has been the target of the most intensive excavations (see the sources cited in chapter 2). It is matched in size, grandeur, and architectural history by the main temple of Tlatelolco, a powerful capital in its own right until conquered by Tenochtitlan in 1473. The double-temple pyramid of Texcoco, known only from a painting and written sources (fig. 1.4B), is described by the chroniclers as 134 meters on a side and 45 meters tall, larger than that of Tenochtitlan (Lesbre 1998).

Azcapotzalco is the only powerful Aztec capital without evidence of a large double-temple pyramid, but as noted in chapter 2, almost nothing survives archaeologically (or historically) of this city. Tlacopan, Azcapotzalco's smaller Tepanec successor, is shown in the *Codex Telleriano-Remensis* with a double-temple pyramid (fig. 1.4A). The size and location of the final example, Santa Cecilia Acatitlan, are unusual. It is the smallest example by far, and if this structure dates to the Early Aztec period (its dating is unknown), it must have pertained to Tenayuca, making that city the only Aztec capital with more than one double-temple pyramid.

The lopsided nature of available evidence about double-temple pyramids—nearly all descriptions pertain to Tenochtitlan, which also has the best archaeological fieldwork and reporting—makes it difficult to discuss the nature and significance of these structures. Many authors have extrapolated the symbolism and meaning of the Tenochtitlan Templo Mayor to the other examples, but this produces speculative and even absurd interpretations. It is amusing, for example, to read the tourist signs at Teopanzolco, which claim that this pyramid was copied from the Templo Mayor of Tenochtitlan, including the patron deities of Tlaloc and Huitzilopochtli. As we know from chapter 2, however, this pyramid was built and used in the Early Aztec period, prior to the founding of Tenochtitlan. There is no surviving evidence on the deities housed in the Teopanzolco temples. Although the ancient Tlaloc is a reasonable guess, it is extremely unlikely that Huitzilopochtli, the Mexica patron god, was worshipped at Teopanzolco at a time before the Mexica had even started building their temple and city.

The surviving double-temple pyramids are similar in form and architectural detail. Two parallel stairways lead from the ground level to a common platform that supported two temples. The change in slope of the alfarda, noted above for single-temple pyramids, also occurred on double-temple pyramids. At a few sites, vestiges of the temples survive for the earliest stages (because they were covered over by later stages), and from this information and documentary descriptions it appears that the two temples were usually similar in size but differed in details of layout and architectural ornamentation. This differentiation is not surprising, since we know that (at Tenochtitlan at least) the two temples housed different deities. All examples faced west; they stood on the east side of a plaza or, as in the case of Tenochtitlan, the east side of a walled precinct (little is known of the setting of the Santa Cecilia Acatitlan temple). The Texcoco main pyramid, known only from written sources, was also said to face west.

The standardization of double-temple pyramids in size and form is probably due to their status as the largest and most central temples at the most powerful capital cities. Once the first large double-temple pyramid was established at Tenayuca, the powerful Early Aztec capital, this form became the prime visual symbol of political might at Aztec cities. It is likely that all of these structures had rich mythological symbolism of the sort known for the Tenochtitlan Templo Mayor (see chapters 2 and 5), although there is no reason to think that each city celebrated the same gods and myths at their central temple. As far as we know today, the same sorts of sacrifices and other activities that took place at single-temple pyramids also occurred at double-temple pyramids. Nicholson (1990) discusses Aztec temples in greater detail.

CIRCULAR TEMPLES

(figs. 2.13, 4.2G, 4.3)

> This was the God of the Air, and he had his Temple in circular form, and it was very sumptuous. . . . These Indians of New Spain formed and devised the Temple of the Air God also round; and the reason that they gave was to say that thus as the Air moves and surrounds all, thus the house had to be, so that in its form it might reveal its meaning. (Torquemada 1975–83: 3:86; translation by Pollock 1936: 8–9)

Whereas the various Aztec single-temple and double-temple pyramids almost certainly housed a wide range of patron deities, all or nearly all circular temples were dedicated to Ehecatl, the wind god. Ehecatl was one of the avatars of Quetzalcoatl, the feathered serpent. During the Epiclassic and Early Postclassic periods (ca. A.D. 600–1100), a cult based on the feathered serpent spread through Mesoamerica, bringing feathered serpent symbolism and circular temples to many areas (Ringle, Gallareta Negrón, and Bey 1998). By Aztec times the feathered serpent's control of the wind had become separated in the form of Ehecatl. Numerous references in the chroniclers and the codices describe the close association between circular temples and Ehecatl (Pollock 1936), and stone sculptures of Ehecatl have been excavated as offerings at several circular temples. The Spanish chroniclers were told that Ehecatl preferred circular temples because the wind could flow around them more easily. Given the existence of a large circular temple at Tula (the El Corral structure), the prominence of this form at Aztec sites could derive from their imitation of the architecture of Tula.

Accounts by several chroniclers state that the entrances to circular temples were painted or carved in the form of giant serpent mouths with fangs (Pollock 1936: 5–18). The rock-cut circular Temple 1 at Malinalco fits this description, as do several images in the codices (for example, fig. 4.2G). None of the freestanding circular temples, however, have traces of this feature. Motolinía suggests that there were two types of circular temple: low temples, perhaps even semisubterranean, without steps that had serpent mouth entrances and tall temples with steps that were dedicated to Quetzalcoatl (Ehecatl) and the wind. Most surviving circular temples have a single stairway on the east side extending out beyond the circular pyramid or platform (this feature must not have disturbed the passage of the wind sufficiently to upset Ehecatl). Beyond this standard feature, however, circular temples showed considerable variation in their sizes and architectural details. Figure 4.3 illustrates some of the largest and best-preserved circular temples. Circular temples are depicted in the codices with pointed roofs (fig. 4.2G). There are a few ceramic models of circular temples (Baer 1996: 74–77). Nevertheless, virtually no information survives in the written sources on the types of activities that took place in these temples. The recovery of a sacrificial altar (fig. 4.8A) at Structure 3, the large circular temple at Calixtlhauaca (chapter 2; see also the discussion of altars below) indicates that human sacrifices were probably carried out at this and perhaps other circular temples.

Circular temples had open courtyards or small plazas in front of the stairs; at Tlatelolco this area was full of burials with rich offerings (Guilliem Arroyo 1999). The locations of circular temples within Aztec cities show an interesting pattern. Some were situated within the epicenter along with most of the other public architecture (at Ixtapaluca, Zultepec, and Tlatelolco, for example), whereas others were built as isolated structures, far from the epicenter and other large buildings (at Huexotla and Calixtlahuaca, for example). This latter pattern could suggest that the Ehecatl cult retained a degree of independence or separation from the state cults that centered on single- and double-temple pyramids that were the central temples at Aztec cities. Pollock (1936) remains the best discussion of circular temples in Mesoamerica.

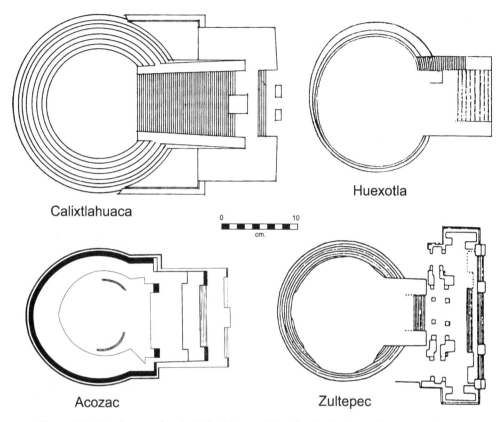

Figure 4.3. Circular temples. A: Calixtlahuaca (after García Payón 1981); B: Huexotla (after Batres 1904: lám. 15); C: Acozac (after Brüggemann 1987: 177); D: Zultepec (after Martínez Vargas and Jarquín Pacheco 1998: 22).

BALLCOURTS

(figs. 2.10, 4.4)

> Ball courts existed in all the illustrious, civilized, and powerful cities and towns, in those ruled by either the community or the lords, the latter stressing [the game] inordinately. . . . The ball courts were enclosed with ornate and handsomely carved walls. The interior floor was of stucco, finely polished and decorated with figures of the god and demons to whom the game was dedicated. . . . The corners were built on purpose so that if the player's ball fell into one it was lost and was considered a foul. (Durán 1971: 314)

Although written descriptions and painted images of Aztec ballcourts are common, very few have been identified on the ground and excavated. Figure 4.4 shows depictions of ballcourts from the codices (Nicholson and Qui-

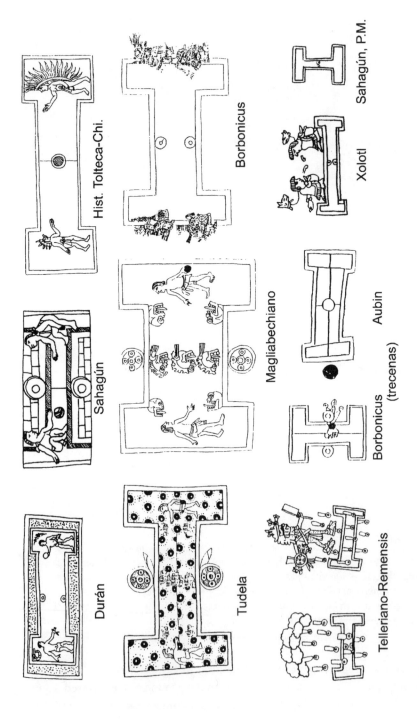

Figure 4.4. Ballcourt images in the Aztec codices. (After Nicholson and Quiñones Keber 1991.)

ñones Keber 1991). The only Aztec ballcourt excavated in its entirety is at Coatetelco (fig. 2.10); partially preserved ballcourts have been excavated near the Templo Mayor (Matos Moctezuma 2001) and at Ixtapaluca (Nicholson 2005). Ballcourts have a long history as fundamental features of city planning in Mesoamerica (Taladoire 2001). In fact, in at least one early colonial central Mexican codex, the *Códice de Nicolás Flores*, images of ballcourts seem to be used to indicate major towns (Lorenzo Monterrubio 2001). Given their prominence in the Aztec codices, at least part of the paucity of actual ballcourts can probably be attributed to issues of preservation and excavation. But the far smaller number of cities with ballcourts compared to pyramids, palaces, and altars (table 4.1) may suggest that not every Aztec city had a ballcourt.

The I-shaped form of Aztec ballcourts is typical of the Postclassic period (Taladoire 2001), when Mesoamerican ballcourts showed more standardization than in earlier times. The two excavated ballcourts at Tula are both of the I shape, and again emulation of the Toltec city may have been responsible for the Aztec use of this form of ballcourt. Unlike the open ends of some Mesoamerican ballcourts, the platforms that formed the I-shaped courts hid the players from sight unless a spectator was standing or sitting on the platform or an adjacent building. Access to the ballcourt itself was quite open, however, as most Aztec ballcourts were located on the central plaza of the city, along with a pyramid and a palace.

Despite a body of documentary evidence and considerable scholarly attention, we know very little about the nature and significance of the Mesoamerican ballgame (Olko 2001; Scarborough and Wilcox 1991). Played with a rubber ball on courts with sloping sides (fig. 2.10), the ballgame combined elements of sport and ritual. Games were watched by an audience who often gambled on the outcome. Many writers have taken as literal a cryptic written reference to the sacrifice of the players on the losing team, an unlikely practice in my opinion. Partial excavation of a large ballcourt in the center of Tenochtitlan revealed a series of rich offerings, including rubber balls and ceramic musical instruments, stone replicas of balls and musical instruments, shell ornaments, and sacrificial knives (Matos Moctezuma 2001). These offerings suggest that the Aztec ballgame, like that played by other Mesoamerican cultures, had a rich symbolic and mythological component. It is likely that there were several different types of ballgames played on the ballcourts at Aztec and other Mesoamerican cities.

Ballcourts probably served as settings for a variety of ceremonies in addition to ballgames. Some authors have suggested that ballgames and ballcourts in Mesoamerica had significance in diplomacy and political relations among polities (Gillespie 1991). Aztec temples provided both small, secluded settings for rituals by priests and open venues for theatrical rites such as human sacrifice witnessed by large audiences in the plaza. Ballcourts and palace plazas, on the other hand, were enclosed, semipublic venues ideal for limited gatherings of elites for socially and politically significant ceremonial activities. Special ballgames and other ceremonies in the ballcourt probably had political importance for rulers or relations between rulers. Although the archaeological record is scanty, the presence of a ballcourt may have signaled that a city served as a capital.

SHRINES

(figs. 2.4, 4.5, 4.6, 4.10, 5.1, 7.2)

> The place of sacrifice, which was next to the base of the great pyramid [in a place] called *temalacatl*, was a platform structure, rectangular, with stairways on all sides, not higher than one could mount with four steps, three *brazos* across, and in the center, a large stone like a large millstone, on which they put the prisoner to be sacrificed. (Pomar 1986; author's translation)

Aztec cities were full of low platforms built in public locations that served as altars or shrines. To avoid confusion I use the term "shrine" for these constructions and reserve "altar" for portable or semiportable features. Built shrines are perhaps the most distinctive feature of the Aztec townscape in comparison with the cities of other Mesoamerican cultures (fig. 4.5). Although such features were part of Mesoamerican townscapes from Olmec times onward, they proliferated significantly in the Aztec period. An earlier central Mexican tradition of shrines built in association with large residential compounds, prominent at Teotihuacan and Tula, was apparently abandoned or used far less frequently in Aztec times. Many Aztec cities had long rows of low platforms situated in prominent positions within the urban epicenter (fig. 4.5A). Although several functional types of shrine have been identified at Aztec sites, our understanding of the forms and significance of these features is still rudimentary. I discuss shrines under four headings: skull racks, tzitzimime platforms, circular shrines, and other shrines. As discussed by Olivier (2003: 172–182), the term *momoztli* was often used to designate small platforms and shrines. In some cases the term was used broadly to describe all temples and altars, and in other cases it referred to a specific type of shrine dedicated to Tezcatlipoca.

Figure 4.5. Shrines at various cities. A: Teopanzolco; B: Tlatelolco; C: Tenayuca; D: Ixtapaluca. Photographs by the author.

Tzompantlis

(fig. 4.10)

A tzompantli was a wood frame that held the skulls of human sacrificial victims. As one of the more gruesome of Aztec urban features, skull racks were the target of much attention by the Spaniards: at first to destroy them and later to describe them as pagan shrines. In the words of Friar Diego Durán, "From pole to pole, through the holes, stretched thin rods with numerous human heads pierced through the temple. Each rod held twenty heads" (Durán 1971: 79). Depictions of skull racks in the codices show the wood framework resting on a low platform of some sort (see fig. 4.10 below). Sahagún's (1950–82: bk. 2, pp. 179–193) catalog of types of temples and religious buildings in Tenochtitlan includes six different entries for tzompantli; it is possible that many or most of the major temples of the capital city had an associated skull rack.

Likely tzompantlis have been excavated by archaeologists at the Aztec cities of Tlatelolco (Pijoan, Pastrana, and Maquivar 1989) and Zultepec (Martínez Vargas 2003; Martínez Vargas and Jarquín Pacheco 1998). At Tlatelolco, the remains consist of a plain stone platform (without decoration) with an associated offering of neatly arranged skulls with lateral perforations (to hang the skulls on the wood rails). The Zultepec example consists only of the offering of perforated skulls; its possible association with a platform is not clear from the reports. These skulls are from Spaniards and their native allies captured and sacrificed during the Spanish conquest. In neither Tlatelolco nor Zultepec have traces of the wood frames survived, and neither site has yielded post holes for the wood frames. These tzompantlis are located in the epicenter near the major temple of their city. Platforms with carved or painted skulls and crossed bones at Aztec sites have likely been misidentified as skull racks by many writers; these are better classified as tzitzimime platforms.

Tzitzimime Platforms

(fig. 4.6)

"Tzitzimime platform" is my term for low platforms or shrines decorated with skulls and crossed bones in relief or painted on the sides of the platform. This type of structure was first identified by Alfonso Caso (1940), who called it an "altar de craneos" (see also Noguera 1937). In place of Caso's interpretation, which links these structures to the New Fire ceremony and rites of calendrical completion, I follow Cecelia Klein's (2000) reinterpretation of this category.

Elizabeth Baquedano (1988) discusses the skull-and-bones motif in Aztec sculpture and codices and relates it to mythological accounts in which bones were used to create the first people. She states, "Bones and skulls have thus had a very important place in Mesoamerican thought as a source for regeneration and life" (193). Furthermore, "skeletonization, then, symbolizes not death, but life giving and life sustaining qualities" (196; see also Klein 2000). The *Codex Tudela* (fig. 4.6E) shows a midwife or curer seated in front of a tzitzimime platform. These features served purposes very different from the tzompantli, and the widespread assumption that platforms decorated with skulls and crossed bones were tzompantlis is almost certainly incorrect.[5]

The earliest tzitzimime platform in central Mexico was attached to Tula's El Corral pyramid (fig. 4.6A) (Acosta 1974). An example from Tenayuca (fig. 4.6C) had carved skulls and bones on the exterior and colorful mural paintings of the same elements on the interior of a central chamber. This plat-

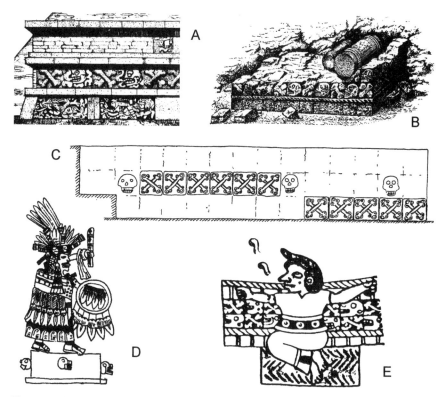

Figure 4.6. Tzitzimime shrines. A: Tula (alter Gendrop 1970: 170); B: Tenochtitlan (alter Batres 1979: 153); C: Tenayuca (alter Marquina 1935: lám. 35); D: *Codex Borbonicus*, 36; E: *Codex Tudela*, f. 50r).

form is attached to the lowest basal platform in front of the double-temple pyramid. Several of these shrines have been excavated in the sacred precinct at Tenochtitlan. The example shown in fig. 4.6B was found with effigy year bundles (related to the New Fire ceremony) on top; Olivier (2003: 175–177) reviews a long-running debate about the symbolism and meaning of this structure.

There are several images of tzitzimime platforms in the codices: the *Codex Tudela* shows a midwife or curer engaged in a ceremony in front of a tzitzimime platform, and the *Codex Borbonicus* (fig. 4.6D) shows the goddess Cihuacoatl on top of the platform (which is labeled a tzompantli by Anders et al. 1991: 229). The iconographic motif of the skull and crossed bones (which has nothing to do with the Jolly Roger images on pirate flags) is not infrequent in Aztec sculpture and the codices. On the basis of this limited sample of archaeological and historical examples, it appears that some tzitzimime platforms were attached to major temples whereas others were freestanding.

Klein (2000) shows how the Spanish friars transformed interpretations of the tzitzimime deities from benevolent female fertility deities to threatening and malevolent causers of harm. Because the friars did not have a good understanding of Aztec women or their activities (Burkhart 1997), they did not grasp the true nature of the tzitzimime, nor did they understand the significance of the small shrines where tzitzimime and other female deities were invoked. Unfortunately it is very difficult to reconstruct the uses and social contexts of tzitzimime platforms today. Their spatial prominence in several cities may indicate a public ceremonial role for midwives and curers that is only hinted at in the writings of the chroniclers (Klein 2000). This suggestion is explored more fully in chapter 8.

Other Rectangular Shrines

(figs. 4.5, A, C, D, 4.8C)
"Other rectangular shrines" is a catch-all category for rectangular shrines that do not fit into one of the above categories. The fact that it is by far the largest category of shrine shows the high level of uncertainty about the nature and significance of Aztec shrines and platforms. Some of these features probably pertain to the so-called momoztlis (altars) described in the sources as dedicated to the god Tezcatlipoca (Olivier 2003: 172–182). Molina's six-

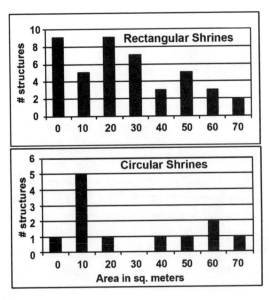

Figure 4.7. Graphs of the sizes of rectangular and circular shrines.

teenth-century Nahuatl dictionary states, "Mumuztli, tlalmumuztli, Altar of the demons, that they placed on the roads, made of earth" (translation by Olivier 2003: 172). In a number of depictions in the codices and written sources (the above quotation from Pomar, for instance), shrines were bases for large cylindrical stone altars known as temalacatl (fig. 4.8C). Although a number of these large stones have been recovered (see discussion of altars below), none have a clear archaeological association with a shrine or platform.

There is a wide variation in the sizes of rectangular shrines (fig. 4.7), but nearly all of these are under 80 square meters in area. Cities such as Teopanzolco (figs. 2.4, 4.5A), Coatetelco (fig. 1.1), and Ixtapaluca (fig. 5.2) had long rows of small platforms (often including both rectangular and circular examples) along their central plazas. Many rectangular shrines consisted of a low rectangular base, only one or two steps in height, on top of which was constructed a slightly higher platform, reached by two to five steps (fig. 4.5 C, D).

Circular Shrines

(figs. 4.5B, 7.2)
Circular stone features are found in a wide variety of sizes at Aztec sites, from very small, low platforms to the large pyramids discussed under circular temples above. The smallest examples of fixed circular structures (less than 80 square meters) are separated and grouped with the shrines here (fig. 4.7), whereas other examples of circular platforms are included in the circular temple category. Portable, although often large, circular stones with carved reliefs are included in the separate category of portable altars below. Most circular shrines resembled rectangular shrines in their size and height.

PORTABLE ALTARS AND SACRIFICIAL STONES

(figs. 4.8, 4.10)
Carved stone altars were set up in front of many temples (on the platform at the top of the stairs) and in other locations in the epicenters of Aztec cities. Although these are best categorized as stone sculptures, not buildings, they were important parts of Aztec townscapes and should be mentioned here.[6] It is likely that most of the freestanding stone altars identified at Aztec cities served as settings for rites of human sacrifice (Graulich 1998). The most elaborately carved (and best studied) examples were large flat cylinders called *cuauhxicalli* ("eagle bowl") or temalacatl ("stone wheel" or "stone spindle whorl") (fig. 4.8A). These were positioned horizontally either on the ground or on top of a shrine platform (fig. 4.8C), and some or all stones served as

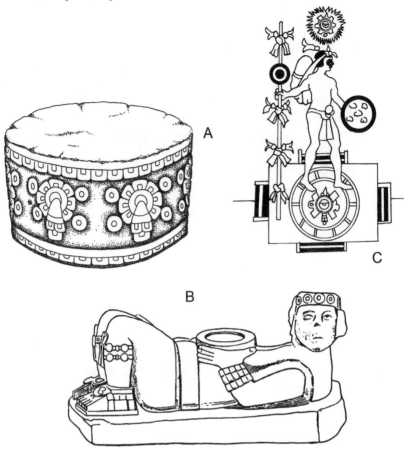

Figure 4.8. Sacrificial stones. A: sculpture from Calixtlahuaca (drawing by Will Russell); B: Chac-Mool from Tlaxcala (after Seler 1998: 74); C: gladiator sacrifice from Durán (image after Heyden 1972: 112).

settings for a ritual known as the gladiator sacrifice. The sacrificial victim, a warrior, was tethered to the stone with a rope and forced to battle (using pretend weapons) with seasoned warriors until he was killed. These stones had complex iconographic texts with cosmological and military themes; the famous "Aztec calendar stone" is the largest and most complex example. They represent public ideological statements about military power and sacrifice by the Mexica rulers of Tenochtitlan, each of whom apparently commissioned at least one large stone of this type (Umberger 1998).

Another class of sacrificial altars consisted of smaller and more simply decorated stone cylinders, known as *techcatl*. The example shown in figure 4.8A was excavated at the circular temple at Calixtlahuaca (chapter 2). Its sides are carved with repeating symbols of blood, confirming its use as a sacrificial stone. Altars like this probably served as bases for the most common form of human sacrifice, the heart sacrifice, which took place at the tops of pyramids, in front of the temples. The victim was stretched out on his back, and a high priest (whose title was quetzalcoatl priest) cut open the chest and extracted the heart.

One of the most unusual types of sacrificial altar was the so-called Chac-Mool, a large stone sculpture of a man reclining on his back, looking to one side and holding a bowl on his stomach (fig. 4.8B). Chac-Mools became popular at Tula and other cities during the Early Postclassic period, and the form was later adopted by the Aztecs. Although these enigmatic sculptures have interested several generations of scholars, only recently has it been established that they served as sacrificial altars (López Austin and López Luján 2001; López Luján and Urcid 2002). A Chac-Mool was excavated in front of one temple from an early stage of the Templo Mayor of Tenochtitlan, and Aztec examples have been reported from Mixquic, Calixtlahuaca, and several other Aztec sites.

PALACES

(figs. 2.9, 4.9)

> *Tecpancalli*: It means the house of the ruler, or the government house, where the ruler is, where he lives, or where the rulers or the townsmen, the householders, assemble. . . . There is honor, a state of honor. . . . It is a center of knowledge, of wisdom. . . . It is the house of artisanship, a product of skill, formed with skill. . . . It stands constantly shining. . . . It is extended, roomy; it has a portal, a servants' hall . . . [rooms] pertaining to women. . . . It is provided with a place of deliberation, an audience room, an eating place, a sleeping place. (Sahagún 1950–82: bk. 11, pp. 270–271)

I use the term "palace" to refer to the residence of a noble household. Aztec palaces show an enormous variation in size and luxury, from the modest compounds of low-ranking country gentry to massive and sumptuous royal palaces at the imperial capitals. All of these palaces, however, conform to a single basic plan. The fundamental attributes of this plan are (1) rooms were arranged around a central rectangular courtyard, (2) rooms were elevated above the level of the courtyard (and above ground level) on platforms, (3) the courtyard had a single entrance to the outside, and (4) a special raised platform was located opposite from the entrance. Although no two palaces had identical forms or plans, they all fit these general rules, including both archaeological buildings and images in the codices. The chronicler Juan de Pomar (1986: 113) noted that the palaces of the nobles of Texcoco had the

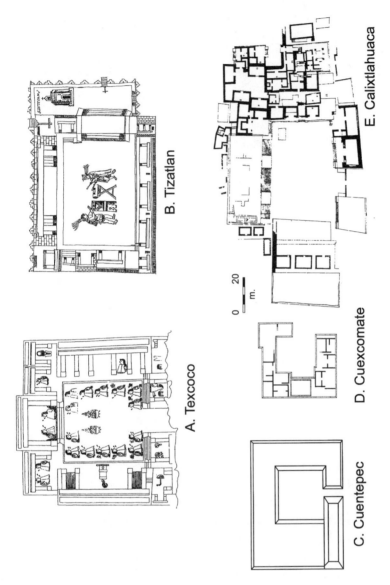

B. Tizatlan

A. Texcoco

C. Cuentepec

D. Cuexcomate

E. Calixtlahuaca

0   20
┤────┤
m.

Figure 4.9. Palaces. A: Texcoco, from the *Mapa Quinatzin* (after Evans 2000: 242); B: Tizatlan, from the *Lienzo de Tlaxcala*, cuadro 16 (after Wake 2002: 94); C: Cuentepec (map by Oxvaldo Sterpone and Michael E. Smith); D: Cuexcomate (Smith 1992: 189); E: Calixtlahuaca (after García Payón 1981). There is no scale for the images from codices.

Table 4.3. The Size of Aztec Palaces

Palace	Area (m²)	Illustration
Imperial palaces		
Tenochtitlan, Motecuhzoma Ilhuicamina	7,950	
Tenochtitlan, Axayacatl	11,439	
Tenochtitlan, Motecuhzoma Xocoyotzin	25,425	
Texcoco, palace of Nezahualcoyotl	843,000	
Tlatoani palaces		
Yautepec royal palace	6,200	
Calixtlahuaca royal palace	6,800	Fig. 4.9
Cuentepec royal palace	2,000	Fig. 4.9
Tecuhtli (high-ranking noble) palaces		
El Conde palace (Tlacopan)	2,400	
Other noble palaces		
Chiconautla royal palace	430	
Cuexcomate, Group 6	540	Fig. 4.9
Cuexcomate, Group 7	200	
Yautepec, Structure 6	430	
Cihuatecpan, Structure 6	360	

Source: Data are compiled from sources cited in chapter 2.

same layout as Nezahualcoyotl's royal palace and were similarly elevated on platforms, although they were much smaller than the king's palace. Figure 4.9 illustrates three archaeological palaces and two examples from the codices. Aztec palaces have been discussed in a number of publications by Susan Evans (1991, 2004) and in my book, *The Aztecs* (Smith 2003a: 139–145).

Some idea of the range of sizes of Aztec palaces is given by the information in table 4.3. The palace of King Nezahualcoyotl of Texcoco may have been the largest Aztec palace. No archaeological traces survive, but a detailed description was given by the chronicler Fernando de Alva Ixtlilxochitl, a descendent of Nezahualcoyotl, a century after the Spanish conquest (Alva Ixtlilxochitl 1975–77). The size listed in table 4.3—843,000 square meters, almost a square kilometer—is clearly exaggerated, and it appears that Alva Ixtlilxochitl was describing the entire epicenter of Texcoco, not just the royal palace (his description of the "palace" included a ballcourt and a market, features not found within any known Aztec palace). Nevertheless, the number of different types of rooms and courtyards in his description of the palace is truly impressive, and even if the structure was one-tenth of the size he reports, it would still be the largest known palace.

Ignacio Alcocer (1935) used early Spanish descriptions to reconstruct the locations and likely sizes of three royal palaces in Tenochtitlan. The best information is on the palace of Axayacatl, since that is where Cortés and his troops were housed during their initial stay in Tenochtitlan. Each of the three known Mexica royal palaces was larger than the previous examples (table 4.3); all three are larger than any of the known archaeological palaces but smaller than Alva Ixtlilxochitl's description of the Texcoco palace.

Large royal palaces excavated at Yautepec and Calixtlahuaca are similar in size and only slightly smaller than the palace of Motecuhzoma I in Tenochtitlan. The Calixtlahuaca structure (fig. 4.9) has been completely excavated, although the poor documentation of the fieldwork prevents any analysis of the uses of different rooms or the construction history of the structure (García Payón 1981). The Yautepec palace has only been partially excavated (de Vega Nova 1996); it is a large platform with steps on the west side and a series of rooms and passageways on top. Unfortunately, not enough of the structure has been excavated to determine whether it fits the standard Aztec palace plan.

A third rank of noble, between the tlatoani and the bulk of the noble class, was the *tecuhtli*. This category of high lord is discussed further in chapter 6. The El Conde platform from the Tlacopan altepetl may have been a tecuhtli's palace (table 4.3). Smaller palaces, included under the label "Other noble palaces" in table 4.3, were probably the homes of low-ranking nobles. Even the most modest Aztec palaces are impossible to confuse with commoner houses; they are much larger, they are elevated above the ground, they use superior construction materials and methods, and they conform to the basic palace plan (see chapter 6).

The two pictorial representations of palaces, Texcoco and Tizatlan (fig. 4.9), follow the same plan as the excavated examples. The size of these structures is not certain, although both were probably quite large. The Texcoco image is a depiction of Nezahualcoyotl's palace discussed above, and the Tizatlan palace may correspond to a large walled enclosure uncovered during excavations of an adjacent temple in the 1920s (Noguera 1927). The locations of palaces on the central plaza gave them high visibility in Aztec cities. Their single entrance restricted access to the courtyard, but once inside the courtyard most parts of the palace were easily accessible (except in the largest royal palaces).

Aztec palaces were multifunctional structures. They served as the dwelling of a noble family, which often included a single male and his multiple wives and concubines. Many servants and attendants also lived in the palace. Palaces housed diverse administrative activities. Royal palaces were the centers of governance in the altepetl, with chambers for officials and warriors, storage facilities, archives, and other administrative features. Palaces also contained altars, shrines, and temples for worship. Diplomatic events took place in palaces, and the courtyards were gathering places for communications between the king and nobles and commoners alike. These activities were scaled down in the palaces of lower ranking nobles, but these too had a variety of administrative, religious, and economic functions.

OTHER PUBLIC BUILDINGS

There is frustratingly little information on types of public buildings other than those discussed above. Written sources mention a variety of specialized religious and civic structures in the sacred precinct of Tenochtitlan (Matos Moctezuma 2002, 2003), but there is little evidence for any of these types of buildings at other cities. The most extensively excavated epicenter, Tlatelolco, does have some structures that do not conform to the types discussed here, but their uses and significance are not clear. Of the various specialized public buildings described for Tenochtitlan, the ones most likely to have existed in other cities are the two types of schools—the calmecac and the *telpochcalli*—and buildings for gatherings of elite warriors.

The telpochcalli was a basic school where boys and girls learned ritual practices (singing, dancing, playing musical instruments) and boys received military training. Although these schools were said to exist in every town, there are no firm descriptions of them outside of Tenochtitlan. The calmecac was a more exclusive school, catering to children of the nobility, which provided training for government, the priesthood, and military leadership (Calnek 1988). Priests lived in the calmecac, as did the students. It was located adjacent to a major temple, which may account for the statement by Zorita (above) that priests lived permanently in the major temples. The calmecac was the place where Aztec elite culture was inculcated into the youth of the nobility. They learned myths and rituals, historical accounts, music and dance, how to read codices, and how to behave like proper Aztec nobles.

Archaeologically, one would expect a calmecac to be a special kind of residence (perhaps with dormitory-type rooms for the resident priests, novices, and students), located next to a major temple, with evidence for extensive ritual activity. The excavator of the royal palace at Calixtlahuaca, José García Payón, believed the structure was a calmecac, and it is still labeled such for visitors to the zone, but it is clear from its form that this was a palace. Calmecacs have yet to be identified archaeologically.

Another likely type of public building was a house for the gathering of elite warriors. One particularly well-preserved example—known as the Eagle Warriors House—was excavated adjacent to the Templo Mayor of Tenochtitlan (López Luján 2006). Another possible example is the circular chamber at the hilltop precinct of Malinalco (fig. 2.17), interpreted by some as a warriors' chamber (Hernández Rivero 2004). Although it would not be surprising to find smaller versions of these structures at altepetl capitals, the only likely candidate to date is a long hall decorated with paintings of shields excavated at a site in southern Puebla on the edge of Aztec central Mexico (Sisson and Lilly 1994).

Finally, the *temazcalli* (sweatbath) is another possible type of public architecture. Many Mesoamerican cities had public sweatbaths (for example, Cresson 1938; Houston 1996), and small domestic sweathouses survive today as important ethnographic features in central Mexico (Soustelle 1993). They are used today for medicinal, hygienic, and ceremonial purposes, uses that can probably be projected back to the public sweatbaths of ancient Mesoamerica.

The fact that calmecacs and warriors' houses have not been identified at altepetl capitals outside of Tenochtitlan could indicate that their activities took place in other locations. The royal palace is the logical place for these. Palaces were large buildings with numerous rooms, and in a small city they may have been the settings where nobles were schooled and warriors gathered. Only in a large metropolis like Tenochtitlan were these activities separated into their own specialized buildings.

URBAN PUBLIC ARCHITECTURE

The Ceremony of Tlacaxipeualiztli

The ceremony of Tlacaxipeualiztli illustrates some of the rituals that took place in and around the temples and shrines described above. Figure 4.10 is a tracing by Eduard Seler (1927) of the painting of this ceremony in the *Primeros Memoriales* of Sahagún (1993: f. 250r). This was one of a sequence of 18 monthly public religious celebrations known as the *veintena* ceremonies, which are discussed in detail in chapter 6. The major themes of Tlacaxipeualiztli focused on two series of human sacrifices dedicated to the god Xipe Totec ("Our lord with the flayed skin"). In one type of ritual, victims were sacrificed at the top of a single-temple pyramid (top center) and then flayed (top left). Priests donned the flayed skins and performed a variety of rites. The second type of sacrifice was the gladiator sacrifice (see above). At top right, a victim is tied to the circular altar, and at his left and below are two eagle warriors and a jaguar warrior who engaged the victim in mock battle.

Figure 4.10. Depiction of the monthly ceremony (veintena) of Tlacaxipeualiztli from the *Primeros Memoriales* of Sahagún. (After Seler 1927.)

Behind the warriors is a tzompantli, which has a double meaning here. First and most obviously this is the shrine where the skulls of victims were displayed. Second, the tzompantli was a spatial marker in the events surrounding the gladiator sacrifice; captives were assembled at the tzompantli while awaiting their turn on the altar. At center left is a smaller temple, probably one of several temples that featured sacrifices and offerings during Tlacaxipeualiztli. Two musicians are shown near this temple, one with a conch shell trumpet and the other with a ceramic flute. Below them a priest dances. At bottom right are three figures dancing with rattles; these may relate to Sahagún's (1997: 57) description that during this ceremony commoners and nobles danced together with rattles. At lower left two individuals carry paper banners or flags; their role in the events is unclear.

This image depicts only a small portion of the numerous activities that made up the Tlacaxipeualiztli veintena ceremony (Broda 1970; Carrasco 1991), but it does suggest something of the busy public activity involved and the different sorts of rites that were practiced. It also situates much of the action with respect to five architectural features in the urban epicenter: a large single-temple pyramid where a victim is sacrificed; a small shrine in front of the pyramid; a smaller temple with musicians and dancers; a circular temalacatl altar, most likely placed on top of a rectangular shrine (fig. 4.8C), and a tzompantli that served as a staging area for the sacrificial rites.

In book 2 of the *Florentine Codex*, devoted to the monthly ceremonies, there are scattered mentions of the uses of public buildings during the veintena celebrations (Sahagún 1950–82: bk. 2). For example, during Tlaxochimalco, musicians, singers, and dancers stood next to a circular altar (p. 110); during Ochpaniztli, when a procession went by the skull rack, they beat a drum (122); during Tepeilhuitl, sacrificed victims were decapitated next to the skull rack and their skulls were mounted immediately (133); and during Panquetzaliztli, branches were spread on circular altars (141).

The surviving descriptions of the monthly veintena ceremonies are rich sources of information about the ceremonial lives of Aztec cities. Sahagún's painting of some of the activities during Tlacaxipeualiztli shows how various temples and religious shrines were arranged to provide settings for major religious rituals. The social and political significance of the monthly ceremonies are taken up in more detail in chapter 6 below. For the present chapter, their importance lies in their use of the public buildings that were arranged together in the downtowns—or epicenters—of Aztec cities.

The Urban Epicenter

Most of the public architecture in Aztec cities was concentrated in the urban epicenter. For all measurable Late Postclassic Mesoamerican cities, the median size of urban epicenters is 2.0 hectares (Smith 2005a: 415). Most Aztec city-state epicenters were between 1 and 2 hectares, and the largest—16.9 hectares—was in Tenochtitlan. Since the median extent of Late Postclassic Mesoamerican cities was 90 hectares (Smith 2005a), these calculations indicate that the average city had most or all of its public architecture concentrated in less than 3 percent of its total area. A few cities did have large buildings located away from the center of town (for example, the circular temple at Huexotla), but in general the temples, ballcourts, and palaces described above were clustered together in the center of the city.

These Aztec urban epicenters and their public architecture were far smaller than their counterparts in large Mesoamerican cities such as Chichén Itzá, Teotihuacan, Monte Alban, Tula, or the Classic Maya cities (Andrews 1975). Nevertheless, the concentration of public buildings created a skyline at Aztec cities that towered over the residential zones and the rural hinterlands beyond. Visitors to the epicenter, whether commoner urbanites from residential neighborhoods or visitors from outside the city, would have encountered Aztec townscapes as impressive built environments. The strong visual effects of public architecture on viewers were produced not just by the individual buildings and their concentration in the epicenter but also by the connections among buildings and their arrangements around plazas. In the next chapter I take up these issues of planning and meaning of Aztec townscapes.

5

Form, Meaning, and Urban Planning

But, whether or not the town plan really derives from traditional cosmological
ideas, it certainly reflects, with quite remarkable fidelity, the pattern of political
realities within each settlement. (Krapf-Askari 1969: 42)

Aztec kings and builders, like their Yoruba counterparts discussed by Krapf-
Askari, took great care in deciding where to build the stone buildings described in chapter 4. They carefully designed and laid out their cities in accordance with widely recognized canons of urban design. The use of these
planning concepts accomplished two things. First, they helped each ruler
achieve a series of political and ideological goals that furthered his power
and control. The townscape of the epicenter was not just a collection of
buildings in a city center; it was a material statement by rulers that helped
strengthen their rulership. The arrangement of buildings, particularly monumental buildings arranged in formal patterns, produced emotional effects in
the people who observed them, and these were designed to legitimize and
further the rule of kings. Second, the adherence to basic canons of urban design also communicated messages about the cultural affiliation and identity
of the city and the altepetl. There were basic ideas about what an Aztec city
should look like, and by making cities conform to this model, kings forged
community identities while sending strong visual messages about their legitimacy and right to rule.

In this chapter I first identify the concepts and models of urban design
and city planning used by Aztec kings and builders. I employ a model of
city planning in the ancient world that focuses on two kinds of material patterns: coordination among buildings and standardization among cities (this
model is described in Smith 2007a). I then turn to the meanings of Aztec
townscapes—their buildings, spaces, and arrangements on the ground—to
explore the social and cultural contexts of buildings and their planned arrangement. The urban built environment can be understood as both an arena
for the communication of messages of royal ideology by rulers and as a setting where the lives of people took place and acquired meaning (Rapoport
1988, 1990a). Urban life is explored in chapter 6.

One thing will become clear in this chapter: the uniqueness of the city of Tenochtitlan. As previewed in chapter 3, the city's Mexica rulers began with the basic canons of Aztec city layout, but as their empire expanded they added new features and concepts to achieve a unique urban configuration very different from other Aztec cities. The common assumption that Aztec city-state capitals imitated the layout of Tenochtitlan[1] is incorrect both descriptively (the two patterns were very different) and historically (the late city Tenochtitlan imitated aspects of other Aztec cities, not the reverse).

URBAN PLANNING IN ANCIENT CITIES

Writing on ancient urban planning has been hampered by reliance upon some simplistic and ethnocentric notions. For many decades most authors employed a dichotomy between planned and unplanned cities and used the criterion of an orthogonal grid layout to identify "planned" cities. Yet the variety of urban forms in the premodern world cannot be classified in this way without seriously distorting the nature of their organization and layout (Lilley 2002: 157; Smith 2007a). A useful approach to ancient urban planning is suggested by historical geographer Keith Lilley in his book on medieval cities:

> Generally speaking, "planning" operates at different levels; it will include deciding where a new urban landscape should be put, and considerations about what form it should take and how it should be laid out on the ground. . . . Urban planning, therefore, was about more than just laying out new towns with regular plans—it was about designing, planning, and building new townscapes. (Lilley 2002: 157)

Urban planning can be a difficult topic for archaeologists, since we seldom have access to the actual ideas, procedures, and contexts of ancient planning and construction activities. My planning model (Smith 2007a) is designed to approach the subject through the material manifestations of ancient planning decisions, using the kinds of data—city plans and architectural reconstructions—to which archaeologists have access. These data are evaluated with respect to two phenomena: the coordinated placement of buildings (the greater the extent to which individual buildings are arranged in relation to one another, the greater the extent of planning) and standardization among cities (the existence of standardized urban forms or phenomena suggests that cities were deliberately planned to achieve this standardization). This model allows the existence of variation in both the nature and degree of city planning, unlike previous studies that divide cities artificially into planned and unplanned examples.

AZTEC URBAN PLANNING

The Planning Process

Following a model presented by Lilley (2002: 157–163; 2005), the planning of historical or ancient cities can be divided into a series of tasks, including (1) selection of the general location of a city, (2) selection of the specific site for construction, (3) design and surveying, and (4) construction. Unfortunately, there is little direct evidence for any of these stages, but some reasonable possibilities can be suggested.

Selection of the General Location

Unlike many of the medieval cities Lilley analyzed, decisions about the general location of Aztec city-state capitals were circumscribed. City-states were small polities, and the capital had to be within the general land occupied by the polity's members. The location of a city-state itself would have been established early on, when the migrants first arrived and settled in an area. But this was not a case of a ruler looking far and wide to find a site for a new capital, a common practice in the ancient Old World.

Selection of the Specific Site

City-state capitals were probably established toward the center of the area inhabited by the polity's members; perhaps whichever early settlement grew fastest and attracted the most nobles was selected by the tlatoani as his capital. Alternatively, the capital may have been selected first, the subjects then settling the surrounding lands.

Design and Surveying

We know next to nothing about the specific personnel or processes involved in designing, surveying, and laying out Aztec cities. Architects are mentioned in a few sources, but other than one noted example, we do not know if architects were nobles, priests, or commoners. The exception was the celebrated "poet-king" Nezahualcoyotl of Texcoco, whose many talents included that of architect. He is reputed to have designed and built many of the temples in Texcoco, as well as palaces, irrigation systems, and aqueducts. Several pictorial codices provide clues about surveying techniques used to lay out and measure agricultural fields (Harvey and Williams 1980, 1986). These sources demonstrate a strong concern with accurate measurement, a feature that probably applied to urban surveyors as well.

Construction

Of all the steps involved in the planning process, we have the most information on construction techniques (this section is based upon Rojas 1986: 142–146). Masons, stonecutters, and carpenters are mentioned frequently in written sources as occupational specialists—and not just in Tenochtitlan. These specialists worked on public construction projects as part of their taxes to the state. One component of Aztec taxation was a system known as rotational labor in which every household contributed a set number of hours of labor per year to the king or another noble (Hicks 1984). Labor taxation programs like this are known as corvée labor (Booth 1998). This was one way that skilled construction workers were recruited for urban building projects. In the words of the chronicler Alonso de Zorita,

> The building of the temples and the houses of the lords and public works was always a common undertaking, and many people worked together with much merriment. . . . Each worked a little and did what he could, and no one hurried or mistreated him for it. . . . Thus they went about their work, cheerfully and harmoniously. (Zorita 1963: 203)

It is possible that such labor exercises were followed by a feast, which could explain the cheerful attitude noted by Zorita; otherwise one may doubt whether people really paid their labor tax so readily and happily. Construction specialists and unskilled laborers also offered their services for pay in the marketplace, where construction materials were also sold.

Plazas and Coordination among Buildings

Aztec urban design began with the plaza, which served as the spatial anchor for the entire epicenter. The formal plaza has been called the fundamental unit of Mesoamerican city layout, the feature that generated and structured urban space (Arancón García 1992). William Ringle and George Bey note that

> rather than being the by-product of building placement, the plaza instead may be seen as a socially and ritually charged field about which buildings were built. In other words, such spaces are owed primacy in understanding site layouts. (Ringle and Bey 2001: 278–279)

The first dimension of my urban planning model is the extent to which the locations and forms of individual buildings are coordinated with one another. In Aztec cities the plaza was the central feature for the coordination of buildings. Cities exhibited a high degree of coordination among buildings in their epicenters but not in their residential zones. In other words, they had planned epicenters but unplanned residential zones. The nature and layout of residential areas are discussed in chapter 6; the present chapter focuses on planning within urban epicenters. This pattern of a planned epicenter coupled with unplanned residential areas is one of the ancient and fundamental principles of city layout in Mesoamerica (Marcus 1983). The adoption of this basic urban structure signaled the participation of Aztec city-state capitals in the Mesoamerican urban tradition.

Of the various types of deliberate coordination that can exist among buildings (Smith 2007a), the epicenters of Aztec cities typically exhibit common alignments, formal layouts, monumentality, and some degree of orthogonality. In short, Aztec cities had extensively planned townscapes. These various elements of planning converged on the central plaza. The plaza was most important at the Morelos cities with the Tula plaza plan (figs. 1.1, 3.5; see the discussion in chapter 3). As noted in chapter 3, Tula's epicenter was perhaps the most formally organized city center in ancient Mesoamerica. The plaza was rectangular and symmetrical, and it gave an orthogonal structure to all of the buildings in its immediate vicinity (figs. 1.5, 3.4). The Morelos Aztec cities reproduced this pattern, although at a smaller scale than at the Toltec capital.

As at Tula, these Aztec plazas created a strongly formal arrangement in which most public buildings shared a common orthogonal layout. Although the buildings were smaller than those at the large Mesoamerican cities such as Teotihuacan, Monte Alban, or Tikal, they created a strong visual impression on people within the plaza. The visitor in the plaza was surrounded by carefully arranged stone buildings. The largest in area was the palace of the ruler, and the tallest in height was the central pyramid, which towered over the plaza.

The basic features of the Tula plaza plan are also reproduced on page 36 of the *Codex Borbonicus* (Anders et al. 1991). This image (fig. 5.1), one of the few surviving pre-Spanish maps of an Aztec urban epicenter, depicts a plaza with five structures and a series of deities. A large single-temple pyramid (with the break in alfarda angle; see chapter 4) dominates the plaza on the east side, and opposite this is a smaller temple with a tzitzimime shrine in front. Another temple is located on the south side of the plaza, and an unadorned shrine sits in the center.[2] Fourteen deities or ixiptla (deity impersonators; see chapter 4) and a bundle of sacred firewood are arranged around the sides of the plaza. The purpose of this image was to illustrate rites in the veintena cer-

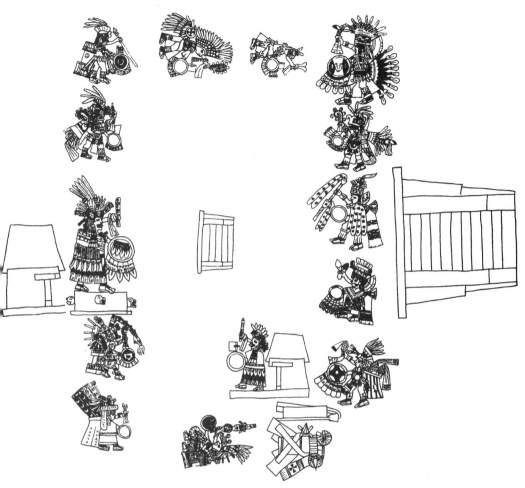

Figure 5.1. Tula plaza plan in the *Codex Borbonicus* (Anders et al. 1991: 36). The image has been rotated 90 degrees clockwise so that east is at the right. (After Séjourné 1983: 168.)

emony of Tititl, whose major event was the sacrifice of the impersonator of the goddess Ilama Tecuhtli. According to Sahagún's (1950–82: bk. 2, p. 156) description of Tititl, after the sacrifice numerous ixiptla marched around the temple in a line; this is probably the scene illustrated in the *Codex Borbonicus* (fig. 5.1).

As noted in chapter 3, Aztec city-state capitals outside of Morelos do not conform as closely to the layout of Tula (fig. 5.2). These city plans are more difficult to evaluate because there are fewer examples and most have only partial preservation of the urban epicenter. Ixtapaluca (fig. 5.2) is probably the best-preserved city-state epicenter in the Basin of Mexico, yet it is difficult to discern an overall design to the public architecture. Some buildings were destroyed by construction activities in the 1960s, however (see chapter 2), and it is possible that some key structures are missing today. The location of the epicenter on a long, narrow ridge probably influenced the layout of buildings. A north-south row of structures, including a series of shrines, a palace, and a circular temple, may have formed the west side of a large plaza, with the large pyramid with an enclosed patio at the south end. This pyramid faces east, with a small enclosed patio on its east side, an unusual orientation for a central Aztec temple. It is possible that the main plaza was originally west of the pyramid, with the ballcourt on the north side and the palace in the northeast corner; unfortunately, the existing excavation results do not allow this possibility to be evaluated.

Aztec Huexotla, another relatively well-preserved city in the Basin of Mexico, has several public buildings concentrated in what is now the modern village of the same name (fig. 5.2). Many other structures have probably been destroyed or have not been located, but the central pyramid does face west, and it probably defined the east side of a central plaza, whose west side may have been marked by a monumental stone wall (see below). Other public buildings at the site are located at some distance from this hypothetical plaza. The plan of Zultepec (fig. 5.2) is even more difficult to interpret, since it is not at all clear whether the excavated and mapped structures comprise the entire epicenter, part of the epicenter, or even a separate compound outside of the city's epicenter. What appears to be a small formal plaza has a circular structure on its west side and a quite modest temple on its east side. A residential complex is located north of the circular temple.

Another example of an epicenter that may not conform to the Tula plaza plan is the depiction of Cholula in the *Historia Tolteca-Chichimeca* (fig. 2.14). This map contains a major temple facing west (assuming that this plan is oriented with east at the top), along with two temples dedicated to Quetzalcoatl, a calmecac, and various other features (see chapter 2). In this map the temples and shrines are contained within a great plaza or open space that is surrounded by the residences of nobles. This is a very different pattern from Aztec archaeological zones, in which the plaza is an open area framed by buildings, not a semi-enclosed space full of buildings. The only Aztec epicenters that resemble the Cholula map are Tenochtitlan and Tlatelolco, with their sacred precincts full of temples and other public buildings. If this map is an accurate portrayal of the Cholula epicenter in Postclassic times, then Cholula was an interesting variant on the basic Aztec epicenter plan. On the other hand, it seems equally likely that the map may not be accurate in the

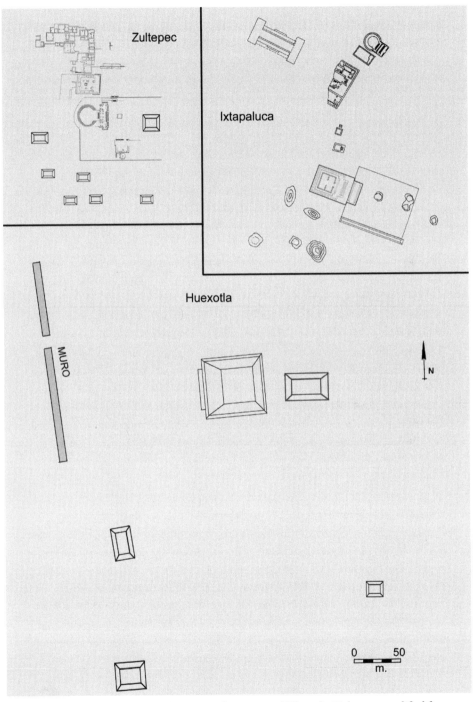

Figure 5.2. Epicenters of cities in the Basin of Mexico and Tlaxcala. Zultepec: modified from
Martínez Vargas and Jarquín Pacheco (1998: 21, 22); Ixtapaluca: after Brüggemann (1987: 160)
and Taladoire (1981: pl. 62); Huexotla: after García García (1987).

spatial arrangement of buildings, in which case its layout could have been based on the plan of Tenochtitlan, or perhaps on Spanish urban planning conventions, which had a large open plaza flanked by a church, other public buildings, and residences of the wealthy (Crouch, Garr, and Mundingo 1982).

Walled Precincts?

As noted above, Huexotla has the remains of several massive north-south stone wall segments to the west of most of the public architecture (fig. 5.2). Although most authors assume that this was part of a precinct wall that once surrounded the urban epicenter (as at Tenochtitlan), I am more struck by the absence of such wall segments in other places at the site. One would think that if these massive walls had formed a rectangular precinct, traces would have been reported in other parts of the town. It would be a relatively simple matter to search for remains of this wall with some targeted excavations, but no one has done this yet.

The wall segments at Huexotla bring up the question of walled precincts at Aztec cities. Based upon the presence of the walled sacred precinct in Tenochtitlan and several ambiguous references in the works of the chroniclers, many authors have asserted that all or most Aztec cities had such precincts, but this was not the case. Much of the discussion can be traced to the chronicler Motolinía (1979: 50–51), whose words suggest that he is generalizing to all cities when he mentions a wall surrounding the central ceremonial district. In addition, Sahagún's (1993: 269r) illustration of the walled precinct of Tenochtitlan has caused much confusion. Following Sahagún, for example, Nicholson (1971b: 437) suggests that "all communities of substantial size" had walled precincts. Based on the evidence discussed in this book, this statement must be seen as incorrect.

I attribute these interpretations to an overemphasis on Tenochtitlan as a model for Aztec cities. Nicholson (2003b) makes the strange and unlikely suggestion that Sahagún's painting represents a (hypothetical) walled precinct at Tepeapulco, not Tenochtitlan, because the painting shows far fewer than the 78 buildings described for Tenochtitlan in Sahagún's (1950–82: bk. 2, pp. 179–93) text. One is hard pressed to imagine how a native painter would include all 78 buildings in a single illustration, however. For fuller discussion, see Heyden's comments on this topic in Sahagún (1993: 117–119, n. 1). In sum, there is little concrete evidence for walled precincts outside of Tenochtitlan and Tlatelolco, and this feature should not be considered a basic element of Aztec urban planning.

Standardization Among Cities

The standardization of buildings and layouts among a series of cities is the second component of my urban planning model (Smith 2007a). The basic idea is that architectural similarities suggest the existence of a model of the proper urban center to which the builders of a series of cities attempted to conform. The Tula plaza plan found at Morelos cities is the clearest case of spatial standardization. In cities that do not conform to the Tula plaza plan, the central role of formal plazas and the eastern location of the (west-facing) central temple pyramid are examples of spatial standardization. The most striking types of standardization among Aztec city-state capitals, however, concern individual public buildings.

As discussed in chapter 4, many of the basic building types show high levels of standardization in form. In some cases structures in different cities are virtually identical: Double-temple pyramids in the major capitals are quite similar, circular temples always have their stairs on the east side, and all known ballcourts have the same shape. In other cases there was more variation, but all examples conformed to a basic layout. Palaces are the best example, but small altars and single-temple pyramids also show great similarity and are easily distinguished from structures of these types built by other Mesoamerican cultures.

Another type of standardization among Aztec city-state capitals is their architectural inventory. Table 4.1 lists the various major building types found in my architectural sample. Nearly all cities with a minimal level of architectural preservation had a large pyramid of either the single-temple or double-temple variety (17 sites). Equally as common were shrines (17 sites), followed by palaces (12 sites). Given the variations in preservation and excavation of Aztec cities, it does not seem unreasonable to infer that these three categories were the fundamental kinds of buildings constructed in Aztec cities, and that they were part of a native model of what constituted a proper Aztec city. This reconstruction matches the model of the proper Aztec city as inferred from native historical sources, with one exception. From the native viewpoint, the royal palace and the temple of the patron god(s) were the dominant urban features, but shrines and platforms are barely mentioned in discussions of urban architecture.

The fact that native historical prose accounts fail to mention shrines as basic urban features can be explained in two ways. First, these were much smaller and less impressive than pyramids and palaces and perhaps less memorable to natives recounting their history to Spanish chroniclers several decades after the Spanish conquest. But a more likely explanation is that

Table 5.1. Types of Buildings Depicted in a Major Ritual Cycle in the *Códice Borgia*

Building	Deities Worshipped
Temples	
Temple of the sky, with conical roof	Quetzalcoatl and Tlauizcalpantecuhtli
Temple of the sky, with roof with eaves	Xolotl
Temple of jade and precious flowers	The sun
Temple of darkness and death	Cihuacoatl
Shrines and altars[a]	
Circular altar for ritual dances	
Jade shrine for ritual dances and sacrifices	
Circular shrine decorated with a serpent wall	
Small shrine	Xolotl
Four eagle houses or temples around a plaza	
Tzitzimime platform[b]	Tlauizcalpantecuhtli
Other buildings and features	
Ballcourt	
Sunken patio or subterranean chamber	Cipactonal
Plaza with a great hearth	
Sanctuary	Tepeyollotl and Chalchiuhtlicue
A river and a crossroads	

Sources: The images are in the *Códice Borgia* (1993: 29–48), and the interpretations are from Anders, Jansen, and Reyes García (1993: 181–187).
[a]I employ my classification of platforms and features here; for example, what the authors call a "jade altar" I label a "jade shrine."
[b]This feature, a platform decorated with skulls, is called a skull rack by the Anders, Jansen, and Reyes Garcia.

many of these shrines or altars were associated with women's rituals, part of a system of "alternative religious practitioners" that was separate from, and perhaps in opposition to, the state religion (Clendinnen 1991: 54–56). This realm was not only poorly understood by the Spanish friars but also feared and repressed (Burkhart 1997; Klein 2000). Thus it is entirely possible that native informants neglected to mention such features and their rituals to the chroniclers, or that the chroniclers chose to leave these out of their texts. In contrast to the written sources, the Aztec ritual codices are full of depictions of shrines (figs. 2.14, 5.1).

The public buildings depicted in the ritual codices provide another perspective on the architectural inventories of Aztec cities. The best example is the *Códice Borgia* (Anders, Jansen, and Reyes García 1993), whose numerous ritual scenes include many temples, shrines, and other buildings. The most elaborate section of this codex—with the largest number of buildings—is a long passage on pages 29–48 of the codex. Anders and colleagues give two labels to this passage: "The nine rites for light, life and maize" and "Diverse ceremonies in a complex of temples, under the supervision of [the priest of the deity] Cihuacoatl" (Anders, Jansen, and Reyes García 1993: 175). In table 5.1 I have listed the various buildings and features that occur in this passage, following the interpretations of Anders and colleagues (which are based ultimately on the work of Nowotny 2005). At least four different temples are depicted, and most appear to be single-temple pyramids. As expected from the archaeological zones, temples are outnumbered by shrines and altars. Other features include a ballcourt, various specialized ritual features, and a river and crossroads. Overall there is good agreement between the inventory of structures in this passage of the *Codex Borgia* and the structures excavated at Aztec cities.

These similarities among Aztec cities in buildings and inventories are an example of canonical architectural communication. There was a basic cognitive model of what an Aztec city should look like: what buildings it must contain, what they should be like, and how they should be arranged. Although no explicit description of this hypothesized cognitive model has survived, the native historical information on cities reviewed in chapter 3 accords with the archaeological data and the codices. The evidence suggests that such a model did indeed exist among the royalty and nobility of Aztec central Mexico.

Urban Infrastructure

One additional aspect of urban planning is the design and construction of urban infrastructure—public features such as roads, bridges, communications, and the supply of food and water to the city. The only Aztec city with much information about infrastructure is Tenochtitlan. The canals running through the city greatly impressed the Spanish conquerors, who remarked on some of the associated features such as bridges and boats in the canals. The causeways that ran from the lakeshore to Tenochtitlan also received some comment, particularly the aqueducts that supplied fresh water from springs at Chapultepec on the shore (Zorita 1963). Bribiesca Castrejón (1958) discusses the aqueducts at some length as part of a treatment of the water supply of Tenochtitlan. Beyond this, there are bits and pieces of information on sanitation and public health in the imperial capital (Ortiz de Montellano 1990).

Outside of Tenochtitlan, there is very little information about such topics as water supply, sanitation, or roads and transport. Xaltocan, situated on an island in salty Lake Xaltocan, also had an aqueduct to bring fresh water from a spring on the shore, but this was to irrigate the chinampas, not for drinking water (see chapter 2). Urban food supply is a major topic of research for Tenochtitlan, whose many thousands of inhabitants may have periodically found it difficult to obtain sufficient grain. It was much easier to supply smaller Aztec cities with grain, however, and this topic is taken up in chapter 7.

LEVELS OF MEANING IN THE BUILT ENVIRONMENT

Given that Aztec cities show multiple evidence for central planning (in their epicenters, at least), what does this imply about the meaning and significance of the buildings and layouts? As discussed in chapter 1, the topic of meaning is difficult to reconstruct, both methodologically and theoretically, for ancient cities. What did ancient buildings mean to the people who built them and the people who used them? Was religious symbolism pervasive in ancient societies, as some writers maintain? How can we investigate this topic rigorously without succumbing to the rampant speculation that all too often passes for scholarly interpretation? Amos Rapoport's model, introduced in chapter 1, provides a path through the difficulties of analyzing ancient meanings. I briefly review his three levels of meaning (high-level, middle-level, and low-level meanings) and then relate them to the architectural data on Aztec townscapes.

Rapoport's *high-level meaning* refers to the explicit symbolism of buildings and cities within a religious or cultural tradition. In Rapoport's scheme *middle-level meaning* refers to the transmission of messages about identity, status, and power. The concept of "architectural communication" focuses on middle-level meanings. Many of the characteristics of Aztec buildings and their arrangements into townscapes can only be understood by attention to their middle-level meanings. Rapoport's *low-level meaning* concerns the influence of the built environment on the thought and behavior of individuals. I use the concept of "townscape interaction" in chapter 6 to analyze low-level meanings of Aztec cities.

HIGH-LEVEL MEANINGS: COSMOLOGY AND THE GODS

It is a commonplace notion that religion was of great importance in most realms of life in ancient civilizations. Although there is much historical and archaeological evidence that accords with this viewpoint (for example, Trigger 2003), the methodological tasks of reconstructing ancient religious concepts from archaeological data alone—without the use of texts—are daunting (Flannery and Marcus 1993). Nevertheless, there seems to be a strong desire among some students of ancient civilizations to see religious symbolism as pervasive, even in the absence of supporting evidence.[3] In the case of high-level urban meanings, this desire manifests itself in speculative reconstructions of cosmological symbolism of cities and buildings. I have previously criticized this trend as applied to Classic Maya cities (Smith 2003b, 2005b), and those criticisms apply equally to speculative accounts of the cosmological significance of Aztec city plans.

Although it is likely that many ancient buildings and cities had religious or cosmological significance, many authors go beyond this observation to claim that this religious symbolism was a source of power for ancient rulers (for example, Reese-Taylor and Koontz 2001). In ancient states, however, religious power is rarely a direct source of social or political power (except in stories like J. R. R. Tolkien's *Lord of the Rings*). The cosmological importance of a building may help a king legitimize his rule, but it does little to contribute directly to his power or rulership (Earle 1997; Kurtz 2001: 63–64; Trigger 2003: 250).

The Symbolism of Individual Temples and Shrines

Most discussion of high-level meanings of individual structures at Aztec cities has focused on the Templo Mayor of Tenochtitlan (fig. 5.3), whose cosmological symbolism and meaning have been much discussed using the concept of "cosmovision" (Broda, Carrasco, and Matos Moctezuma 1987; Carrasco 1999b; Matos Moctezuma 1988). Thanks to the preservation of numerous

Figure 5.3. Artist's reconstruction of the sacred precinct of Tenochtitlan with the Templo Mayor. (Marquina 1951: lám. 55.)

Aztec myths and religious texts, we have a good idea of the specific symbolic meaning and significance of the Templo Mayor, its offerings, and the rituals that occurred there. The two temples atop the Templo Mayor were dedicated to the deities Tlaloc and Huitzilopochtli. The pyramid was often referred to as Coatepec, a setting for one of the key Aztec origin myths. The Mexica patron god Huitzilopochtli was born at Coatepec, and his first action was to slaughter his siblings, an act that included the dismemberment of his sister Coyolxauhqui. A large buried sculpture of the dismembered Coyolxauhqui was excavated in front of the Templo Mayor, confirming the temple's symbolic association with this myth. The rich offerings at the Templo Mayor provide abundant details of the symbolism and rituals dedicated to Tlaloc (López Luján 2005).

In short, we have considerable information about the specific high-level meanings of the Templo Mayor of Tenochtitlan, and there is a large body of scholarship on this topic. Unfortunately, this rich evidence is not matched for the single- or double-temple pyramids at other Aztec cities. Sources suggest that each temple had a patron god, but we rarely have evidence on the identity of such deities for individual temples.

On the other hand we know quite a bit about the religious significance of circular temples (chapter 4). Their association with Ehecatl is abundantly confirmed in the chronicles, in the codices, and in offerings of Ehecatl sculptures excavated in association with circular temples. We also have some information about the symbolism and deity associations for at least two categories of shrine—the tzitzimime shrine (Klein 2000) and the momoztli shrine dedicated to Tezcatlipoca (Olivier 2003: 272–82). It is clear that Aztec religious structures had rich symbolic associations with individual deities and mythological events, and in some cases we can reconstruct these high-level meanings from texts (see also the discussions of the mountaintop temples at Tepozteco and Huixachtepetl in chapter 2). When we turn to symbolic interpretations of whole cities, however, we move from the realm of empirical scholarship to the realm of speculation.

City Symbolism

Some of the cosmovision scholars have attempted to extend the well-documented high-level meanings of the Templo Mayor to the entire city of Tenochtitlan (for example, Carrasco 1999b), claiming that the entire city was a sacred place whose formal attributes—its orthogonal layout, the division into quarters, the four major avenues—had cosmological significance (fig. 5.4). I have pointed out elsewhere (Smith 2003b) that there is no textual basis for this interpretive extension. Universalistic theories of the sacred na-

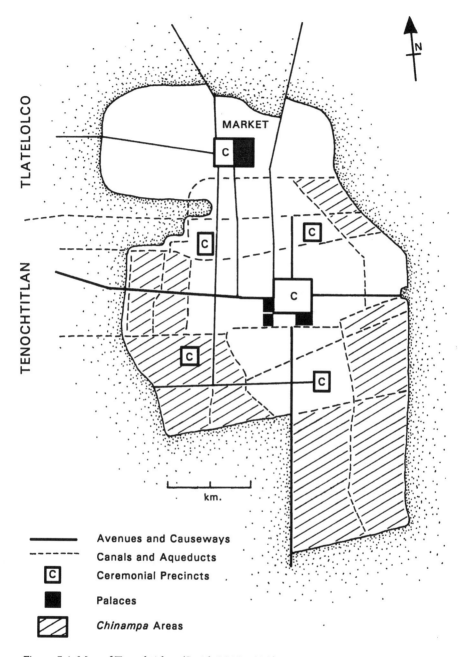

TLATELOLCO

TENOCHTITLAN

MARKET

N

C

C

C

C

C

C

km.

——————— Avenues and Causeways

- - - - - - - Canals and Aqueducts

C Ceremonial Precincts

■ Palaces

▨ *Chinampa* Areas

Figure 5.4. Map of Tenochtitlan. (Smith 2003a: 186.)

Figure 5.5. Cosmogram from the *Codex Féjerváry-Mayer*, 1. (After Šprajc 2004: 169.)

ture of ancient settlements (Eliade 1959; Rykwert 1988; Wheatley 1971) are naïve and inadequate, and in the absence of written texts there is no way to determine whether the layout of Tenochtitlan, or any other Aztec city, had specific high-level meanings to their inhabitants. If such high-level meanings did exist for the entire city, they were most likely only known to a restricted group (members of the nobility and priests) who had studied at the calmecac; they would have been part of Aztec elite culture.

Mesoamerican cultures, including the Aztec, had a spatially based four-directional cosmology with elaborate symbolism and calendric attributes (Aveni 2001: 148–152; Smith 2005b; Thompson 1934). A number of graphic representations of this directional cosmology, known as cosmograms, are found in the codices and sculptures. For example, an image from the *Codex Féjerváry-Mayer* (fig. 5.5) shows four directions (with east at the top), each with specific sacred trees, birds, deities, and other cult paraphernalia. The 260 days of the ritual calendar are arranged as small circles around the entire diagram.

In light of this cosmogram and the known importance of directional symbolism in Aztec thought, it is reasonable to suggest that the striking quadrilateral formality of the epicenter design of Tula and many Aztec cities may have had cosmological significance or symbolism. But there is currently no way to confirm or deny this inference. None of the chroniclers mention any such symbolism for an entire city or an entire urban epicenter. There is simply no empirical basis for extending our knowledge of the high-level meanings of the Templo Mayor of Tenochtitlan to the entire city, much less to other cities.

One can make a stronger argument, on the other hand, that key buildings in Aztec cities were laid out in accordance with astronomical phenomena, and this was a kind of high-level cosmological symbolism of its own. But like the basic associations of temples with deities, high-level astronomical meanings most likely operated on the level of individual buildings, not entire cities or epicenters.

HIGH-LEVEL MEANINGS: ASTRONOMICAL ALIGNMENTS

Considerable evidence exists to show that the peoples of ancient Mesoamerica were accomplished astronomers. Priests tracked the movements of the sun, moon, planets, and stars and used their observations to calculate calendric cycles quite accurately (Aveni 2001; Broda 1993; Šprajc 2001). Indeed, astronomy was an important part of Mesoamerican religion (Milbrath 1999). One chronicler, Motolinía (1971: 51), stated that the Templo Mayor of Tenochtitlan was oriented in line with sunrise on a key date in the Aztec calendar. When this alignment was off after an expansion of the pyramid, according to Motolinía, King Motecuhzoma ordered the building torn down and rebuilt to get the alignment right. Archaeoastronomers have yet to determine just how the sightings and other details of the process were carried out (Aveni and Calnek 1999; Aveni, Calnek, and Hartung 1988; Šprajc 2000a).

Although there is no textual evidence for astronomical orientations at other Aztec buildings, many archaeoastronomers posit solar (and other astronomical) alignments for such structures. Because there is no single consistent alignment for Aztec temples or other buildings (see below), some archaeoastronomers argue that individual structures were aligned with the direction of sunrise over key peaks and other visible features of the eastern horizon in what is called a horizon calendar or an orientation calendar (for example, Broda 1993).

Archaeoastronomer Ivan Šprajc (2001) has made numerous measurements of orientations of key buildings at central Mexican cities, including measurements of key horizon markers such as mountain peaks. He finds that a good number of the measured orientations match key calendric intervals for sunrises and sunsets and concludes that such orientations produced horizon calendars that were crucial in designing buildings and cities. In other words, builders selected the sites for temples and carefully oriented the temples in order to create orientation calendars that marked key intervals and dates in the annual solar cycle. He compares the buildings to Aztec cosmograms (fig. 5.4) and argues that

> by incorporating astronomical alignments into their architecture and urbanism, the ancient Mesoamericans reproduced and perpetuated the cosmic principles and heavenly order in their earthly environment. (Šprajc 2004: 173)

I find Šprajc's interpretation—that most Aztec temples were astronomically aligned—difficult to accept on both empirical and theoretical grounds. Empirically, his conclusions require far too many distinct orientations. If all or most major Aztec temples were aligned with sunrise on an important date—for example, if most Aztec temples shared the orientation of the Templo Mayor of Tenochtitlan—one might conclude that there was pervasive astronomical influence on building orientations. This is clearly not the case, however; the measured alignments for structures at the Aztec cities described in chapter 2 above are not at all consistent with one another. Although it is possible that each temple was aligned astronomically, using different principles and different orientations, this suggests a chaotic situation. We know that myths, rituals, and deities were widely shared among Aztec altepetl, largely due to the influence of calmecac training and the social networks that constituted Aztec elite culture. If astronomy were such a pervasive influence on temple alignments, I would expect far more uniformity among cities and buildings.

Theoretically, Šprajc's conclusions rest on the unlikely assumption that priests needed to mark important calendric dates in order to help farmers plan their agricultural activities throughout the year (Šprajc 2001: 71–88). He states that orientation calendars "were necessary for predicting important seasonal changes and for an efficient scheduling of the corresponding agricultural activities" (Šprajc 2004: 164–165).

There is no doubt that the Aztec annual calendar was tied to the agricultural cycle,[4] but it is unlikely that Aztec farmers needed the annual calendar to schedule their planting, harvesting, and other seasonal activities. Ross Hassig notes that "many agrarian societies lack the complex calendars of states and yet function perfectly well" (Hassig 2001: 70). Further, "everyday life, especially among farmers, does not depend on a calendar. Is there a farmer anywhere so ignorant as not to know when to plant or when to harvest?" (71). Traditional farmers use various clues in the natural environment to schedule their activities. For modern Mayan farmers of Yucatan, for example, "the beginning of the planting year is announced by the Bright-rumped Attila, a bird whose wild, loud, exquisite song carries a mile over the silent forest. The bird is sometimes called *pak' sak'ab* 'plant your fallow field'" (Anderson et al. 2005: 52). Sometimes the direction of sunrise is used to schedule planting. The Hopi of the U.S. Southwest observed the horizon to determine when to plant crops, but this was a simple observation of nature that did not involve priests, rituals, or temples (Titiev 1938).[5]

Although some Aztec temples were aligned with key features of the horizon and with directional astronomical events (Aveni 2001, 2003), current evidence is insufficient to infer that all or most temples were so aligned. Even if it could be shown that many buildings were astronomically aligned, however, the explanation for this practice is far more likely to lie in the workings of the Aztec calendar and the use of esoteric knowledge by priests than in the need to tell peasants when to schedule their agricultural activities.

ARCHITECTURAL COMMUNICATION
AND MIDDLE-LEVEL MEANINGS

Aztec buildings and cities were designed and built with at least two types of architectural communication (middle-level meanings) in mind: statements of identity and memory that made reference to Tula and the Toltecs and statements of monumentality and formality that proclaimed the power, glory, and legitimacy of kings. These messages were forms of political ideology,[6] created by the tlatoani and disseminated through visual and perceptual attributes of urban planning and design on the one hand, and through the forms and activities at public buildings on the other. Archaeologists use the term "materialization" to describe the process by which such messages were transformed into material form (DeMarrais, Castillo, and Earle 1996).

History and Memory

Aztec cities can be viewed as material statements about the adherence of their builders to the models of the Mesoamerican past. On the most general level, the inventory of public buildings and the use of the planned epicenter/ unplanned periphery spatial model signaled the participation of Aztec cities in the ancient Mesoamerican urban tradition. Not all central Mexican cities followed these principles. The Classic period metropolis of Teotihuacan clearly violated the basic canons of Mesoamerican urban design; for example, there was no central plaza, the basic design was structured by a single ceremonial street or way, the entire city was rigidly planned (not just the epicenter), and there were no ballcourts (fig. 5.6). The uniqueness of Teotihuacan culture within Mesoamerica has been much discussed (for example, Cowgill 1997; Pasztory 1997), although its urban features have yet to be fully analyzed from the perspective of Mesoamerican urban traditions.

After the fall of Teotihuacan, central Mexican city builders returned to earlier Mesoamerican roots by stressing epicenters planned around plazas coupled with unplanned residential zones, and prominent roles, spatially and culturally, for ballcourts. Tula's urban design was part of this trend (figs.

Figure 5.6. Teotihuacan from the air. Courtesy of the Companía Mexicana de Aerofoto.

1.5, 3.4). Tula's epicenter, with its symmetry and regularity, exhibits perhaps the most strongly formal plan of any Mesoamerican city. I have suggested elsewhere (Smith n.d.d) that Tula's builders may have deliberately rejected the idiosyncratic layout of Teotihuacan in an effort to proclaim their strong adherence to ancient Mesoamerican principles.

The adoption of Tula's urban plan by the builders of Aztec cities in Morelos may be seen as an example of urban social memory. Susan Alcock's (2002) concept of "memory theater" refers to architectural spaces designed to invoke specific memories of a glorious past (chapter 3). The use of the Tula plaza plan in Aztec altepetl capitals is a good example of this phenomenon. These references to Tula were strengthened by the adoption of such Toltec architectural features as circular temples, tzitzimime platforms, and palace plans. Such direct material references to Tula and the Toltecs would have been clearly understood by Aztec nobles trained in the calmecac, although it is less likely that commoners would have understood such messages.

Monumentality and Formality

In ancient cities, the size, decoration, and position of particular buildings communicated information about the power, status, and wealth of their builders and their owners or sponsors (Trigger 1990). Although the kings of Aztec altepetl had the largest palaces and temple pyramids in their realms, these features may have communicated the message that their sponsors had only limited power and influence. There were many city-states in Aztec central Mexico, each with its capital city with modest public architecture. These structures were significantly smaller than earlier urban architecture at Tula, Teotihuacan, Xochicalco, or, indeed, most of the large cities of ancient Mesoamerica.

The largest temple in the Early Aztec period was the double-temple pyramid at Tenayuca. Its contemporary, the double-temple pyramid at Teopanzolco, was much smaller in size. Thus in the Early Aztec period the hierarchical relationship between these two cities, as inferred from the native historical record (see chapter 2), was measured by the size of their pyramids. In the Late Aztec period, three cities had large double-temple pyramids: Texcoco, Tenochtitlan, and Tlatelolco. The first two were the major capitals of the Triple Alliance empire. While Tlatelolco's political status is not well understood, it may have been more powerful than Tenochtitlan prior to 1473, but after its conquest by Tenochtitlan in that year, its historical legacy was repressed. In any case, these three cities stood out among Aztec altepetl as the most powerful and influential polities. The decisions of their rulers to build double-temple pyramids may have signaled deliberate attempts to differentiate their cities from the mass of smaller altepetl (see the discussion below). Perhaps the very choice of this architectural form was an archaizing feature selected to invoke memories of the powerful ancestral city of Tenayuca.

Aztec kings made grander ideological claims about their power and influence on the level of the urban epicenter. The invocation of Tula was an ideological claim directed at the nobility, both within the altepetl and in other peer polities. The Toltec origins of Aztec city layout may have been unknown to most people, however. To commoners, the formality of urban epicenter design and the size of the plaza sent messages about power, stability, and control (Rapoport 1990a) in what could be called a secular political ideology.

The layout of Aztec urban plazas fits the requirement of "political stages," or settings for public political performances. Murray Edelman (1964: 95–99) notes that the common physical characteristics of political stages include massiveness, ornateness, and formality. He suggests that political stages are particularly important in the political process in situations where it is important to impress large audiences and when legitimation is an important public goal. Large crowds probably gathered in the plaza periodically to witness religious ceremonies or to hear oration from the king or priests. The formal plaza thus played a clear role in the political process (see also Goodsell 1988; Inomata and Coben 2006).

The Case of Tenochtitlan

Tenochtitlan was the most divergent Aztec city in form and planning, and this was not an accident. The Mexica kings deliberately made a series of planning decisions to emphasize the grandeur of the imperial capital and distinguish it from other Aztec cities. These changes pertain to the realm of middle-level meaning because they were material statements of identity and power.

We know next to nothing of the layout of Tenochtitlan and its epicenter during its first century, prior to the founding of the Triple Alliance empire in 1428. It seems reasonable to hypothesize that the Templo Mayor (whose earliest stages date to the early years of the city) was originally part of an epicenter with a plan similar to other Aztec cities. The temple faced west, like most other Aztec central temples, and thus the plaza would have been in the area immediately to its west. At some stage in its history, however, the Mexica rulers made a radical break with the Aztec city plan by enclosing the central area in a walled precinct and filling it with buildings (fig. 5.3). By the time of the Spanish conquest the sacred precinct was full of temples, shrines, altars, a ballcourt, and numerous other structures used in the state religion of Tenochtitlan (Marquina 1960; Matos Moctezuma 2003; Nicholson 2003b).

The rulers of Tlatelolco also built a walled precinct. Tenochtitlan did have a modest plaza, located immediately south of the walled precinct (Calnek 1976, 2003). This space served as a permanent marketplace, however, and not as a formal ceremonial plaza (fig. 5.4).

The Mexica kings drew inspiration and legitimacy from the ancient city of Teotihuacan (fig. 5.6), and the ideological aspects of this legacy were materialized in a number of practices, including placement of Teotihuacan objects into Mexica offerings and imitation of Teotihuacan styles in ritual objects and architecture (López Luján 2005; Olmeda Vera 2002; Umberger 1987). Teotihuacan became the setting for important Mexica creation myths. Explicit material references to Teotihuacan near the Templo Mayor occur late in its history. Most date to construction stage VI, most likely dating to the reign of Ahuitzotl (1486–1502; see López Luján 2005: 52–54). Particularly prominent are the Teotihuacan-style "red temples" (Olmeda Vera 2002: 55), which are typical Aztec shrines with decoration and details in the fashion of Teotihuacan, and Offering 5 at the Eagle Warriors House with its Teotihuacan thin orange vase (López Luján, Neff, and Sugiyama 2000).

Distant Imperial Provinces

A few examples of Aztec style pyramids have been identified in distant imperial provinces, well outside the central Mexican homeland of Aztec culture. These suggest that provincial builders were emulating or imitating the Aztec architectural style, most likely in an effort to create middle-level meanings to reinforce their local power. Unlike the Inka empire of Peru, the construction of Aztec style buildings in the provinces was not a strategy of the Triple Alliance empire (Berdan et al. 1996), and such examples are not frequent. Perhaps the most striking example is at the city of Quauhtochco, an imperial administrative center near the Gulf of Mexico in the modern state of Veracruz (fig. 5.7A). This pyramid is not the only Aztec material referent at this city; the basic epicenter plan (fig. 5.7B) conforms roughly to the Tula plaza plan. Furthermore, Quauhtochco has yielded high quantities of imported Aztec pottery, much more than most provincial cities (Medellín Zeñil 1952).

One interpretation of this city is that a group of Mexica administrators and soldiers founded Quauhtochco and built the city and buildings in their native architectural style. A more likely scenario, however, is that the local ruler of Quauhtochco created these Aztec style buildings and plans in order to make a political statement (to his subjects, to his peers in other cities, and perhaps to imperial administrators as well) about his affiliation with the empire. This kind of politically motivated emulation of imperial styles has been

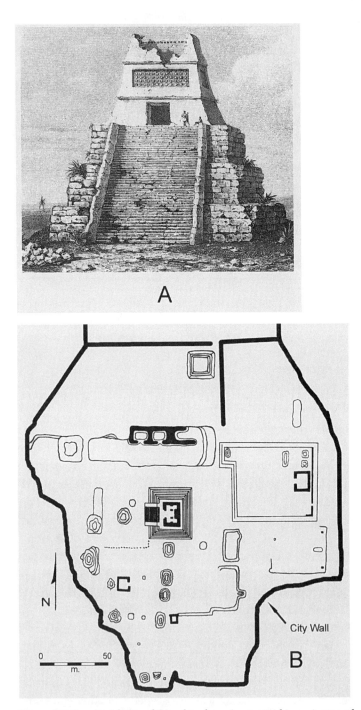

Figure 5.7. Provincial city of Quauhtochco. A: pyramid in a nineteenth-century lithograph (Dupaix 1834: pl. 9); B: map of the epicenter (modified after Medellín Zeñil 1952: 24).

documented at Cuetlaxtlan, a city not far from Quauhtochco (Ohnersorgen 2006). Another example is from the site of Castillo de Teayo, also along the Gulf Coast, whose main pyramid was built in the style of an Aztec single-temple pyramid. In addition, numerous Aztec style stone sculptures have been recovered from the site (Solís Olguín 1981).[7]

FORM AND MEANING IN THE AZTEC TOWNSCAPE

Although architectural historians fixated on the orthogonal layouts of Greek or Roman cities may not characterize Aztec cities as "planned" settlements, there is in fact considerable evidence for the use of a variety of planning principles in the design and layout of Aztec city-state capitals. They conform well to my cross-cultural model of ancient urban planning (Smith 2007a), which emphasizes two dimensions of city layout: coordination among buildings and standardization among cities. The builders of the epicenters of Aztec cities employed common alignments, connections between buildings, orthogonal arrangements, and principles of formality and monumentality. They employed a common inventory of public buildings in each city, and many of the buildings followed standard forms and orientations.

Ethnohistoric sources suggest that the central pyramid in each city housed the patron deity or deities of the altepetl. These patron gods are clear examples of high-level meanings, although in most cases we cannot identify the specific gods worshipped in particular excavated temples. We know that at least some Aztec temples were aligned astronomically, but the extent of this practice has yet to be established with confidence. Astronomical alignments provide another example of high-level meaning of individual buildings.

When we move to the level of the entire city, however, there is no clear evidence for high-level meanings. Among the thousands of pages of text that the early Spanish chroniclers wrote on Aztec religion, there is not a single statement that cities were planned or laid out with cosmological principles in mind. This has not stopped modern scholars from speculating about such religious significance for Aztec cities, particularly Tenochtitlan. It is certainly possible that Tenochtitlan and other cities had esoteric cosmological symbolism known to priests and kings, but in the absence of evidence I prefer to avoid speculating about the topic.

The topic of architectural communication, Rapoport's middle-level meanings, can be studied on a much firmer empirical basis. Unlike high-level meanings, which are esoteric and culturally specific, middle-level meanings are more universal among human cultures. Nearly all ancient rulers, for example, employed principles of monumentality and formality to make political statements. Some of the principles involved, such as the use of height to draw visual attention and to create emotional responses, appear to be universal human patterns (Rapoport 1990a) rooted in the human brain (Betz 2002).

I have identified two realms of architectural communication employed by Aztec kings to make ideological statements and to promote their power and legitimacy. First, they explicitly drew on the past, particularly the Toltec city of Tula, in designing their cities. The use of the Tula plaza plan (chapter 3) is the clearest example of this. Aztec kings also copied the plans of palaces from Tula and employed the tzitzimime platform as an element of urban design. Second, kings used the universal principles of monumentality and formality to promote their political agenda. Rapoport's third level, low-level meanings, concerns ways in which people moved about the city. In the next chapter I discuss this level as part of an exploration of the nature of life in Aztec cities.

6

Life in Aztec Cities

Public life in the city was, is, a political process, and should be studied as such.
Here in the streets there is not only noise and odor, but meaning.
(Trexler 1980: 552)

The lives of Aztec urban residents were lived both in private and in public. Most social interactions took place within families and household groups, in houses, compounds, and neighborhoods. But crucial social activities took place on a more public stage in the streets, paths, and plazas and gardens of the city. Some of these were prosaic events, such as attending the weekly market, and some were sacred ceremonial events, such as participating in the monthly religious celebrations. Amos Rapoport's concept of low-level meaning concerns the ways in which the activities of individuals intersect with the built environment. I use the term "townscape interaction" to describe those built-environment interactions that took place in public contexts.

In this chapter I examine the nature of life in Aztec cities. The first factor to consider is the size of cities; urban population and population density have strong effects on the nature of urban life. I next review the nature of Aztec social classes and the archaeological evidence for nobles and commoners in urban settings. The following sections are devoted to urban public life and urban private life. These two realms intersected in the elaborate religious ceremonies that took place each month, with rituals in both public and private settings. The chapter closes with a comparison of urban and rural contexts. One surprising finding of recent research is that there was little difference between city and countryside in the lives and activities of Aztec commoners.

THE SIZE OF CITIES

The size and density of urban populations are perhaps the most important factors influencing the nature and dynamics of urban life cross-culturally. As noted in chapter 2, Tenochtitlan was the only Aztec city with a large, dense population. The typical Aztec altepetl capital, in contrast, had a population of

Table 6.1. The Sizes of Aztec Cities

City	Altepetl Capital				Second Largest Site	
	Population	Area(ha.)	Density	Sources	Population	Percentage of Capital
Imperial capitals						
Tenochtitlan	212,500	1,350	157	a		
Texcoco	25,000	450	55	a	8,000	32
Altepetl capitals						
Amecameca	10,000	400	25	a	100	1
Calixtlahuaca	5,000	100	(50)	b		
Chalco	12,500	250	50	a	4,000	32
Chimalhuacan	12,000	260	45	a	480	4
Chiautla	600	115	40	c	300	50
Coatepec	2,500	85	35	c	180	7
Coatlan Viejo	800	15	30	a		
Coatlinchan	11,000	210	25	c	450	4
Cuitlahuac	4,500	90	50	a	725	16
Culhuacan	4,400	65	70	a	160	5
Huexotla	23,000	300	75	a	750	3
Ixtapalapa	2,800	28	100	a	963	34
Ixtapaluca	1,600	90	20	a	100	6
Mixquic	2,300	45	50	a	30	1
Otumba	10,700	220	50	a		
Tepetlaoztoc	13,500	450	30	a	1,200	9
Tlalmanalco	4,000	80	50	a		
Xaltocan	1,300	26	(50)	b		
Xochimilco	10,700	214	50	a	2,000	19
Yautepec	13,300	209	64	a		
Median	4,750	108	50	465		7

Sources: a = Smith et al. (1994: 8); b = Smith (2005); "Second Largest Site" data are compiled from Blanton (1972); Hodge (1997); Parsons (1971); Parsons et al. (1982); Parsons, Kintigh, and Gregg (1983).
Note: The "Percentage of Capital" is the size of the secondary city as a percentage of the size of the capital city in that altepetl. The "Median" does not include the imperial capitals.

around 5,000 people living in an area of one square kilometer (100 hectares). Data on city sizes are presented in table 6.1.[1] Altepetl capitals ranged from a low of 600 inhabitants to a high of 23,000. For most of the cities in table 6.1 we have both population estimates from documentary sources and area measurements from archaeological fieldwork.[2] Within a given altepetl, no other settlement comes close to the capital city in population size (table 6.1); the implications of this pattern are explored more fully in chapter 7.

In a study of city size (surface area) in all of Late Postclassic Mesoamerica (Smith 2005a: 410), central Mexican cities, including Aztec altepetl capitals, were quite close to the overall median size for all of Mesoamerica (90 hectares). Cities in western Mexico and on the Gulf Coast were larger, whereas cities in the Maya region were smaller than central Mexican cities. Tenochtitlan stands out greatly from the altepetl capitals in all measures of size: population, area, and population density. These facts alone signal the uniqueness of the imperial capital as an Aztec urban center; no other city comes close to its size.

In contrast to the modest variation among altepetl capitals in their populations and areas, the population densities of these cities are quite consistent. Most are close to the median density of 50 people per hectare (or 5,000 people per square kilometer). This suggests that Aztec cities (outside of Tenochtitlan) may have had comparable residential settlement patterns. None of these cities had the densely packed housing of Tenochtitlan or the earlier Teotihuacan. There was considerable open space within these cities, and in many cases the open areas were used for agriculture. Life for the inhabitants of altepetl capitals must have been quite different from life in the imperial capital, and in many ways urban life resembled rural life in the countryside.

SOCIAL CLASSES

So far this book has been concerned mainly with the actions of Aztec kings and their builders. The commoner inhabitants of cities have only been considered in terms of how their labor constructed large buildings and how they used or viewed such structures. It is time to take a closer look at the people who lived in cities and whose actions helped shape the city and its dynamics. Different categories of people lived different sorts of lives, and these need to be examined separately. The lives of slaves, for example, were quite different from the lives of nobles; men and women spent their time differently; and merchants experienced urban life much differently than priests. The fundamental social divide in Aztec society was that of social class, a fact that provides a good way to organize the discussion of life in urban settlements. Although wealth, power, and status had complex gradations with many different categories, a threefold division of Aztec society works well. Most people were commoners, a small percentage of people were nobles, and a very few nobles were part of the royal family. The following discussion of Aztec social classes is based upon Smith (2003a: chap. 6) and Lockhart (1992: chap. 4).

Commoners

Although commoners dominated Aztec cities demographically, their archaeological and historical traces are less visible than those of nobles. We have information about commoners from sixteenth-century administrative documents and from archaeological fieldwork in the residential areas of a few Aztec cities. There was considerable variation within the Aztec commoner social class, but two kinds of variation stand out: occupation and dependency status. The most abundant occupational category within the commoner class was the peasantry. Peasants were rural farmers who grew most of the food and provided taxes in labor and goods to support both nobles and the institutions of government. Urban commoners, another important category in Aztec society, worked in a wide variety of occupations, including as artisans, merchants, priests, and bureaucrats (see chapter 7). Interestingly, farming was perhaps the most common occupation among urbanites. Some urban farmers cultivated plots within town, and many others walked out to their fields in the countryside each day.

Another way to describe Aztec commoners was in their degree of dependence upon nobles. All commoners were subjects of the tlatoani, and most were also subjects of a lower-ranking noble. Beyond this, however, there was a scale of dependency that had a major impact on the lifestyle and quality of life of commoners. At the "low" end of the scale were slaves, or *tlacotin*. Slavery was not hereditary; rather, people became slaves for reasons of extreme debt or poverty, or as punishment for crimes. The owner, who controlled the labor and life of the slave, was responsible for a slave's feeding and housing. Slaves were not a large group in Aztec society, and they were not organized into large gangs for purposes of heavy labor. Most slaves were domestic servants or workers.

Just above slaves on the scale of freedom and well-being were commoners directly subject to a noble. Called *mayeque* in some sources, they were similar to European serfs—landless laborers who had to work directly for an elite patron. Their lack of land or other independent resources gave them few options, and their life was probably a hard one. Still higher up on the scale were commoners who belonged to a calpolli. Calpolli consisted of households (from several dozen to more than one hundred) who lived near one another and were subject to the same noble. The noble typically owned the land inhabited and farmed by calpolli members. Calpolli members had access to land for housing and farming, and members of rural calpolli could decide for themselves how to farm their land. The simple status of belonging to a calpolli gave one access to land and other resources and greater control over one's economic activities than noncalpolli commoners. Although calpolli members had lighter obligations than some other commoners, they were still under the control of a noble. Calpolli members are called *macehualli* in some documents, and historians sometimes refer to them as "free commoners."

At the top of the scale of wealth and status within the commoner class were the *pochteca* merchants and luxury artisans. These economic specialists, most of whom were based in the imperial capitals and several other large cities, often worked for the king and other noble patrons. The more successful merchants and artisans could amass quantities of wealth that surpassed that of some nobles.

Nobles

All ancient states and empires had commoners and elites, but in some cases, such as the Aztec, the elites formed a social class of nobles. A noble class is an elite class that is hereditary and defined by law (Bloch 1961). Although there were far more Aztec commoners (about 95%) than nobles (about 5%), the nobles controlled many aspects of society and government. Cities were particularly important in Aztec class structure, partly because most nobles lived in cities and partly because the institutions controlled by nobles—the royal palace and other branches of altepetl government—were based in cities.

Nobles were firmly in control of Aztec society. They assisted the king in running the city-state government and they owned all of the land in each city-state. Their preeminence in wealth and power led nobles to build large impressive residences, and as noted in chapter 4 these palaces were major components of the townscape. Just as Aztec commoners could be arranged along a scale from slave to free commoner, so too could nobles be assigned places on a scale of wealth and power. The tlatoani, or king, was at the top of the hierarchy (chapter 3). As discussed in chapter 3, from the Aztec viewpoint a city was defined as the place where the king lived.

The title *tecuhtli*, which can be loosely translated as "high lord," was used for powerful nobles with important positions in the city-state government. Some of these nobles lived in the city, some lived in the countryside on rural estates, and many probably had residences in both settings. The rest of the nobles were included in the category of *pilli*, the largest subdivision of the noble class. Some pilli were powerful and wealthy individuals with considerable prominence and influence, while others were their poor country cousins, less wealthy even than some commoners, struggling to maintain the lifestyle of a noble.

Although most cities only had a relatively small number of resident nobles, these individuals were highly influential in shaping the contours of urban life. As noted in chapter 1, the Aztec noble class throughout central Mexico was linked together into a single group through intermarriage, through visits among city-states, and through their common participation in elite activities and practices. Such practices included writing, ritual, and specialized knowledge of things from court etiquette to calendars. These activities and prac-

tices constitute Aztec elite culture. Nobles most likely supervised the design
and construction not only of their own residences but also of the temples,
ballcourts, and other public architecture. The basic canons of architectural
style and form were created and maintained through communication among
nobles in the scattered city-states of Aztec central Mexico.

PUBLIC LIFE: TOWNSCAPE INTERACTION

Urban public life—that is, the activities of individuals in the city outside of
houses—can be divided into two components: the everyday public life of
commoners, most of which took place within residential zones outside of the
epicenter, and public life in the epicenter. Most nobles' public life occurred in
the latter setting, and commoners participated in epicenter life periodically
for marketing, civic tasks, and ceremonial events. To understand urban public life, we need to look more closely at the spatial organization of epicenters
and residential zones.

The Spatial Organization of Residential Zones

Urban life was influenced by the layout and population density of cities. As
described in chapters 4 and 5, Aztec cities were divided into two basic zones:
the epicenter with most of the monumental architecture and the surrounding residential neighborhoods. The public buildings in the epicenter were
carefully designed and built following Aztec and Mesoamerican principles
of city planning, whereas the houses in the residential areas were built in a
seemingly haphazard fashion with little evidence of central planning. Nevertheless, these chaotic settlement patterns led to a general consistency of
population density across cities and probably to similarities in urban life.

Cuexcomate (fig. 6.1) and Ixtapaluca (fig. 6.2) are among the only Aztec
urban settlements where large numbers of houses have been mapped. Cuexcomate has a small epicenter consisting of two elite residences, a temple,
and another special building, all arranged around a formal square plaza that
conforms to the Tula plaza plan (chapter 5), although Cuexcomate was only
a small town (see chapter 2). The houses at the site, on the other hand, are
arranged along a ridgetop in seeming random fashion. Ixtapaluca, a major
city-state capital, was much larger than Cuexcomate but had a similar layout.
On its west ridge houses were scattered along the ridgetop on either side of
the epicenter, whereas the eastern ridge did not have an epicenter. The epicenter is marked on figure 6.2 by the large circle and stars; a more detailed
architectural map is shown in figure 5.2.

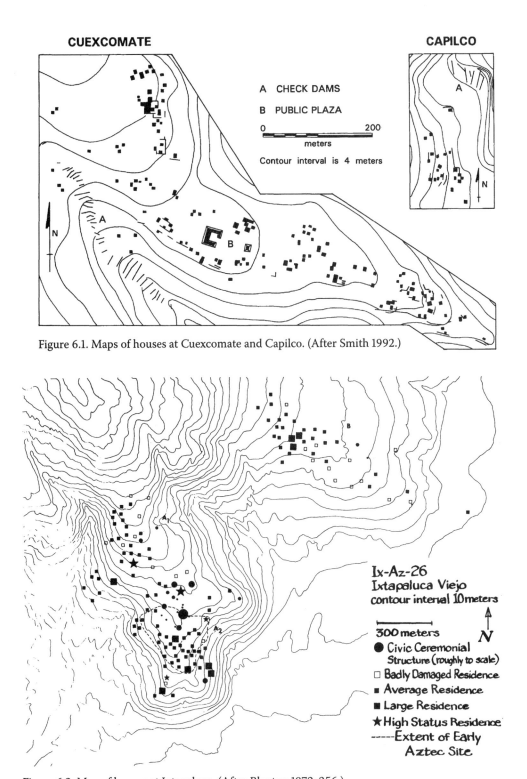

CUEXCOMATE

A CHECK DAMS
B PUBLIC PLAZA

0 ————————— 200
meters

Contour interval is 4 meters

CAPILCO

Figure 6.1. Maps of houses at Cuexcomate and Capilco. (After Smith 1992.)

Ix-Az-26
Ixtapaluca Viejo
contour interval 10 meters

300 meters   N

● Civic Ceremonial
   Structure (roughly to scale)
□ Badly Damaged Residence
■ Average Residence
■ Large Residence
★ High Status Residence
-----Extent of Early
        Aztec Site

Figure 6.2. Map of houses at Ixtapaluca. (After Blanton 1972: 256.)

In cities, members of a calpolli often comprised a neighborhood. The neighborhoods of Tenochtitlan are described in various documents (Calnek 2003), and there are scattered references to calpolli neighborhoods at other cities. Archaeologists, however, have found it difficult to identify neighborhoods or calpolli at Aztec urban sites. Cuexcomate (fig. 6.1) may have had three or four clusters of houses that correspond to calpolli or neighborhoods, but this cannot be proven. At Ixtapaluca there are two settlement clusters, each on a separate ridge. Within these large clusters, however, it is difficult to identify potential neighborhood divisions. Perhaps the best evidence for neighborhoods is found at Otumba, where the distribution of craft activities at the site suggests specialization by district or neighborhood (fig. 2.8).

Cuexcomate and Ixtapaluca illustrate the layouts of Aztec cities and towns located in piedmont or hilly regions. The epicenters and most houses were located on the level ridgetops, and the hillslopes were covered with agricultural terraces. Terrace walls on the steeper slopes were substantial walls of stone, and terraces on more gentle slopes often consisted of a row or two of stones held in place by the roots of maguey plants (Donkin 1979; Evans 1990). The terraced areas included some houses and they should be considered part of the urban settlement. It is very likely that some of the ridgetop areas were also cultivated (there are traces of possible field walls at Cuexcomate), perhaps as kitchen gardens adjacent to houses. This pattern probably held true for cities located on more level surfaces, although the residential zones at these sites have not been mapped due to the destruction or burial of the houses.

Aztec cities had low population densities (low in comparison to ancient cities in many other areas)[3] because houses were not packed tightly together and a considerable portion of the urban land was probably cultivated. Thus urban agriculture was a major part of the lifestyle of Aztec city dwellers (even at Tenochtitlan; see chapter 2), just as it was in other parts of ancient Mesoamerica (Stark and Ossa 2005). Although Aztec cities were modest in their overall size and population density, the regional population density was quite high (Sanders, Parsons, and Santley 1979: 216–219). Settlement occupied virtually every available corner of central Mexico. In the piedmont zone, settlement was nearly continuous across the landscape to the extent that archaeologists have found it difficult to define where one settlement ends and another starts (Sanders, Parsons, and Santley 1979: 163–171).

Movement through urban residential zones was relatively open and unimpeded. Much of the land was taken up with gardens and open spaces, and movement was probably channeled by an irregular system of paths or lanes between rough stone field walls, much like those found in central Mexican dispersed peasant villages today (Charlton 1970). In the epicenter, on the other hand, there were more barriers to movement and more buildings and areas with limited access.

Movement through the Epicenter: Access and Visibility

The interaction of people with the townscape can be approached through a consideration of access to spaces and visibility. Where could people go, and what could they see in the city? For the urban epicenter, these issues can be examined on two levels: the individual structure and the entire epicenter townscape. On the level of the individual structure, the palace is the only type of Aztec building sufficiently complex and sufficiently well published to address questions of movement and access. Aztec palaces, royal and other, had a single entry point (fig. 4.9). Although this suggests restrictions on who could enter, these structures were far more open than royal palaces in many cultures. Features such as tall stairways, gates, protracted entryways, and outer compound walls are common attributes of royal palaces in many pre-industrial cultures (for example, Gates 2003; Inomata and Houston 2000; A. T. Smith 2003). In comparison, it appears to have been easy to gain access to an Aztec palace. Once inside the central courtyard, visitors or inhabitants generally had a very short trip to enter the various rooms, many or most of which opened onto the courtyard. In the language of formal access analysis (Blanton 1994; Hillier and Hanson 1984), this feature is termed "low depth value."

These attributes of access may relate to the use of palace patios for gatherings and meetings of nobles who carried out the administrative business of Aztec city-states (Evans 2004). Such design features may suggest that commoners, apart from palace staff, rarely entered the central courtyard, unlike Yoruba royal palaces (Ojo 1966) or royal palaces in Bali (Geertz 1980), which included large courtyards where subjects gathered periodically for civic and ceremonial events.

Although Aztec temples had very simple layouts, typically one or two rooms with a single entrance, access was limited by their placement on top of pyramids. These pyramids lacked additional physical barriers, and theoretically anybody could walk right up the stairs and into the temple. Nevertheless, it is almost certain that there were unwritten cultural barriers that prevented widespread admittance into the interiors of temples. Written sources mention priests entering temples, but rarely other types of people.

The fact that sacrifices took place on altars located in front of the temple, at the top of the stairs, indicates that these were public events meant to be watched from the plaza below. Public performance and theatricality are now recognized as important components in the political dynamics of ancient states (Inomata and Coben 2006). Rulers and nobles undertook public ceremonies and spectacles to demonstrate their power, to reinforce their legitimacy, and to send various ideological messages to their subjects. When these performances took place at specific locations in the townscape, they can be considered part of the low-level meaning of the urban built environment.

On the level of the entire epicenter townscape, one of the notable characteristics of Aztec cities was the lack of enclosed precincts around temples or palaces, and the lack of architectural barriers to movement (see note 6 to chapter 4). Most central plazas were open at all four corners and sometimes at additional points along one or more sides. We cannot know from current evidence what kinds of rules or prohibitions may have prevented people from entering the plaza, but the lack of enclosing walls means that it could not have been too difficult for commoners to enter or to see what was going on there.

Plazas were probably used for a variety of kinds of activities. These were very formal settings, surrounded by religious and civic buildings. Many ceremonies took place within the plaza (see the discussion of civic ritual below), and during such events entrance into the plaza was probably regulated by priests or other officials. Other ceremonies, particularly rites of human sacrifice, were carried out in front of the temple that sat atop the central pyramid on the plaza. For these rituals, people probably gathered in the plaza to witness the events. At other times, plazas served as marketplaces. Temporary stalls were set up on market day, and the plaza was filled with throngs of people buying, selling, and enjoying themselves. Thus the central plazas were multifunctional spaces whose uses and meanings were radically distinct on different days.

As noted above, the walled sacred precincts at Tenochtitlan and Tlatelolco were radical innovations in urban planning. Although we lack specific textual descriptions of who was allowed access to these areas, information on the imperial capital suggest that entry was limited and controlled. Tenochtitlan and Tlatelolco were the only Aztec cities where a visitor was physically prevented from approaching the central temple or ballcourt. While some of the Mexica innovations in planning may have been esoteric and known only to elites (in other words, high-level meanings, such as cosmological models for temples), the enclosure of a central zone of temples was quite obvious to the inhabitants of and visitors to the city. A provincial commoner did not have to know anything about cosmological schemes or claims of political legitimacy to understand that he or she could not enter the sacred precinct of Tenoch-titlan.

Visual perception is another important component of low-level meanings. What did people see as they moved about an Aztec city? Although formal spatial analyses directed at this question have only started to be conducted at Aztec cities, some preliminary observations can be made. As one approached an Aztec city from the hinterland, the central temple pyramid would have stood out as a prominent feature, as at most Mesoamerican cities. No other building approached that structure in height. In comparison to Tenochtitlan and earlier Mesoamerican capital cities, however, Aztec altepetl capitals presented only a modest urban skyline. The lack of precinct walls and enclosures meant that the exteriors of most public buildings were visible to the public. Beyond the palaces of nobles and the temple chambers atop pyramids, non-domestic space that was secluded and private was not very common in the urban townscape.

Some architectural features were apparently placed in locations of maximum visibility. This certainly appears to be the case for shrines and platforms, most of which were located in the middle of the plaza, along the sides of the plaza, or adjacent to a large pyramid. Some stone sculptures—images of deities, altars, and other large monuments with imperial iconography—were probably placed in locations that were seen by people as they moved about the city. Unfortunately, few of these have been recovered in situ at Aztec sites, but such monuments are common at other Mesoamerican cities (for example, stelae and altars at Classic Maya cities and carved reliefs at Tula, Xochicalco, Monte Alban, and many other cities).

Carved stone sculptures, altars, and murals communicated messages on all three of Rapoport's levels of meaning. High-level meanings of their religious symbolism and significance may have been known most completely by priests and nobles, although commoners could probably identify various deities and understand some of the iconography. They certainly understood the general religious significance of sculptures and altars. Middle-level meanings about the public presence of the state or other cults were probably understood, at least partially, by most people. Low-level meanings clear to everyone included the fact that people could see these altars and sculptures as they walked about the city. Their placement may have influenced foot travel through town. As people stopped to witness or participate in a public ceremony near buildings or features, they interacted with one another, with priests and perhaps with state officials. During the major monthly ceremonies, public sculptures and altars took on an added significance as they contributed to the nature of peoples' interaction with the built environment and with other people; this theme is explored further below.

Building and Rebuilding the City

Construction work on public buildings and infrastructural features was nearly continuous in most Aztec cities (just as it seems to be in many cities today). As noted in chapter 4, temples and other structures were periodically rebuilt and enlarged. All stone structures needed regular maintenance, particularly their roofs and other parts built of perishable materials. Corvée labor for this work was drawn from the rotational labor tax system (chapter 5), and at any given time there must have been teams of laborers toiling away in the urban epicenter. Apart from the utilitarian ends of this work, participation in such labor projects was an important part of urban public life in several respects. Indeed, Inomata (2006) identifies construction projects as one of the two major occasions when the majority of the urban populace at Classic Maya cities gathered together; the other occasion was periodic public spectacles (whose role at Aztec cities is discussed below).

Socially, these collective labor projects were a chance for people to work together on a common project in a type of social interaction and activity outside of one's household and neighborhood. These activities thus helped generate social integration among normally separate households and neighborhoods. Politically, the process of constructing temples, palaces, and other public buildings helped forge a collective identity for the members of the altepetl. This process has been studied for the early colonial period in central Mexico, when documentation is more extensive:

> Whether it was in the same place or not, the Nahuas took the Christian church as the analogue of the preconquest temple. They enthusiastically participated in its construction and decoration in the same spirit as with its predecessor, looking to magnify the central tangible symbol of the altepetl's sovereignty and identity. (Lockhart 1992: 206)

Although evidence is scarcer for the Aztec period, it is likely that a similar process operated for labor on public building projects (see the quotation from Zorita in chapter 5).

This kind of process, in which the act of laboring on civic construction projects generated social and political allegiance and an ideological affiliation with the ruler, has been identified in a number of other ancient societies (Cowgill 2003; Pauketat 2000; A. T. Smith 2000). The implications go far beyond social interaction and integration, however. The act of participating in labor on temples and palaces helped generate feelings of identification with the tlatoani and the altepetl. On the one hand, the construction of taller and more elaborate pyramids can be seen as an ideological message from the tlatoani to his subjects about the glory of the city and the altepetl. On the other hand, the participation of commoners in these tasks sent another kind of message about their support for the king and the city-state. Timothy Pauketat (2000: 123) suggests that the very process of constructing large buildings was part of the constitution of political authority: "In monuments, we see not the consequences of political actions to legitimize centralized authority but these formations in the process of becoming."[4] Mass construction projects can be viewed as a form of political ritual, and in the words of David Kertzer (1988: 25), "Ritual is used to constitute power, not just reflect power that already exists" (see also Bell 1997: 129). Political rituals of all types, and the monuments that result from public construction projects, are examples of the process by which ideology was materialized—fashioned into material form—in ancient societies (DeMarrais, Castillo, and Earle 1996; Earle 1997). The process of working collectively on civic projects was thus an important part of public life for urbanites and an important part of political legitimation, ideology, and power for the tlatoani.

PRIVATE LIFE: HOUSES AND HOUSEHOLDS

The clearest archaeological evidence of differences between nobles and commoners is in their housing. The palaces of nobles were much larger than commoner houses, they employed finer and more expensive construction materials, and they were differentiated from commoner houses through many aspects of form (for example, they were built on platforms) and decoration. Palaces are discussed in chapter 4; this section reviews the nature of commoner housing in Aztec cities.

Commoner Houses

Nonelite houses have been excavated at only a few sites, including Cihuatecpan and Otumba in the Otumba altepetl; Mexicaltzinco near Tenochtitlan; Yautepec and Cuexcomate in Morelos; and Calixtlahuaca in the Toluca Valley (see chapter 2 for citations). Surface mapping of houses at a few sites provides additional information (Blanton 1972; Evans 1985), and some early colonial documents from Mexico City include plans and descriptions of conquest period houses in Tenochtitlan (Calnek 1974). Additional house excavations are urgently needed (see chapter 8), but at this point these sources suggest some of the basic patterns in urban commoner housing. Figure 6.3 shows some

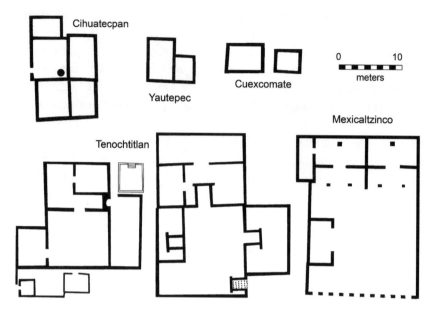

Figure 6.3. Commoner houses. The scale applies to all drawings except for Tenochtitlan; the latter plans are from documents without a secure scale. (Sources: Yautepec and Cuexcomate, author's data; Cihuatecpan, after Evans 1988: 59, 88; Mexicaltzingo, after Ávila López 2006: 251; Tenochtitlan, after Alcántara Gallegos 2004: 183, 186.)

representative house plans from these contexts, and data on the average sizes of houses are given in table 6.2.

At the Aztec sites I have excavated in Morelos, most commoner houses were small, one-room structures. They were built of adobe (sun-dried mud) bricks set on top of stone foundation walls. The foundations are all that survive today (figure 6.4 shows one of these houses I excavated at Cuexcomate). When originally built, the foundations were buried 30 to 60 centimeters below the ground surface and extended up less than a meter above the ground level. The walls, 30 to 40 centimeters wide, had two rows of stones. The top of the foundation wall provided a solid flat base for the rectangular adobe bricks. Although most of the adobe was turned back into mud by rain when the houses were abandoned, fragments of the bricks survived in several excavations. There is no direct evidence for the kinds of roofs on these houses, but modern peasant houses in the region provide some clues. Traditional rural houses in Morelos are very similar to the Aztec houses: small, one-room buildings of adobe bricks constructed on stone foundations (Moya Rubio 1982). The modern houses have thatched roofs, with dried leaves laid over a

Table 6.2. The Size of Aztec Commoner Houses

Context and Site	Mean Area	Number of Houses with Size Data
Urban commoners		
Yautepec	35.1	8
Ixtapaluca	>100.0	Many
Tenochtitlan	23.6	8
Rural commoners		
Cuexcomate	23.1	29
Capilco	21.0	15
Cihuatecpan	88.1	6

Source: Data are compiled from sources cited in chapter 2.

wood frame. These roofs do not require any tools or technology not available in Aztec times, so the simplest suggestion is that the Aztec houses also had thatched roofs. Modern roofs extend beyond the walls to protect the adobe bricks from rainfall damage.

The commoner houses I have excavated at Yautepec, Cuexcomate, and Capilco show little variation in size or form. The major architectural difference among these sites is the use of sand-covered stone for floors at the latter sites and lime plaster at Yautepec; plaster floors are limited to elite houses at the other sites. Many of the houses at these sites are arranged in groups of two to four houses built around a common patio. Early colonial census documents provide a name for the inhabitants of these patio groups

Figure 6.4. Commoner house excavated at Cuexcomate. Photograph by the author.

(*it hualli,* "people of a yard") and indicate that these were important social groups between the levels of the household and the calpolli (Smith 1993).

At the Morelos sites, the distinction between the houses of commoners and nobles is clear; commoner houses are smaller, built at the level of the ground, and use coarser materials and techniques than elite houses. At Calixtlahuaca, on the other hand, my initial impression is that it may be more difficult to distinguish commoner and noble houses. Only portions of most of the excavated houses have survived, and thus it is hard to reconstruct the sizes of houses with confidence. Most structures, large and small, employ fine stonework, so this trait cannot be used to measure social class. Our analyses of these structures have just begun, however, and with more study it will probably become easier to analyze the nature of social class distinctions in the houses of Calixtlahuaca (see fig. 8.1).

The Cihuatecpan houses excavated by Susan Evans are more varied than houses in Morelos; they range from small one-room buildings to larger multiroom structures, a pattern also found in houses mapped by Richard Blanton at Ixtapaluca. The differing climates in Morelos and the Basin of Mexico may explain part of the differences in house form. Morelos has a semitropical climate, and it is warm all year round. Most domestic activities probably took place outside in the patio, with the house used primarily for sleeping and storage. The Basin of Mexico is considerably higher in elevation, with many cool days. In the Otumba area, there is frost at night during the winter. If more domestic activities took place indoors, this may explain why many of the commoner houses were larger, and had more rooms, than the houses in Morelos.

Only a few small portions of commoner houses have been excavated in Tenochtitlan. Fortunately, a series of early colonial wills and testaments provide information on houses in several parts of the city. Many of the archival documents include drawings of the houses (fig. 6.3), and they often describe their sizes as well. Some houses were built of wood and others of stone and adobe brick. Many houses are rectangular multiroom compounds, and others appear to be smaller buildings grouped around a patio. Unlike Morelos, however, the houses around patios are so close together that they touch, making these look like more of a single compound than separate structures. In either case, the Tenochtitlan houses seem to have been designed to save space, an important consideration in the very densely settled island city. The houses excavated at Mexicaltzinco, a city close to Tenochtitlan, resemble those of Tenochtitlan.

Household Activities

Whereas the term "house" refers to a building, "household" refers to the group of people who live in a house. In Aztec society some households consisted of nuclear families and others were extended, or multigenerational, families (Kellogg 1993). In many cases unrelated people lived with families. Whether servants, slaves, or distant relatives, these individuals were members of the household. The archaeological remains of a household include the house itself, often one or more related buildings—such as kitchens, granaries, or shrines—features such as hearths or burials located in or near the house, and the artifacts used and discarded by the members of the household (Nichols 2004).

My excavations of commoner houses in Morelos provide information not only on houses and architecture but on domestic activities and conditions at these sites.[5] The excavations did not stop at the outer house walls; indeed, exterior areas were a prime target. The inhabitants of these houses threw their trash out in their back and side yards (but not in the front, or patio side, of the house). These trash deposits or middens are rich sources of evidence for the activities that took place in and around the house. They allow us to reconstruct something of the households that once inhabited the house.

One of the ways anthropologists identify households, in both modern and ancient settings, is through meals. Typically the members of a household cook and eat together, and archaeological traces of the preparation and serving of food can help identify an ancient household. When we located midden deposits full of potsherds from cooking and serving vessels at each structure in a patio group, this suggested that each building was a house with a separate household. It helped rule out an alternative interpretation—that one single household occupied the entire group using the different structures for different purposes (a kitchen, a granary, and sleeping quarters, for example).

Each household had a basic set of kitchenware, including ceramic cooking jars, storage vessels, and tortilla griddles of fired clay. Knives and other cutting tools were made from the imported volcanic glass obsidian, which was abundant in commoner middens. Metates to grind maize and mortar bowls, called *molcaxitl*, to prepare sauces were made of basalt and other locally available volcanic stone. Carbonized bits of maize and beans are sometimes found associated with houses. Bones from turkey, deer, dog, rabbit, and other animals show that meat was a regular part of the diet, as were tortillas and tamales made from maize dough.

Food was served in ceramic plates, bowls, and cups. Although most serving vessels were undecorated, a good number were finely painted with geometric designs. Each region of central Mexico had its own distinctive patterns of painted ceramic vessels in the Aztec period. Most of the decorated serving vessels at any site were painted in the local style and were probably produced within the altepetl or an adjacent polity. But the typical household also had access to vessels from a number of foreign sources, and these are evidence of active networks of commercial exchange between regions (see chapter 7). What is interesting is that nearly everyone had access to some imported painted pottery. Archaeologists sometimes assume that nicely painted vessels were elite items, or perhaps ritual vessels, but it turns out that virtually all Aztec households, including commoners at both urban and rural sites, had access to such wares. Not everyone had the same amount of decorated and imported pottery, however, and the frequencies of these items serve as measures of domestic wealth levels. Elite households had much more imported and decorated pottery than commoners, and wealthy commoners had more than their poor cousins.

Not all domestic artifacts had a utilitarian function. Middens from commoner houses contain abundant evidence for ritual activities. People may have had small altars within their homes, just as traditional Mexican families do today. They burned incense using the same kinds of long-handled censers that priests used in ceremonies at temples (fig. 6.5A), and their broken fragments are regular components of domestic middens. Small ceramic figurines are also common in domestic contexts (fig. 6.5B). These small images of people, deities, and animals were used in rites of divination and curing, probably by female curers and midwives who worked in the home. These two types of ritual object, censers and figurines, suggest that two very different traditions of domestic ritual intersected in commoner homes. The censers provide a link with state religion and public rites by priests (see below), whereas the figurines represent a separate realm of curing and divination independent of, and perhaps deliberately hidden from, the state cults (Smith 2002; Olson 2007).

In Aztec society cotton textiles were used for both utilitarian purposes, such as clothing, and as a form of money. People paid their taxes in cotton cloth, and they used cloth to make purchases in the marketplace. According to written sources, textile production was an important part of gender identity for Aztec women, and all women, from nobles to slaves, spun thread and wove cloth (McCafferty and McCafferty 1991; Nichols, McLaughlin, and Benton 2000). Archaeological excavations confirm the importance of textile production by Aztec women. Virtually every excavated house has furnished evidence for this in the form of clay spindle whorls (fig. 6.5C) (Smith and Hirth 1988).

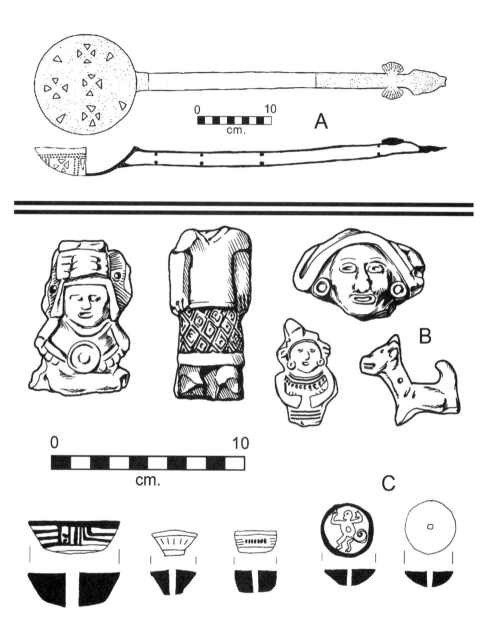

Figure 6.5. Domestic ceramic objects from public and private contexts. A: long-handled censer from a ballcourt offering at Coatetelco (Smith 2008); fragments of censers like this were excavated at commoner and elite residences at Yautepec and Cuexcomate. B: figurines from commoner houses at Yautepec; C: spindle whorls from commoner houses at Yautepec. Note difference in scale between A and B/C. Drawings by Ben Karis and Ruth Fauman-Fichman.

Members of some households also produced other craft items. In Aztec society, as in other Mesoamerican societies, most artisans worked in their homes, not in large, spatially separated workshops. The two largest craft industries were the manufacture of obsidian tools and ceramic vessels. At Yautepec a few households specialized in obsidian production and several worked in ceramic production, whereas at Cuexcomate the only crafts were the ubiquitous textiles (made by all households) and bark paper, produced in a few locations. Otumba is unusual in the extent and intensity of its craft production (see chapter 7), much of which was destined for export to other communities. Most of the goods produced at Yautepec, in contrast, were almost certainly intended for local consumption within the altepetl.

PUBLIC LIFE, PRIVATE LIFE, AND CIVIC RITUAL

> Regardless of whether a townsperson was literate or not, visual displays and enactments of biblical stories staged in the streets of a town would have been understood by all. Such storytelling, rooted within particular places within the townscape, such as market places and street corners, and performed at certain times of the year, usually in association with religious feast days, inscribed moral virtues onto the medieval townscape. (Lilley 2002: 243)

In the passage above, urban historical geographer Keith Lilley describes one component of townscape interaction in medieval European cities. A parallel process occurred within Aztec cities: popular participation in urban ceremonies and spectacles served to bind people to their townscape and to provide a context for the architectural communication of religious and ideological (political) messages by kings and priests. The pattern is seen most clearly in the 18 monthly veintena ceremonies (see chapter 4 for a partial description of one such ceremony, that of Tlacaxipeualiztli). The Aztec solar calendar divided the year into 18 months of 20 days, plus 5 additional days. Each month featured an elaborate series of celebrations based upon one or more mythological themes. These ceremonies lasted several days and involved activities throughout the city: music, ceremonial dancing, offerings, and sacrificial rites in temples, plazas, and other public locations; processions around the city and sometimes into the countryside; and feasting and ritual activities within houses and compounds.[6]

The veintena ceremonies are examples of what historians call civic rituals (Inomata and Coben 2006; Muir 1997; Trexler 1980), events that "draw people out of their households and kin groups and into participation in the wider world of civic life" (Parish 2005: 482). Everyone, from kings to slaves, participated in one way or another. The monthly celebrations tied together the public and private lives of nobles and commoners. In most of the activities of the veintena ceremonies, individual groups—including social classes, occupational groups, and neighborhoods—had specific roles or actions. Nobles, for example, gathered together for one type of rite while commoners participated in another, all under the supervision of priests. In other activities, nobles and commoners participated together. In the month of Tlacaxipeualiztli, for example, Sahagún (1997: 57) tells us, "Everyone, all the noblemen and commoners, danced with their rattles" (see fig. 4.10).

Most of the ceremonies involved processions in which ixiptla (deity impersonators), prisoners, priests, and others paraded through the streets of the city.[7] Sometimes people watched the processions, and at other times people performed sacred dances and other rites during a procession. The high points of the veintena ceremonies were the enactment of one or more human sacrifices, typically witnessed by large crowds. The very public participation of people from all walks of life in these events generated social solidarity and integration across urban society. As noted by Kertzer (1988), common participation in public ritual events is a powerful means of forging political identity and social solidarity.

At the same time, however, the veintena ceremonies reinforced social class differences and made public the power of the state (Broda 1976; Brumfiel 2001). Distinctions between nobles and commoners were clearly marked at all times, and the entire ceremonies were orchestrated by the priests, who can be seen as agents of the tlatoani. Massive resources from the royal treasury were expended at each ceremony. Broda notes that "the ceremonies demonstrated the ritually sanctioned power of the king. The participation of different social groups in the cult exposed the economic and political inequality that existed among them, while at the same time assigning each group its place within society" (Broda 1976: 54; author's translation). This statement parallels interpretations of civic rituals in European cities of the Renaissance: "Civic ritual both represented the utopian ideal of a harmonious community and reminded citizens of the possibility of coercion if they failed to accommodate themselves to those in power" (Muir 1997: 238).

A further political role of the veintena ceremonies was the forging of explicit connections between domestic ritual and the state religion (Smith 2002). In some cases this involved domestic rituals that related to, or even duplicated, the public state ceremonies conducted by priests. For example, during the ceremony of Tepeilhuitl, public offerings were made to the mountains and mountain gods while people venerated small models of the mountains in their homes, and during the ceremony of Tititl, "all this food and drink was offered up in the temples, and each person offered the same in his domestic shrine" (Durán 1971: 463). The occurrence of long-handled censers in domestic contexts (fig. 6.5A) probably signals other types of duplication between public and domestic ritual. During the ceremony of Toxcatl, the intrusion of state religion into the home was even more direct as priests entered homes to carry out rites:

> Early in the morning the minor priests from the wards went from home to home with incense burners in their hands, and even though the master of the house was most humble, [the priest] would incense the entire house all the way from the threshold to the last corner. . . . The house owners were obliged to give alms to these priests. (Durán 1971: 427)

The monthly veintena ceremonies served as a mechanism for linking public and private life together into an integrated urban social experience. People participated in the streets, in plazas, and in their homes and house lots. The use of music and burning incense made these ceremonies rich sensory experiences (a "great sensory assault," in the words of Clendinnen 1991: 258) that heightened their effects on all participants. Many of the commoner houses I have excavated yielded fragments of whistles, flutes, bells, drums, and rattles. These musical instruments were probably used during the veintena ceremonies. At other times people kept them in their homes, discarding them with the trash when they broke. In sum, the veintena ceremonies not only served the gods but also served the tlatoani, reinforced social classes, and contributed to the identity and success of the city as a social institution.

RURAL AND URBAN

Peasants came into town to participate in the monthly ceremonies and other public ritual events alongside urban residents. Many urbanites were farmers, just like their rural cousins; they just had a longer walk to their fields each morning. In a variety of realms the lives of Aztec urbanites were not very different from the lives of their country cousins. We can start with the houses. At all three sites I excavated in Morelos—a village (Capilco), a town (Cuexcomate), and a city (Yautepec)—the basic commoner house was the small, one-room adobe structure (figs. 6.3, 6.4). More of the urban commoner houses in Yautepec had lime plaster floors than at the other sites, but this is a minor difference. The basic set of domestic artifacts—ceramics, chipped stone, ground stone, and other objects—was almost identical at all three sites. Ceramic vessels and figurines imported from other parts of central Mexico were present at all houses, and painted serving vessels were significant parts of the domestic inventory in all cases. Imported obsidian was abundant at all houses, as were the remains of domestic ritual behavior. Items of jewelry—such as greenstone beads, obsidian ear spools, and rock crystal lip plugs—were rare artifacts, but these items were regularly recovered in commoner middens at both rural and urban sites, as were bronze needles imported from the Tarascan realm of western Mexico.

This is not to say that there were no differences between urban and rural contexts. Part-time craft specializations were more common at Yautepec than at Capilco, and urban households had slightly greater access to imported goods, although they did not have any imports or valuable goods that their rural counterparts lacked. Moreover, if we consider features that do not show up in the archaeological record, it is easy to imagine differences between urban and rural lifestyles. For example, urbanites had far more opportunities to interact with foreigners (merchants and others) and with kings and nobles. It would have been much harder for them to shirk on their taxes or avoid participating in corvée labor projects called by the palace. They had more opportunity for recreation than did peasants, including ballgames, public ceremonies, and just going to market to hear the latest gossip. As noted above, the veintena ceremonies were crucial events in urban life, and the differential participation of rural and urban residents in these occasions may have been one of the more significant differences between rural and urban life.

Nevertheless, the similarities between urban and rural life in Aztec society are striking. Although cities, with their monumental buildings and large populations, were quite different from rural villages and towns, in many ways urban residents lived the same kinds of lives as Aztec peasants.

AZTEC URBAN LIFE

As in nearly all ancient societies, most Aztecs lived most of their lives within the settings of their household and their neighborhood or village, and because lifestyle was heavily conditioned by social class, the lives of nobles and commoners were different in almost every way. Some of the differences were in the domestic realm of private life—houses, domestic activities, and lifestyles all varied between social classes. Other differences were expressed more in the realm of public life—nobles and commoners had differential participation in urban ceremonies and they had different levels of access to palaces and temples. Nobles were bound much more closely to the ruler and the government than were commoners. For nobles, these ties included attendance at the calmecac, frequent feasts, and other social events with the ruler and other nobles. For commoners, ties to the king and state were more exploitative—payment of taxes in labor and goods and participation in construction programs. The monthly ceremonies provided a setting for the joint participation of both nobles and commoners in public activity.

Whereas the great differences between social classes are not at all surprising, another kind of social variation is perhaps unexpected: The lives of rural and urban peoples were not very different. Leaving aside Tenochtitlan for a moment, my archaeological fieldwork in Morelos shows that rural and urban nobles had similar small palaces and similar domestic artifacts and rural and urban commoners had very similar small adobe houses and almost the same basic inventories of domestic goods.

Although it is difficult to explain the rural-urban similarity in activities, conditions, and lifestyle with confidence, several contributing factors can be suggested. First, most altepetl were small in size, so rural and urban peoples lived close together and rural peasants probably came into town often. Second, the marketing system tied rural and urban together and furnished all people in an altepetl with the same kinds of goods. Market channels were also conduits for the movement of information about goods, styles, and customs; as such they helped tie the altepetl together into a cohesive social unit. Many of these activities and institutions that bound rural and urban together can be considered urban functions of Aztec city-state capitals, the topic of chapter 7.

7

Cities and Their Hinterlands

Urban Functions

Cities do not grow up of themselves. Countrysides set them up to do tasks that
must be performed in central places. (Jefferson 1931: 453)

No city exists as an isolated space of its own; cities are connected to areas
outside their limits by a variety of linkages, from the economic to the religious. Goods, people, and information all move between cities and their
hinterlands. One of the most important links between cities and their wider
social contexts is the urban function. As discussed in chapter 1, an urban
function is an activity or institution within a city that affects a wider hinterland. Some of the common urban functions in preindustrial cities include
craft production, regional and long-distance exchange, political administration, and religion (Fox 1977; Marcus 1983). Each of these can be further
subdivided into more detailed functions. It is important to stress that urban
functions are activities that tie cities to their hinterlands. The urban production of pottery to sell or distribute outside the city is an urban function, for
example, whereas the urban production of pottery for sale to urban residents is not.

In chapter 1 I argue that a functional definition of cities and urbanism better fits Aztec city-state capitals than does the alternative, and more popular,
demographic definition. The public architecture and layout of Aztec cities
provide clear material evidence for administrative and religious urban functions. But what about economic activities? Were Aztec cities nodes of craft
production and market exchange for their hinterlands? The archaeological
and historical data suggest that whereas market exchange was probably an
urban function at all Aztec cities, craft production played such a role at only
a few.

A key theme of this book is that political power and administration were
the dominant urban functions of Aztec city-state capitals. The role of Aztec
cities as capitals of city-states influenced the nature and expression of all
other urban functions. To start with, these cities were the only large urban

settlements within their altepetl. There is no documented case of an altepetl that contained more than one major urban center. Table 6.1, which lists
the population size of altepetl capitals, also indicates the population of the
second-largest settlement in each polity. The small size of these secondary
settlements is striking; the median second-largest settlement had only 7 percent of the population of its capital.

Several implications flow from the dominant sizes of capitals within their
altepetl. First, there was no alternative political center to challenge the capital
for power or influence. Second, the rural farmers of the altepetl only had to
support a single urban center, not a series of cities with their nonfarming
populations. Third, most urban-based activities or institutions in the realm
of economics or religion—markets, craft workshops, large temples, or organized cults, for example—were by necessity concentrated in the capital and
not in potentially competing secondary urban centers. These altepetl capitals
dominated their hinterlands in every possible way, and it is not surprising
that they were the settings for a variety of urban functions beyond politics
and administration.

In the functional urban perspective that I employ in this book, the concept of "rural" has a distinctive denotation. In contrast to traditional models,
in which rural is presented as the opposite of urban (for example, Redfield
1941), I argue that rural and urban can be seen as spatial sectors of an urban-
ized society. I borrow this perspective from Anthony Leeds, who notes that

> any society which has in it what we commonly call "towns" or "cities"
> is in *all* respects an "urban" society, including its agricultural and ex-
> tractive domain. . . . The terms "urban" and "rural" come to stand to
> each other not as opposites and equivalents. Rather, the inclusive term
> describing the whole society is "urban" while the term "rural" refers
> only to a set of specialties of an urban society characterized by being
> inherently linked (under any technology known) to specific geographi-
> cal spaces. (Leeds 1980: 6–7)

Leeds was echoing an earlier functional approach to rural and urban described by geographer Mark Jefferson (1931): "Urban and rural, city and
country are one thing, not two things." This concept of rural has an important implication for the study of Aztec urbanism. The degree of rural-urban
differentiation among households is an empirical topic for research, not a
fixed datum established by theory. In Redfield's (1941) influential model of
twentieth-century Mayan peasantry, for example, rural and urban life and
society were fundamentally different by definition. As discussed in chapter
6, however, there were numerous close similarities in domestic activities and

conditions between Aztec rural and urban areas; this situation is inexplicable in traditional approaches such as Redfield's.

FARMING AND URBAN FOOD SUPPLY

The supply of food to urban residents is a crucial logistical problem that all cities have to solve. In ancient Mesoamerica, where goods were transported by human porters, it was costly and difficult to obtain grains from distant areas (Sanders and Santley 1983). This is probably one of the reasons for the small size of most Aztec cities, and, for the relatively large Tenochtitlan, food supply presented serious organizational problems. Furthermore, the problems of urban food supply in Aztec central Mexico were exacerbated by the large size of the overall Aztec population and a growing inability of farmers to produce enough food. Several million people lived in central Mexico at the time of the Spanish conquest (Smith 2003a: 57–61). The Aztec period witnessed one of the largest demographic surges in the entire prehistory of the New World (chapter 3). This led to episodes of famine and hunger, as reported in codices and historical accounts. One incident in particular, the famine of 1452–54, was so severe that thousands of people starved, leading to chaos and unrest in the Basin of Mexico (Hassig 1981).

In order to keep up with the food needs of this exploding population, farmers and collectors intensified their food production by every conceivable means. The ancient Mayan swamp-reclamation technique of raised field construction was revived in the southern lakes and around Tenochtitlan; the Aztec term for such fields is *chinampas*. Rivers were dammed and canals built to irrigate virtually all of the valley lands where this was feasible. But the most extensive system of intensive agriculture was hillside terracing. Stone terrace walls covered virtually all of the hillsides of central Mexico, and eroding ravines were crossed with check dams. As noted in chapter 6, even the open land within cities was put to work to produce food. These changes—construction of chinampas, terraces, and irrigations systems—are examples of the process known as agricultural intensification, which involves increased effort in production in order to raise yields (Stone 2001).

At harvest time, maize was stored in household granaries, using proven methods still employed by traditional central Mexican peasants today. Maize on the cob was stored in wood corn cribs (fig. 7.1A) and shelled maize was put into a *cuezcomatl* granary (fig. 7.1B–C). Maize in both forms was also stored within the house, either in a special storeroom or hung from the rafters or walls. There is no evidence for large-scale granaries apart from the stores kept in royal palaces for court consumption.

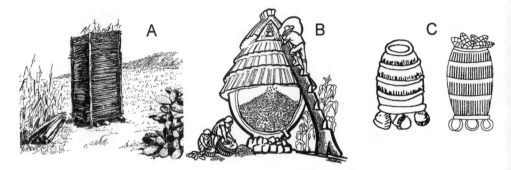

Figure 7.1. Domestic granaries. A: modern corn crib (after Soustelle 1970: 100);
B: modern cuezcomatl granary (after Florescano and Moreno Toscano 1966); C:
cuezcomatl granaries from the *Historia Tolteca-Chichimeca* and the *Lienzo de
Tlaxcala*. See Smith (n.d.c) for discussion.

In the salty lakes of the Basin of Mexico, collectors gathered insect larvae
and algae for human consumption. In fact, they even introduced methods
to promote and manage the growth of these rich protein sources (Ortiz de
Montellano 1990: 102–119; Parsons 1996). How successful were Aztec farmers and collectors in their intensification efforts? Although some authors
suggest that sufficient food was produced to feed people adequately (Ortiz
de Montellano 1990: 72–97), various types of evidence cast doubt on this
interpretation. Documentary research combined with field mapping and demographic simulations by Thomas Whitmore and Barbara Williams (1998)
in the region of Temazcalapa (north of Texcoco) indicate that the food supply
at the time of Spanish conquest was precarious. Their quantitative models
indicate that in a year of poor agricultural yields, up to 60 percent of the
population was at risk of famine, and even in good years 16 percent of the
population experienced some form of food poverty. Furthermore, codices
and native historical accounts make it clear that droughts and pests leading to food shortages and famines became increasingly common in the final
century before the arrival of Cortés (Kovar 1970).

Given these bleak demographic and agricultural conditions, urban food
supply must have been a serious problem. The imperial capital Tenochtitlan, with its 200,000 inhabitants, had the greatest food needs of any city
in ancient Mesoamerica. There is a body of ethnohistorical research on the
methods and institutional arrangements of the city's food system (Parsons
1976; Rojas 2001, 2006; Smith n.d.b). Food was obtained through at least
four mechanisms. First, a minor amount was grown in the chinampas cultivated on the edges of the city. Second, large quantities of grains arrived in

Tenochtitlan through the imperial tribute system. The tribute records are accurate enough to reconstruct the amounts, and it is clear that such tribute only accounted for a portion of the food consumed in the capital.

A third channel for the movement of food into Tenochtitlan was rent paid by farmers to urban landlords. Nobles owned or controlled Aztec farmland, although many aspects of field allocation and use were decided by calpolli councils (chapter 6). We do not know how many of the nobles who owned farmland in the Basin of Mexico lived in the imperial capital, nor do we know the levels of rent that were charged farmers, and thus it is difficult to determine the significance of rent as a source of grains for the imperial capital.

The fourth, and probably most significant, mechanism for getting maize and other foods into the city was the market system. Because we lack evidence for grain merchants or large-scale storage facilities, the most likely channel was sale by petty vendors who offered foods grown by their families in the immediate hinterlands of Tenochtitlan in the Basin of Mexico. Most of this grain must have been stored initially in domestic granaries (like those shown in figure 7.1) in farming villages throughout the Basin of Mexico. Once urbanites obtained grain from the market or other sources, they probably stored it in small rooms within the house.

Unfortunately, there are few historical documents describing the food supply of Aztec cities beyond Tenochtitlan, and archaeologists have yet to carry out the kind of detailed quantitative productivity studies that can illuminate the food-supply systems of individual cities. Even though many Aztec cities had urban land devoted to gardens and agricultural fields (chapter 6), most food for urban residents had to be obtained from hinterland areas. Since many urbanites were farmers who walked out to their fields, their families probably obtained their food this way. But town dwellers whose families were not farmers had to purchase their maize, beans, and other foods in the market.

MARKETS AND COMMERCE

Ethnohistoric evidence suggests that periodic markets were held at most or all Aztec cities and towns (Berdan 1985, 1988), and archaeological evidence points strongly to commercial marketplace exchange as the major mechanism moving goods among settlements (Garraty 2007; Nichols et al. 2002; Smith 2003c). Although we can therefore conclude that most city-state capitals probably had important regional commercial functions, there is unfortunately little direct evidence for such functions at specific Aztec cities. The suite of obsidian types ("types" referring here to geological sources) used at

Yautepec was duplicated at smaller sites in its hinterland (Smith et al. 2007). Although this suggests the operation of a regional market system centered at Yautepec, the evidence cannot be considered strong and unambiguous. The best evidence for the operation of a market system within an altepetl is Otumba, whose craft industries are discussed below.

We know that regional market systems centered on altepetl capitals supplied obsidian and ceramics, both locally made and imported vessels, to settlements in their hinterland (Garraty 2007), and it is likely that other utilitarian goods such as ground stone tools were also circulated through regional markets. Most evidence for the sale of grains and other foods in the markets comes from the imperial capital, but it is logical to infer that grains were also sold in the marketplaces of other altepetl. Similar inferences can be made for luxury goods such as jewelry made from greenstone, rock crystal and obsidian, or tools of obsidian.

Each altepetl capital had a marketplace that served as the commercial hub for the entire polity (fig. 7.2). In addition, at least some altepetl had smaller, low-level markets at hinterland settlements. Markets met periodically, most commonly once every five-day week. The markets within an altepetl were tied to the central capital market by merchants who traveled among them, visiting each market on its weekly market day. The markets from nearby altepetl were also linked together by traveling merchants, and consumers probably shopped at markets at different altepetl for special goods. The market at Acolman specialized in dogs, for example, and several other market specializations are known. Chemical sourcing of ceramics in the Basin of Mexico has confirmed that ceramic vessels were exchanged among altepetl (Garraty 2007; Minc 2006; Nichols et al. 2002), a cross-border trade that almost certainly included numerous additional goods. The existence of active channels of trade among nearby altepetl makes sense given the fluid political boundaries discussed in chapter 3.

CRAFT PRODUCTION

Craft production as an urban function is closely tied to commercial exchange systems. If craft goods were not moved from cities to their hinterlands, craft production could not be an urban function. The spinning and weaving of textiles was perhaps the most important craft in Aztec society because of its extensive and widespread distribution and because of the social importance of the end product. The textile industry was not an urban function, however, because women in all households (nobles and commoners) and at all settlements (rural and urban) produced textiles. One possible exception, however,

Figure 7.2. Marketplace with slaves for sale. There is a circular shrine in the center. (After Durán 1971: pl. 29.)

is Otumba, where dense clusters of spindle whorls in the surface collections suggest the possible existence of specialized workshops for the production of cloth from maguey fiber (Nichols, McLaughlin, and Benton 2000), perhaps for the regional market.

Among the other goods produced at Aztec settlements, the best evidence for regional circulation (that is, for urban function) is obsidian. Archaeologists are learning more every year about the production and exchange of Aztec ceramics, but we do not yet have comparable fine-grained evidence for obsidian production locations and regional exchange systems.

Obsidian Tool Production

The production of obsidian tools was a major craft industry in central Mexico, in part because of the abundance of geological sources in this area. There are six urban settlements with sufficient data to evaluate the extent and implications of obsidian production activities, and these exhibit a wide range of patterns. Otumba was a category of its own as a major production center for several types of obsidian tools as well as textiles and ceramics (see below). At Huexotla, Cuexcomate, and Coatlan Viejo, on the other hand, there is virtually no evidence for obsidian tool production (Brumfiel 1980; Mason 1980b; Smith 2003c). Residents of these towns must have obtained obsidian tools from knappers in other settlements.

Yautepec and Xaltocan occupy positions intermediate between Otumba and the other cities. At Yautepec certain households appear to have specialized in obsidian production, and their middens contained abundant evidence for the production of prismatic blades from cores (Norris 2002). The lack of evidence for obsidian production in Yautepec's hinterlands (Smith 2006) suggests that obsidian production was one of Yautepec's regional economic functions. Xaltocan was the setting for some tool production, probably less than Yautepec (Brumfiel 2005). The evidence from Yautepec and Xaltocan follows widespread patterns of craft production in ancient Mesoamerica in which most goods were produced in domestic settings, not in specialized workshop buildings.

Otumba

Fieldwork at Otumba has produced the most extensive evidence for crafts of any Aztec site (Charlton, Nichols, and Charlton 1991, 2000; Otis Charlton 1993; Parry 2001). The analysis of the production and exchange of obsidian, ceramics, and textiles at Otumba furnishes many details of urban functions in the realms of crafts and commerce. At the level of the altepetl, goods produced in Otumba, the capital, were traded to hinterland settlements (Parry 2001), probably through a regional market system based in the capital. On a broader level, Otumba almost certainly supplied other parts of central Mexico with finished goods. Tools produced from a geological source of obsidian within the Otumba altepetl, for example, have been identified at sites at least as far away as Yautepec.

The largest industry at Otumba was the production of prismatic blades of obsidian by pressure flaking. To supplement the supply of obsidian from local outcrops, people also brought in obsidian from the nearby source area of Cerro de las Navajas to work at Otumba. Areas with high concentrations of obsidian blades and debris from their manufacture signal the existence of a number of production areas at Otumba. These production areas probably represent neighborhoods where part-time or full-time blade production was carried out at the household level. Production areas for bifacial tools of obsidian were also present, but not in the urban center; these tools were made at outlying rural villages. Some nearby rural settlements, such as the site of Cihuatecpan, also have limited evidence of obsidian tool production.

Another major craft industry at Otumba was lapidary work. Partially used obsidian cores, byproducts of the production of prismatic blades, were reworked into various types of jewelry, including lip plugs, beads, ear spools, and disks. Lapidary workshops, identified by cutting and polishing tools and objects broken during manufacture, were located within the urban zone, but not in the same areas as the obsidian blade workshops. A variety of ceramic objects were produced at Otumba, including figurines, censers, spindle whorls, and other small items (see figure 6.5 for examples of these types of objects). Molds for these items are concentrated in two parts of the urban center. Used spindle whorls provide evidence for the spinning of thread. Small whorls used to spin cotton thread are found in all parts of the site, pointing to household-level production of thread and cloth by all families, whereas large whorls used to spin the coarser maguey thread were found in several discrete concentrations, suggesting possible workshop production.

CITIES AS RELIGIOUS CENTERS

Temples were not by any means limited to urban centers. The chronicler Motolinía (1979: 51) pointed out that every town and every neighborhood had one or more temples. Small rural towns such as Cuexcomate (chapter 2) had temples that were small-scale versions of larger single-temple pyramids (fig. 7.3), and archaeologists have located the ruins of similar temples (most likely small single-temple pyramids like Cuexcomate) at nonurban Aztec sites in the Teotihuacan Valley (Sanders and Evans 2001). Cities like Calixtlahuaca had small, neighborhood temples in addition to their large central temples. This wide distribution of temples suggests that they were the settings for frequent ceremonies involving the widespread participation of people. As such, small neighborhood temples in cities pertained to the nearby population, but they were not the basis for urban functions. But several types of urban religious architecture did serve as focal points for religious urban functions: central temples, circular temples, ballcourts, and altars.

The central temple of an altepetl, whether of the single-stair or double-stair form, was typically located on the plaza in the urban epicenter (chapter 4), where it towered over the city. Although we lack complete architectural data from individual altepetl, there are no known cases in which hinterland

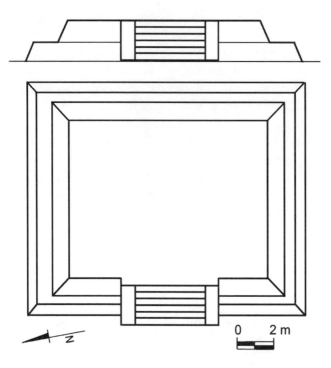

Figure 7.3. Reconstruction drawing of a small rural temple at Cuexcomate.
Drawing by the author.

settlements had temples larger than those in their capital city. The fact that these large temples were only found in capitals points to an urban religious function. The patron gods worshipped at these temples protected the entire altepetl. The altepetl's population, rural and urban, probably gathered periodically for ceremonies at these central temples, most likely for one or more of the monthly veintena ceremonies (chapter 6). Circular temples and ballcourts had a similar distribution to large central temples: They were only built in capital cities. Thus these structures, or more precisely, the activities and institutions centered on them, were the bases for urban functions in the realm of religion. Although altars were built at both capitals and smaller towns, only capital cities had large numbers of altars along their plazas, suggesting urban functions for at least some of the activities based on these features.

Some cities had religious functions of greater scope than the typical city-state capital. The imperial capital, Tenochtitlan, is the clearest example of this. Much of the ceremony at the Templo Mayor had an empire-wide significance (if we choose to believe Mexica state ideology, that is), and this temple thus functioned on a much larger spatial and social scale than any temple in a city-state capital. Another example is Cholula, known throughout central Mexico as a religious city. As the destination of pilgrimages and a recognized seat of religious authority for much of Mesoamerica, Cholula had higher-level religious functions than most cities (McCafferty 1996).

EDUCATION AND ELITE CULTURE

As in most preindustrial societies, education was largely a family affair for the commoner class. All young people attended school for a short time (chapter 4), but most acculturation and training was done within the family. The specialized knowledge that formed the core of Aztec elite culture, however, was transmitted to nobles (and to some commoners) in the calmecac schools (Calnek 1988). I suggest in chapter 4 that calmecacs in altepetl capitals might have existed either as special buildings (as in Tenochtitlan) or as part of the royal palace, where certain rooms or courtyards may have provided a location for calmecac education. Regardless of the physical setting for this training in writing, oratory, history, music, and other elite arts and concerns, it was probably offered in every altepetl, and it almost certainly took place within the capital and not in smaller hinterland settlements.

The people who were trained in the calmecac became the leaders of the altepetl—government officials, priests, elite warriors, landowners, and other influential and powerful individuals. As such, the calmecac training had effects, if indirect, on all inhabitants of the altepetl, and it can be considered an important urban function. Since much of the training was in religious affairs—myths, ceremonies, the interpretation of ritual codices, and other religious lore—this can be considered a kind of religious urban function.

More to the point for this book, however, is the fact that the calmecac was the means for the transmission of information about urban design and urban meaning. The training of nobles in myth and history focused extensively on Tula and the Toltecs, and this probably included information about urban layout and architectural patterns. Young nobles from rural towns like Cuexcomate almost certainly traveled to their local altepetl capital to attend the calmecac. This is most likely where they picked up information about such topics in urban design as proper temple form (fig. 7.3) and the Tula plaza plan. Given the role of the calmecac in the intellectual, conceptual, and religious integration of the noble class, it is not surprising to find the Tula plaza plan even at a rural town like Cuexcomate, which had just a small palace compound (chapter 4).

URBAN FUNCTIONS AND THE ALTEPETL

Most of the administrative, economic, and religious activities that affected the lives of people throughout an altepetl were concentrated in the capital city. Within a given altepetl, the existence of multiple urban functions within a single settlement went hand in hand with the large size of these capitals in comparison with other settlements. Although the altepetl capitals were multifunctional cities, like most ancient cities around the world, not all urban functions were of equal importance. As summarized in the following chapter, the available documentary and archaeological evidence points very strongly to administration and religion as the dominant functions of these cities. Most were probably also commercial centers for regional trade in grains and other foods, utilitarian goods, and luxury goods. But not all altepetl capitals were centers for craft production. Except perhaps for the imperial capital, Otumba had no equal among altepetl capitals in the extent and intensity of its craft industries. Some cities had moderate craft industries, while others appear to have seen no production at all beyond ubiquitous domestic textile production.

Although urban functions were strongly concentrated in the altepetl capitals, they were not limited to those cities. Many smaller settlements also had urban functions, albeit on a much smaller scale than the capitals. Cuexcomate is a good example. Although its population was under 1,000 people (table 2.1), this settlement had three architectural features not present at nearby villages such as Capilco: a small palace, a modest temple, and a formal plaza. The palace and temple signal low-level urban functions in the realm of administration and religion. The activities centered on these buildings affected people outside of Cuexcomate (such as the residents of Capilco), but their spatial reach was much smaller than the equivalent buildings at an altepetl capital.

The formal plaza at Cuexcomate is particularly important. The fact that the Tula plaza plan was implemented at such a minor center indicates that the spatial reach of Aztec elite culture was extensive. Even a low-ranking noble family at a rural town understood the symbolism and architectural messages communicated by the Tula plaza plan (chapter 5). The use of this principle of urban design was probably part of this family's strategies and techniques of control and legitimation. This case illustrates the hierarchical nature of urban functions. The most public and wide-ranging urban functions—such as political domination and religious leadership—were concentrated at the altepetl capital, whereas lower-ranking urban functions were present at smaller rural towns (but not at villages and hamlets).

8

Cities, City-States, and Aztec Urbanism

Urbanization is not a simple, unitary, universally similar process. . . . It assumes
different forms and meanings, depending upon the prevailing historic, economic, social, and cultural conditions. (Lewis 1952: 39)

Oscar Lewis, in the quotation above, indicates the main advantage of the
functional approach to urbanism taken in this book. As discussed in chapters
1 and 7, cities in different cultural traditions are rarely identical, and there can
be different kinds of cities within a single cultural tradition. The main argument of this book is that the primary functional emphasis of Aztec cities and
towns was in the realm of political administration. Cities were the capitals of
the altepetl, ruled by kings who used urban design and public architecture to
further their own agendas. I begin this chapter with a review of the evidence
supporting my claim for a political role for Aztec cities. I then describe an exploratory model, based upon principles and insights from political economy
and collective action theory, which helps account for the forms, functions,
meanings, and historical trajectories of Aztec city-state capitals. I close by
comparing these cities with other ancient Mesoamerican urban centers.

AZTEC CITIES AS POLITICAL CAPITALS

Dynasties are prior to towns and cities. Towns and cities are secondary (products) of royal authority. . . . The life of the dynasty is the life of the town. If the
dynasty is of short duration, life in the town will stop at the end of the dynasty.
Its civilization will recede and the town will fall into ruins. On the other hand,
if the dynasty is of long duration and lasts a long time, new construction will
always go up in the town, the number of large mansions will increase, and the
walls of the town will extend farther and farther. (Khaldûn 1958: 2:235)

Ibn Khaldûn, the fourteenth-century Islamic historian and philosopher, es-
poused a political theory of urbanism that accords well with the model of Aztec city-state capitals developed in this book. These were administrative cities, founded and built by kings and nobles as part of their efforts to promote
and legitimize their rule. Aztec cities had a strong religious component as

well, involving myths, ceremonies, and beliefs focused on temples and professional priests. But in Aztec society, as in most ancient states and empires, the state religion did the work of politics. Many of the religious activities in Aztec cities, from sacrificial rites on the central pyramid to games in the ball-court to public processions through the streets, served the interests of kings. These ceremonies were supported and promoted because they strengthened and legitimized dynastic rule, helped maintain public order, and served to reinforce the bonds between ruler and subjects.

The available documentary and archaeological evidence shows quite clearly that Aztec cities were political capitals, and a strong argument can be made that this urban function dominated other roles of cities. In most descriptions of the founding of a city and its altepetl in the native historical accounts, cities were founded by kings. For example, Xolotl founded Tenayuca, Icxicuauhtli founded Tepechpan (fig. 3.2), and Tezozomoc of Azcapotzalco sent his sons out to found cities around his domain. Tenochtitlan is an exception here, a case in which a city was founded by the settling of a migrating ethnic group that did not yet belong to an altepetl. The initial acts of city foundation included the staging of sacrifices and ceremonies, the construction of a royal palace and a state temple, and the division of subjects and land among leading nobles.

Various native concepts and models illustrate the dominance of political and administrative urban functions at Aztec cities. The people-centered administrative model presented in chapter 3 as an alternative to Western notions of territoriality shows the preeminence of the king in the structure and operation of the altepetl. By extension, this model suggests the dominant role of the king's capital in structuring the altepetl. Furthermore, evidence reviewed in chapter 3 points to the palace and temple as the most important buildings and institutions in the native Aztec view of cities.

The fact that the entire altepetl and the capital city shared the same name in native sources is another line of support for the importance of political functions at these cities. As pointed out in chapter 3, this practice is common in ancient city-state cultures around the world (Hansen 2000a). Unlike eighteenth-century France, where Louis XIV is credited as saying that the king was the state and the state was the king ("L'état c'est moi"), in city-state cultures the capital is the state and the state is the capital.

The archaeological evidence of buildings and their placements (chapters 4 and 5) supports the idea that administration was the primary urban function of Aztec cities. The two largest buildings in each urban epicenter were the palace (the largest in area) and the main temple (the tallest structure). Typically located on adjacent or opposite sides of the central plaza, these two stone structures had equivalent structural positions within the townscape. If cities primarily served religious functions, one would expect a smaller size and reduced focus for the palace. This could easily have been accomplished by making the main temple the single central focus of the epicenter (that is, located at the formal center, not on the edge of a central plaza) or by filling the sides of the plaza with temples and religious buildings and placing the palace away from the plaza. This kind of temple-centered city design is found in urban traditions in which cities have a stronger religious role, such as in India and Cambodia (Brown 1965; Dumarçay and Royère 2001), but not in Mesoamerica.

The use of the Tula plaza plan at some Aztec cities further supports the importance of political dynamics as forces that generated Aztec city form and function. Tula was looked at as the great urban capital of the past, the central seat of legitimate royal power in central Mexico. Aztec kings traced their descent from the Toltec kings. By incorporating aspects of the buildings and layout of Tula into their altepetl capitals, the Aztec kings were making clear and explicit, if nonverbal, political claims about their cities. Furthermore, the formality of urban epicenters, with their use of monumentality and orthogonal principles of design, points to central planning and a prominent role for political dynamics in the establishment and operation of cities.

In sum, archaeology shows that politics and religion were of utmost importance for understanding urban dynamics. My reading of the evidence suggests that in Aztec central Mexico kings and the altepetl played more of a role in structuring the state religion than religious principles and forces played in structuring political dynamics. Finally, the fact that the strength of economic functions was much more variable among Aztec cities than were political or religious functions suggests a lower prominence for economic forces in generating urban forms and dynamics. Again, however, Tenochtitlan was different; its economic role and importance grew rapidly as the Triple Alliance empire expanded (Garraty 2007; Rojas 1986).

KINGS, NOBLES, COMMONERS, AND CITIES: INSIGHTS FROM POLITICAL ECONOMY

Why was the political role dominant in Aztec cities? Why was there such a high degree of similarity in building types and city layouts among the capitals of altepetl? Why were Aztec townscapes laid out using more formal designs than other cities in Mesoamerica? How and why did these patterns develop through time? The only way to properly answer these and other questions about the nature of Aztec urbanism and its historical trajectory is through the comparative method. Although a theoretically informed comparative analysis is beyond the scope of this book, it is possible to suggest some of the factors that likely played important roles in generating the patterns described in the preceding chapters. In this section I outline an admittedly speculative model based on principles from the fields of political economy (Allen 1997; Domar 1970; North 1981) and collective action theory (Fargher and Blanton 2007; Hirschman 1978; Levi 1981; Olson 1965). This model is not a full explanatory account of Aztec urbanism; rather, its purpose is to identify some of the relevant processes and to stimulate research and thinking on these topics.[1]

Land, Labor, Intensification, and Exit

My speculative model begins with the relationship between land and labor in agrarian societies. In order for elites to thrive and kings to build cities, peasants must produce a surplus of food over their household consumption needs. This obviously requires more effort than just farming to meet household needs. Ethnographic research shows that people in noncapitalist economies typically do not invest much extra effort to produce a surplus unless there is a compelling reason to do so (Allen 1997; Carneiro 1961; Netting 1993). The increased effort required to produce a surplus is part of the process known as agricultural intensification: the investment of additional labor or energy in order to raise productivity per area of land. In her landmark study of agricultural change, Ester Boserup (1965) assembled evidence suggesting that people only intensify their production if forced to do so by population pressure or by the demands of the state or elites (Netting 1993).

As discussed in chapter 7 (see also Smith 2003a: 65–73), the Late Aztec period was a time of major agricultural intensification throughout central Mexico. Rapidly growing regional populations, coupled with the demands of kings and nobles, forced farmers to intensify their agricultural practices through irrigation, terracing, and other techniques. There was little empty land, no new areas to colonize, and there were many peasants struggling to make a living. In the language of political economy, this was a time with a low land-to-labor ratio. Farmers had little choice but to intensify if they wanted to feed their families and avoid the legal consequences of failing to pay taxes and rent.

But why would farmers want to produce a surplus to support cities and elites during the Early Aztec period? This was a time of open land and much lower population; in other words the land-to-labor ratio was much higher than in Late Aztec times. Getting peasants to produce a surplus under such conditions has always presented problems for elites and kings (Domar 1970;

North 1981: 129–133). If they feel exploited by local nobles or the king, peasants can simply leave and find new land to settle and farm. In the language of collective action theory, it was easy for peasants to "exit" the system (Fargher and Blanton 2007; Hirschman 1978). If kings and elites could not exploit peasants, how did they manage to build cities and rule city-states?

Interests, Strategies, and Predatory Kings

In order to understand the dilemma posed above, we need to consider the interests, strategies, and social conditions of different categories of people in the altepetl: commoners, kings, and nobles.

Commoners

Most commoners were peasants: rural farmers who were part of a state polity and thus subject to rulers and elites. In comparison with peasants in other Mesoamerican societies, Aztec peasants at the time of the Spanish conquest were both disadvantaged and privileged. On the negative side, they were more dependent upon nobles and more strongly subject to nobles. In Postclassic Mixtec city-states, for example, local commoner groups owned farmland collectively (Terraciano 2001: 205–206), whereas the members of Aztec calpolli were dependent upon a noble who owned the land (chapter 6). On the positive side, the extensive development of Aztec regional marketing systems gave commoners greater economic opportunities (for petty crafts and exchange) than in many other Mesoamerican societies.

It was in the interests of Aztec commoners to affiliate more strongly with the king than with lower-ranking nobles. The king had more influence in the market system, and both king and commoners benefitted from smoothly operating commercial exchange networks. The king could also protect his subjects from overexploitation by local nobles. Furthermore, the king had more influence over the gods and religious forces than did other nobles. Although some peasants might have preferred to flee to open, uncontrolled regions instead of paying rents and taxes, those peasants who were settled would have found it in their interests to cooperate and interact with their king as a buffer against predatory local elites.

Nobles

From their structural position between the king and commoners, the Aztec nobility strived to maintain and extend their own power, wealth, and status. Their ownership of land and control of blocks of commoners gave then a significant power base independent of the king. It was in their interests to exploit their commoners as much as possible (with higher rents and more extensive use of corvée labor), but like the king, nobles had to keep their dependent commoners from rebelling or fleeing. Nobles also had to support the king, who could act against individual nobles in various ways. Their most natural alliance was clearly with the king, however. The practices and concepts that made up Aztec elite culture (chapter 1) were clear signals of the shared interests of the king and the nobles, both within individual city-states and among independent city-states throughout central Mexico.

Kings

Aztec kings may have had fewer independent resources and less power than many ancient kings in Mesoamerica and elsewhere. Their domains were small and they engaged in constant competition and strife with their peers. They depended on commoners for labor, for taxes in goods and money, and for military service in their constant wars. In addition, commoners served kings as pawns in royal struggles with nobles. Kings also depended on nobles for political support and for help running the altepetl. Kings were elected from within the royal family by a council of high nobles. Thus kings needed to keep their commoner subjects satisfied and tranquil, and they needed to keep their nobles from usurping power or exiting to a rival altepetl. Not surprisingly, it has been shown that much of the elaborate ideological production at the Templo Mayor of Tenochtitlan was directed not at commoners but at the nobility, in order to keep them satisfied and affiliated (Brumfiel 1998).

The strategies and actions of Aztec kings in relation to commoners and nobles fit well with what has been called "the predatory theory of rule" (Levi 1981; North 1981: 21–24):

> All rulers are predatory in the sense that they, as much as they can, design property rights and policies meant to maximize their own personal wealth. My thesis is not only that the ruler is predatory in that he attempts to formulate policies that maximize his personal objectives but that his success is dependent on his bargaining power vis-à-vis his subjects, agents, and external actors. In this approach, policies are seen as the outcome of an exchange between the ruler and various individual groups. (Levi 1981: 438)

Mancur Olson (2000: 1–11) presents a similar model, although he objects to the metaphor of predation: A king "is not like the wolf that preys on the elk, but more like the rancher who makes sure that his cattle are protected and given water" (Olson 2000: 11). In Olson's model, kings have a wide "encompassing interest" in their realm. Their successful negotiations with nobles and commoners, including the provision of public goods for widespread consumption (see the discussion below).

A basic conclusion of my exploratory model is that the design, construction, and use of cities were parts of this process of exchange or negotiation among kings, commoners, and nobles. An examination of political and economic dynamics in the Early and Late Aztec periods will clarify this point.

The Early Aztec Period: The Founding and Spread of Capitals

The Early Aztec period began with the arrival and settlement of the Aztlan migrants from the north. The earliest of these immigrants encountered a situation of small villages, widely dispersed across the landscape. During the Early Postclassic or Toltec period, Tula had been the only major urban center, and this was the most ruralized era since the initial development of states and cities in central Mexico over a millennium earlier. The new immigrants spread across central Mexico, and populations started to grow rapidly (due to both immigration and natural population increase). But for most of the Early Aztec period the ratio of land to labor was high, and it was easy for commoners and nobles to move from one struggling altepetl to another. To re-pose the questions asked above, how did kings manage to build cities and how did nobles manage to control commoner subjects under these conditions? Recall that the Early Aztec period was the time when most Aztec cities were founded.

Comparative historical analysis by political economists has shown that this kind of high land-to-labor ratio often provides the conditions for the establishment of unfree labor, such as slavery and serfdom. If it is easy for commoners to exit the system, then the only way elites can get commoners to work for them is to create institutions of unfree labor. And the only way to do that successfully is for kings to cooperate with elites by creating and enforcing new rules or laws concerning labor and property relations (Domar 1970; North 1981: 21–24, 129–133). Thus it is very likely that the various forms of commoner subjugation to nobles documented from the time of the Spanish conquest had their origins in the Early Aztec period. Kings supported these forms of unfree labor (chapter 6) as part of their program of alliance with the nobility. The discussion between the king and nobles depicted in the foundation scene of the *Tira de Tepechpan* (fig. 3.2) may have involved just this sort of cooperation or collusion.

Although the establishment of laws for labor and taxation provided some incentives for peasants to accept their lot and pay their rents and taxes, kings also provided benefits or incentives for cooperative peasants and urban commoners. Periodic markets have already been mentioned as one such benefit, but perhaps the most effective incentive of this type was the state religion. In the language of political economy, Aztec state religion can be considered a public good. A public good is something open to consumption by all members of a given community such that its use by one member does not detract from its use by another (Hirschman 1978; Olson 1965: 14; 2000: 1–11). In modern societies public goods are typically offered by governments, and they include law and police protection, defense, and some kinds of infrastructural facilities.

By promoting state religion as a public good, Aztec kings furnished their subjects with supernatural protection, personal satisfaction and emotional fulfillment, and feelings of identity with the community and the city. Commoners received numerous benefits from the state religion: protection by the altepetl's patron deities; intercession by priests with the rain gods; divination services of priests; the chance to witness sacrifices, sacred games, and other theatrical ceremonies; and the satisfaction of participating in civic ceremonies such as the veintena rituals.

Aztec state religion—as materialized in temples, ballcourts, and shrines, and in censers, flutes and other cult objects—can be seen as a factor attracting commoners to cities. Through large-scale construction projects using corvée labor, commoners helped build temples and palaces while developing forms of emotional identification with their cities, their communities, and their king (chapter 6). Perhaps the increasing construction of small platforms and shrines, particularly the tzitzimime platform, was a specific mechanism directed at commoner participation. In ancient Mesoamerica the kind of female-associated rites of curing, fertility and divination carried out at these features (Klein 2000) were more commonly part of the domestic realm than the public arena of state religion. The proliferation of shrines at Aztec cities may have been part of the king's negotiation with his commoner subjects. The design and construction of aspects of these cities in imitation of the ancient city of Tula, on the other hand, was directed more at an audience of nobles, not commoners. Kings used principles of social memory, formal training in the calmecac, and exclusive state ceremonies to help bind nobles to the altepetl.

In sum, the social and demographic conditions of the Early Aztec period generated processes that led to the construction of public architecture and the growth of cities, even in a condition of abundant land and limited labor. First, kings and nobles probably colluded to establish a number of types of commoner subjection to nobles and the laws required to enforce them. Second, a growing population coupled with an expanding system of periodic markets helped create conditions of economic prosperity and growth, particularly for commoners. Third, the provision of state religion as a public good by kings contributed directly to commoner support and to the construction of public architecture in the urban epicenter.

The Late Aztec Period: Urban Growth or Stagnation?

By the start of the Late Aztec period in the early fourteenth century, nearly all Aztec cities had already been founded. Only Tenochtitlan and Cuexcomate, the largest and smallest urban centers discussed in the book, show evidence of being founded in the Late Aztec period (and as discussed in chapter 2, that evidence is equivocal for the imperial capital). Although cities continued to serve as capitals of altepetl, it appears that the growth trajectories of many or most examples may have leveled off in Late Aztec times. Outside of Tenochtitlan no Aztec city grew into a large metropolis, in spite of an overall population explosion. Furthermore, there is some indication that construction activity on public architecture may have slowed down considerably in Late Aztec times.

The social trends identified above continued into the Late Aztec period, but as populations continued to grow, the land-to-labor ratio declined throughout central Mexico. Land became more valuable and labor less costly, which probably strengthened the laws and customs of dependent labor. The growing population led to agricultural intensification, and the entire landscape of central Mexico was transformed by terracing, irrigation, and chinampa construction. Farmers fought a losing battle for adequate yields, and a series of droughts had catastrophic consequences for society. Given the important multifunctional roles of cities, one might expect to see them grow into large, dense settlements by the time of the Spanish conquest, yet with one important exception this was not the case. A key question for Late Aztec urbanization is, Why did Aztec cities remain relatively small settlements in the face of growing populations and increasing economic activity?

One reason for the small size of urban populations was a lack of economic opportunities in cities. Tenochtitlan, Texcoco, and perhaps Otumba were the only Aztec cities with sufficient craft activity and commerce to attract settlement. Although all cities had markets and were visited by regional merchants, most of the commercial exchange seems to have been devoted to supplying urban consumers, rather than exporting craft goods for profit. Cross-culturally, commerce and production are often the major factors contributing to significant population growth within ancient cities (Modelski 2003; Storey 2006; Wrigley 1990).

Another reason for the small sizes of altepetl capitals was the nature of Aztec intensive agriculture. One way that Late Aztec settlement patterns differed from those of earlier periods in central Mexico was in the heavy distribution of household settlement throughout the countryside (chapter 6). Although there were cities, towns, and villages, many people lived dispersed in hilly rural areas because of the labor requirement of terrace agriculture. Terraces require constant maintenance and upkeep, and cross-culturally terrace farmers tend to live close to their fields, not concentrated in towns (Drennan 1988; Netting 1993). As noted in chapter 6, terracing was the dominant form of intensive agriculture in Aztec central Mexico.

The operation of regional marketing systems assured that rural households had ready access to most goods that they needed (chapter 6). Thus among commoner consumers, peasants were not disadvantaged relative to urbanites. From the perspective of nobles and kings, having many of their subjects living in rural areas was not a problem for collecting taxes, rent, or labor drafts because of the small sizes of most altepetl. If goods could circulate in large numbers in both urban and rural areas, as the archaeological record clearly shows, then information and people could also move easily throughout the altepetl. Under these conditions, there were few advantages to large urban populations.

The imperial capital Tenochtitlan is the big exception here, and its huge size can be attributed directly to its political role as capital of the Triple Alliance empire. The amount of wealth entering the capital, through both tribute and commerce, was staggering (Berdan 1987), and the demand for craft goods, both luxury and utilitarian, was significant. Furthermore, its island location made transport from the lakeshore both easy and efficient. In order to meet the growing capital's food needs, the central part of the Basin of Mexico was turned into the city's breadbasket. Brumfiel's fieldwork at Huexotla (chapter 2) shows that peasants and urbanites gave up craft production (except for textiles) and devoted their energies to the production of grains for the capital.

Most cities continued to expand their public architecture in the Late Aztec period, rebuilding their pyramids and expanding their epicenters. Nevertheless, there is some evidence that the scale of construction may have leveled off in Late Aztec times. After four or five stages of enlargement of the Tenayuca pyramid in the Early Aztec period, only one construction stage was completed in Late Aztec times (yet the pyramid continued in use through the Spanish conquest). The Teopanzolco pyramid had at least two major stages of construction in Early Aztec times, and then the urban epicenter was moved several kilometers in the Late Aztec period, but no large temple has been located for the new site. At Cuexcomate, the modest palace of the Late Aztec–A period was abandoned and replaced by a much smaller palace in the Late Aztec–B period. No such slowing of construction happened in Tenochtitlan, however, providing yet another example of the uniqueness of this city among Aztec urban centers. The continuing physical, economic, and political growth of Tenochtitlan may have come at the expense of other Aztec cities.

Aztec cities continued to serve kings in the Late Aztec period (chapter 5), but they may have had a less dynamic and generative role within the altepetl than in their early decades. Given a shrinking land-to-labor ratio, major agricultural intensification, and growing problems of drought and hunger, the options of Aztec commoners were greatly reduced in Late Aztec times. Kings and nobles did not have to worry so much about attracting followers, and thus the impetus to constantly rebuild pyramids and other public buildings may have declined.

The growing populations, however, probably contributed to the development of state religious ceremonies in a more elaborate and exuberant direction. The veintena ceremonies may have expanded from small-scale celebrations of a day or two to the massive productions that lasted a week or more as described by the chroniclers for Tenochtitlan. The scale of human sacrifice probably expanded as well. It may be that the various components of the state religion—priests, temples, calmecac training, public ceremonies, myths, cosmological schemes, and the like—took on lives of their own to develop into the complex, sophisticated, and elaborate religious system described by the chroniclers after Spanish conquest. Cities continued to provide the physical setting for most of these activities in Late Aztec times, but the state religion may have become less strongly coupled to rulership and the altepetl than in the early days of Aztec urbanism.

Carrots, Sticks, and Cities

This admittedly speculative model rests upon a contrast between the Early and Late Aztec periods in the dynamics and organization of urbanism.[2] Cities were founded in Early Aztec times by petty kings on the heels of waves of immigration from Aztlan. Cities were intimately bound up with the establishment of altepetl. Given the demographic and social situation in central Mexico, early kings and nobles likely had difficulty attracting and controlling commoner subjects. In order to build their cities and expand their power and wealth, kings offered both carrots (the benefits of the state religion and the regional marketing system) and sticks (laws and the threat of punishment for wrongdoing). Kings established systems of land tenure and labor institutions that gave nobles a degree of control over commoners. One result was the creation of urban epicenters as we find them at archaeological sites today (chapter 2). Another result was the flourishing of numerous independent petty city-states—the altepetl—linked together by the ties of Aztec elite culture and other economic and social channels.

By the Late Aztec period, institutional systems of labor control were more entrenched, and the exploding Aztec population meant that the ratio of land to labor declined considerably. As a result kings and nobles had less need to attract and control commoner workers and supporters. The demands of terrace agriculture kept many commoners "on the farm," contributing to a relatively slow rate of demographic growth of cities. Although, other than Tenochtitlan, cities did not grow into huge population centers and their rates of temple rebuilding in the epicenter may have declined, Aztec state religion became more elaborate and extensive and came to play a major role in structuring life in cities. After 1428, the growing power of Tenochtitlan as the imperial capital served to further reduce the options of kings, nobles, and commoners alike, perhaps inhibiting urban growth in its subject cities.

MODELS, REALITY, AND THE DESTRUCTION OF ARCHAEOLOGICAL SITES

Does the model presented above match the archaeological and historical data on Aztec cities? Unfortunately this question cannot be answered yet in a satisfactory fashion since there is still too little relevant evidence. These concepts from collective action theory and political economy are consistent with current evidence, but that is a long way from saying that they can be empirically verified. Readers should not conclude that I believe, for example, that kings established temples and public rituals in order to win the allegiance of commoners, although this seems a reasonable hypothesis. Without new research we will never be able to achieve the desired goals of scholarly hypotheses: either to be elevated to a more strongly confirmed interpretation or to be discarded on the back-dirt pile of history.

The best way to move these and other hypotheses along toward acceptance or rejection is to carry out more research. Archaeological fieldwork at Aztec urban sites is badly needed if we are to advance our understanding of Aztec cities and their social roles. On a more basic level, however, fieldwork is also necessary just to gather and preserve information about Aztec cities and society. Most Aztec urban sites that have not already been destroyed by historical and modern urban expansion and economic development are now threatened by those processes. Even at relatively well-protected archaeological zones such as Calixtlahuaca (fig. 8.1), the archaeological remains of many houses, terraces, and workshops continue to be destroyed as a byproduct of modern demographic and economic expansion.

Another source of threat to the archaeological record of Aztec cities is the thriving commercial market for ancient art. Art collectors like to buy the fancy pottery and stone sculpture produced by the Aztecs, Mayas, and other ancient peoples. Although the sale and export of these objects are illegal in Mexico, their high commercial value makes room for them in the shadowy world of the illegal international antiquities market. In order to feed that market, antiquities sellers sponsor the destruction of archaeological sites through both organized looting and the purchase of objects looted by local residents.[3]

For all of the reasons outlined above, it is urgent for archaeologists to continue excavating Aztec sites. Because we know more about pyramids and other public buildings than we do about houses and workshops, residential archaeology is particularly critical right now (fig. 8.1). The preservation and study of Aztec sites is important not only for advancing our understanding of ancient urbanism and other topics but also to keep alive an appreciation of the achievements of past civilizations.

Figure 8.1. Excavation of a commoner house at Calixtlahuaca in 2007. Although this structure is within the government archaeological zone, parts of it had been destroyed by recent farming activity.

AZTEC CITIES AND THE MESOAMERICAN URBAN TRADITION

Aztec cities make more sense if we place them within the broader context of the Mesoamerican urban tradition. Urban centers had a long period of development in Mesoamerica prior to the Aztec period. From the demographic perspective, the first major Mesoamerican cities originated in the Classic period: Teotihuacan, Monte Alban, and some of the large Maya centers. If we take the functional perspective, however, the origins of Mesoamerican urbanism are found earlier than this in the towns of the Middle Formative (or Olmec) period (Clark 2004; Grove and Joyce 1999; Joyce 2000). In spite of a high level of variation among Mesoamerican cities and towns, many or most of these settlements shared a number of key characteristics that allow us to talk of a "Mesoamerican urban tradition" (Sanders and Webster 1988; Smith 2001). Aztec cities were part of this tradition, and many of their material and social characteristics can be found in other ancient Mesoamerican cities.

Aztec and Maya Cities

In this section I briefly note some of the similarities and differences between Aztec and Maya cities. The Classic Maya is one of the few other urban subtraditions in Mesoamerica comparable to the Aztec case in having a large number of well-documented cities; most comparative work in Mesoamerican urbanism has focused on a small number of very large, and usually atypical, cities (for example, Sanders and Webster 1988). I use the topics of chapters 3 through 7 to organize this discussion.

The Founding of Cities

Hieroglyphic and archaeological evidence for the founding of Classic Maya cities parallels the data for Aztec cities. Political foundation events are attested in the written record, where kings claimed credit for founding cities (or, more typically, later kings claimed that their dynastic ancestors had founded cities), and religious foundation events are signaled by offerings and the construction of special religious buildings (Chase and Chase 1995; Ciudad Ruiz and Iglesias Ponce de León 2006). Maya texts unfortunately provide little information about the conceptual basis for city foundations, so it is difficult to evaluate the distinctiveness of Aztec references to the past glories of ancestral peoples, such as Chichimecs and Toltecs, in the foundation process.

Table 8.1. Types of Public Buildings in Aztec and Maya Cities

Aztec	Maya
Single-temple pyramid	Temple
Double-temple pyramid	Temple
Circular temple	
Ballcourt	Ballcourt
Shrine	Altar or ceremonial platform
	Shrine or sanctuary
Palace	Palace
	Stelae

Sources: Aztec: chapter 4; Maya: Andrews (1975).

Architectural Inventory

Most ancient Mesoamerican cities were composed of one or more examples of a standard suite of public buildings: temples, ballcourts, shrines or platforms, and palaces. Table 8.1 compares Aztec public building types with those identified for the Classic Maya by George Andrews (1975). My division of temples into three categories is straightforward; at Aztec sites the three major types are quite distinctive and standardized. Maya temples, on the other hand, exhibit much more variation that is less easily characterized by types (Andrews 1975, 1995–99). Similarly, Maya cities exhibit more variation in their ballcourts and palaces than do Aztec cities, but this may be due in part to the much larger sample of known structures at Maya sites. One difference between the two urban cultures is the prevalence of standardized groups of buildings at Maya cities. In addition to describing building types (table 8.1), Andrews also describes several types of groups, including temple groups, quadrangle groups, and acropolis groups; this level of architectural arrangement does not seem nearly so prevalent or important at Aztec cities.

Planning and Meaning

In chapter 1 I list three ancient and fundamental Mesoamerican principles of urban planning: (1) public architecture was concentrated in a central zone, the epicenter; (2) a variety of planning techniques were applied within the urban epicenter but not in the rest of the city (that is, residential zones show little planning); and (3) the public plaza was the basic feature used to structure urban space. These principles originated in the Olmec period (Clark 2004; Clark and Hansen 2001; Grove and Joyce 1999) and characterized all of Mesoamerica from lowland Veracruz (Stark 1999) to highland Oaxaca (Balkansky, Pérez Rodríguez, and Kowalewski 2004), including the Classic

Maya lowlands (Andrews 1975; Marcus 1983). As shown in this book, Aztec cities fit right in with other Mesoamerican cities in this respect.

Compared with these very general planning principles, the meanings of cities and their townscapes are much more difficult to analyze. High-level meanings of Mesoamerican cities have been hotly debated (Ashmore 1991; Ashmore and Sabloff 2002; Aveni 2001; Carrasco 1999b; Smith 2003b, 2005b), and it is fair to say that Mesoamericanists have yet to reach consensus on this issue (see chapter 5). Because high-level meanings are almost always culturally specific and esoteric (Rapoport 1988), they probably differed among Mesoamerican cultures. Middle-level meanings, referred to here as architectural communication, show more similarity among Mesoamerican cities. Monumentality and formality were common themes in these settlements, and numerous cases of the invocation of past kings and cities have been identified at Mesoamerican cities. Again, Aztec altepetl capitals fit well with basic patterns of Mesoamerican urbanism.

Urban Life

The private lives of Mesoamerican urbanites probably differed greatly depending upon local social organization, economy, climate, and environment. But all Mesoamerican cities contained both elites and commoners, and the differences between these social classes in lifestyles, wealth, and status were significant, even if the details differed from one city to another. The social and spatial importance of neighborhoods is one of the universal characteristics of ancient and preindustrial cities around the world (Keith 2003; Sjoberg 1960), but these have been difficult to define in Aztec, Maya, and other Mesoamerican urban cultures (except at Teotihuacan; see Cowgill, Altshul, and Sload 1984). The basic similarity of Mesoamerican religions probably gave a measure of commonality to public urban life in different areas. Periodic civic ceremonies involving sacrifices, processions, music, and dance probably took place in all ancient Mesoamerican cities.

Urban Functions

Sanders and Webster (1988) suggest that most Mesoamerican cities were examples of Richard Fox's (1977) functional category, the "regal-ritual city" (see also Marcus 1983). This urban type describes capitals of small states in which the dominant urban functions are political administration and religion. Although there has been debate by Mesoamericanists over the usefulness of this characterization, and of the related "segmentary state" model (for example, Fox et al. 1996), the regal-ritual type does capture the basic functional qualities of Mesoamerican cities, including the Aztec cities described in this book.

Just as economic activity was far more variable among Aztec cities than was religion or administration (chapter 7), so too did economics differ greatly in its importance within and among other Mesoamerican urban cultures.

Historical Trajectories

The above summary points to numerous similarities in form and function between Aztec cities and other ancient Mesoamerican cities, particularly Classic Maya cities. Another similarity with some Mesoamerican urban cultures concerns the historical trajectory of urbanization. Balkansky et al. (2004) propose what they call the "synergism model" to explain the development of urban centers in the Mixteca Alta of Oaxaca. This model describes the urbanization process as one of "co-development and concordant change over a broad macroregion" (40); in other words, a series of interacting settlements all develop into urban centers more or less simultaneously with part of the impetus being their mutual interactions. This describes the Aztec developmental trajectory well: Numerous interacting cities developed at the same time in the Early Aztec period.

The high level of similarity among Aztec cities is one way in which this urban culture stood out compared with others in Mesoamerica. Classic Maya cities seem to show far more variation in city layout and architectural forms than do Aztec cities (although this is difficult to establish empirically due to the lack of systematic comparative research on Maya cities). For the Mixteca, Balkansky, Pérez Rodríguez, and Kowalewski (2004: 48) note that "no two Mixtec urban centers looked the same." By contrast the Aztec cities described in this book resembled one another greatly in their design and layout, in their formality and monumentality, in their architectural inventories, and in the forms of specific building types. One reason for this high level of standardization was the emphasis on copying the urban design and architecture of Tula. Another reason was the operation of Aztec elite culture as a force that provided links among cities and a series of shared concepts about urbanism. Although elites in all Mesoamerican states participated in some form of elite culture, the highly formalized training provided in the Aztec calmecac may have given Aztec elite culture more coherence as a social force than in earlier Mesoamerican cultures.

THE FUNCTIONAL APPROACH TO ANCIENT URBANISM

The quotation from Oscar Lewis that opens this chapter offers one of the main arguments in favor of the functional approach to urbanism: It allows for different kinds of cities, both within and between urban cultures. In Aztec society there were three types of urban settlements: the imperial capital Tenochtitlan, altepetl capitals, and small towns. They were differentiated by the number and types of urban functions and by their population and area. One of my goals in this book has been to point out the extent to which Tenochtitlan was different from most Aztec cities. This observation, which should be clear to readers by now, requires the reassessment of many prior discussions of Aztec urbanism that looked to the imperial capital as a model for other Aztec cities.

I have tried to show that Aztec altepetl capitals constitute a distinctive kind of urban center, one that needs to be considered in its own right, independently of Tenochtitlan. There are three main reasons our knowledge of these cities has remained in the shadow of the imperial capital for so long. First, the written record is heavily biased in favor of Tenochtitlan. It is only by looking closely at archaeological remains that we can appreciate the nature of altepetl capitals. Second, the archaeological record for altepetl capitals is not widely known beyond specialists in central Mexican archaeology. Most of these sites are published only in Spanish, and many of the publications are obscure and difficult to find; indeed, it has taken me many years to assemble the information presented in this book. Unfortunately, too few English-speaking scholars and students take the time to track down these sources and read about the archaeological sites. Many of the urban epicenters are protected as government archaeological zones, but visitors will find little solid information in guidebooks or at the sites.

The third reason that knowledge of altepetl capitals has been overshadowed by information on Tenochtitlan is the continuing reliance of scholars on the demographic definition of urbanism. From that perspective Tenochtitlan was the only true Aztec city, so there is little need to consider the altepetl capitals in discussions of Aztec urbanism. But recall the quotation that opens chapter 7: "Cities do not grow up of themselves. Countrysides set them up to do tasks that must be performed in central places" (Jefferson 1931: 453). In Aztec period central Mexico, those tasks were primarily in the administrative and religious realm. Kings needed places to rule their small realms, so they gathered people together and consolidated their power in central places, creating the urban epicenters that survive today as archaeological zones. Although these cities had only modest populations, they were planned cities, created to achieve political and ideological ends. The functional approach asserts that they can only be understood within their regional social context; that is, they only make sense in reference to their altepetl, their kings, and wider social realms that included the Triple Alliance empire, Aztec elite culture, and the interplay among kings, nobles, and commoners.

Notes

Chapter 1. City and Society in Aztec Central Mexico

1. In some approaches the term "city" is used for large urban settlements with numerous urban functions and the term "town" is used for smaller urban settlements with fewer urban functions (Braudel 1981: 479–509; Sanders and Price 1968: 46). If applied to Aztec central Mexico, Tenochtitlan and perhaps a few other capitals would be termed cities, whereas most capitals of altepetl would be called towns. Although this is a useful distinction, for convenience I use the term "city" for all Aztec urban settlements.

2. The functional approach to urbanism should not be confused with functionalism, a theoretical approach common in mid-twentieth-century anthropology and sociology. Functionalist accounts stressed the interdependence of social institutions and practices and their roles in maintaining the unity or integration of cultures (Harris 1968). The scope of the functional approach to urbanism is much smaller; cities can be defined and analyzed in terms of their urban functions without assumptions that societies are well integrated or that particular institutions contribute to the maintenance of society.

3. See Sanders and Webster (1988) and the ensuing debate (Chase, Chase, and Haviland 1990; Smith 1989).

4. Unfortunately there is no comprehensive study of cities and urbanism in ancient Mesoamerica, although there are numerous studies of individual urban sites. Some of the most useful comparative studies are Marcus (1983); Andrews (1975); Sanders, Mastache, and Cobean (2003); and Ciudad Ruiz, Ponce de León, and Martínez Martínez (2001).

5. A number of theoretical perspectives derived from or allied with postmodernism have become popular among some archaeologists in the past two decades (Hodder and Hutson 2003), and these are often grouped together today as the "social archaeology" approach (Preucel and Meskell 2004). While not denying that this work has produced some insights, I find that in most cases it has done little to advance our understanding of archaeological data. Much theoretical work in the postmodern and social archaeology approaches consists of theory-driven speculation: Large doses of fashionable theory are applied to small bits of data to produce speculative interpretations that owe more to the theory and the author than to the data.

6. In an earlier publication (Smith 2003d: 4–5, 177–183) I use the phrase "social archaeology" (following Renfrew 1984) to contrast with the monumental archaeology approach. Because that phrase was later co-opted by postmodern archaeologists to refer to theory-heavy and data-poor research (Preucel and Meskell 2004), I now prefer the phrase "residential archaeology."

7. See discussion of this issue in Smith (2006g) and Gillespie (1989).

Chapter 2. The Roster of Aztec Cities

1. Unless otherwise noted, the city-name glyphs in this chapter are from the *Codex Mendoza* (1992). Texcoco is from the *Codex en Cruz* (Dibble 1981), Zultepec is from the *Codex Telleriano-Remensis* (1995), Huexotla is from the *Codex Xolotl* (Dibble 1980), Cholula is from the *Historia Tolteca-Chichimeca* (Kirchhoff, Odena Güemes, and Reyes García 1976), and the Ixtapaluca glyph is a modern invention, part of an effort to provide a name glyph for every town in the State of Mexico (Robelo, Olaguíbel, and Peñafiel 1966). The bird glyph for Calixtlahuaca is from stone reliefs at the site (Umberger 2007).

2. For information on these sites (beyond the specific works cited for each site), see Marquina (1964) and Umberger (1996) as well as Emily Umberger's other chapters in *Aztec Imperial Strategies*. Joyce Kelly's (2001) guidebook also has summaries of many of these sites along with information on how to visit them.

3. José Luis de Rojas is in the process of writing a book on Tenochtitlan for the University Press of Florida's Ancient Cities of the New World series.

Chapter 3. The Founding of Cities and Dynasties

1. Pedro Carrasco (1999: 16) lists the following terms for city as found in the basic sixteenth-century Nahuatl dictionary (Molina 1970): *altepenayotl* (principal city, which is the head of a kingdom), *totecuacan* (mother city or metropolis; literally "place of our lords"), *altepeyolloco* (the heart or middle of the city), and *altepetlianca* (subject settlement, region, or a city or town).

2. Another possible explanation for the presence of Early Aztec artifacts in Tenochtitlan is that they may have been contained in loads of soil brought from the shore area as construction fill.

3. The Aztec understanding of Mesoamerican prehistory may have been rudimentary, but given the strong empirical and historiographic orientations of Aztec scholars, it is difficult to accept that they actually believed traits such as the calendar and crafts to have been invented by the Toltecs. The Mexica knew about a number of ancient cities in addition to Tula (e.g., Teotihuacan and Xochicalco), and they collected stone masks from the still earlier Mezcala culture of Guerrero to bury in offerings, suggesting that they had some knowledge of earlier cultures besides the Toltecs of Tula (Umberger 1987).

4. This has not prevented some scholars from trying to draw discrete territorial boundaries around Tepechpan, Acolman, and Teotihuacan (Hirth 2003; Sanders and Evans 2001). Berman (2005: 131) comments on the same situation in scholarship on Chinese polities: "Any attempt to draw a distinct boundary that separated land-holdings according to their parent jurisdictions would results in an impossibly complex border, gerrymandered in every direction, with numerous enclaves. Is it reasonable to believe that such a boundary really existed in the minds of the local administration? Or did they only care about the relationship of the landholder to the tax collecting office?"

5. Many traditional definitions of the state emphasize territoriality (e.g., Mann 1986: 37), but this is a limited and even misleading perspective. Steven Grosby's (1995) claim

that modern notions of territoriality are universal in human societies is clearly incorrect (Dyson-Hudson and Smith 1978; Smith 2003: 153–154). The capital-centric model proposed here fits well with the definition of polity given by Ferguson and Mansbach (1996: 34): "A polity has a distinct identity; a capacity of mobilizing persons and their resources for political purposes. . . ; and a degree of institutionalization and hierarchy." This definition does not include territory and boundaries as inherent components of polities; indeed, these authors point out that in some cases distinct polities shared the same space: "Each polity had a territory in the sense of a space occupied by persons who identified with it, but that space was neither contiguous nor often exclusive" (393). Some Aztec capitals had more than one tlatoani (Hicks 1986). These were not single altepetl with multiple kings but separate altepetl that shared a single capital city. Other authors who have described preindustrial polities based on personal relations rather than territory include Hilda Kuper (1972), Monica Smith (2005), and Merrick Berman (2005). Berman, for example, argues against territorial conceptions of the state for ancient China: "It is therefore much more realistic to think of the state (guo) as an aggregation of subordinate localilties under the rule of a walled capital city, the influence of each diminishing as distance from their walled administrative center increased" (123).

Chapter 4. Public Architecture and the Urban Townscape

1. See Andrews (1975) for a similar classification of public architecture at Classic Maya cities.

2. A securely dated potsherd or other object from undisturbed fill inside a platform provides what is called a "terminus post quem" date; the building can be assigned a date at least as old as the object, but not older. Although this kind of dating is not very precise (construction could have occurred any time after the object's date), it is often the only available information for assessing the age of a building.

3. An important figure in Aztec ritual was the *ixiptla*, or deity impersonator. These individuals, most commonly sacrificial victims prior to their sacrifice or priests dressed for a specific ceremony, put on the clothing of a god and conducted activities as if they were a living incarnation of the god. It can be difficult or impossible to distinguish a deity from its ixiptla in representation in the codices, murals, or sculptures; the individual in figure 4.2A could be either a god or an ixiptla.

4. There are platforms and pyramids with two temples at a number of Postclassic cities in the highland Maya region (Smith 1955). These are much smaller than the Aztec examples, and they are part of a distinctive Postclassic Maya architectural type consisting of one or more small temples situated on long rectangular platforms, often with multiple stairways. There are far more of these Maya structures than there are Aztec double-temple pyramids, and there is no evidence that the Maya examples were copied from Aztec models, a common assertion. There are double pyramids consisting of two adjacent temple pyramids joined in the middle at several sites in west Mexico, including the Late Postclassic Tarascan city of Ihuatzio and the earlier site of Tepehuajes in Jalisco (Weigand and García de Weigand 1996), but their formal and historical connections with Aztec double-temple pyramids are uncertain.

5. The confusion between tzompantlis and tzitzimime platforms is common (e.g., Anders, Jansen, and Reyes García 1993: 186; Baquedano 1988: 194; Miller 1999). For example, Anders, Jansen, and Reyes García (1993: 181) identify a platform whose base is decorated with skulls in the *Códice Borgia* (p. 45) as a tzompantli. This feature, however, is portrayed differently from a true tzompantli depicted on page 19 of the same codex that clearly shows perforated skulls mounted on a horizontal rod.

6. In discussing archaeological studies of the built environment, Amos Rapoport (1990b) distinguishes between fixed-feature elements (buildings and other relatively unchanging fixtures), semifixed-feature elements (furniture and large portable fixtures that can be moved around but typically not on a daily or short-term basis), and non-fixed-feature elements (portable items that are frequently moved around). Although my discussion of architecture, like most, focuses primarily on fixed-feature elements, semifixed-feature elements such as sacrificial stones and large sculptures contributed greatly to the form and human perceptions of the urban built environment and need to be taken into account in any description of Aztec townscapes. This and other aspects of urban meaning and perception are discussed in chapter 5.

Chapter 5. Form, Meaning, and Urban Planning

1. For example, "in some respects this physical configuration of smaller centers reproduces in miniature, and in a much more simplified form, the settlement configuration of greater Tenochtitlan" (Sanders, Parsons, and Santley 1979: 163).

2. There is some confusion about the proper orientation of this image. Most authors orient the image with large temple on the right side, as shown in figure 5.1 (e.g., Anders et al. 1991: 229). Nevertheless, there are two opposing reasons to suggest that the proper orientation has the large temple at the top. First, this page is located in a sequence of the monthly veintena ceremonies (chapter 6), and the orientation with the large temple at the top matches nearly all of the other ceremony images (most of which are more easily oriented to the reader). Second, the placement of east at the top is a widespread convention in Aztec cartography (Galarza 1990: 95–96; Sellen 2003), and we have seen that the main temples are almost always on the east side of the plaza. In figure 5.1 I have rotated the image 90 degrees to match the cardinal directions of Western cartography (e.g., with east at the right) so that the image is comparable to the site plans shown in this book.

3. This view, when carried to an extreme, leads to portraits of ancient peoples as obsessed with death and the gods, thinking more about the afterlife than about their life on Earth. This is one way in which ancient peoples are distanced from modern peoples conceptually and portrayed as exotic "Others" rather than as ordinary people like us. Hervik (1998) and Klein et al. (2002) criticize this way of thinking.

4. The precise way in which the monthly veintena ceremonies were aligned with the natural/agricultural seasons is a topic of heated debate, much of which centers on the question of whether days were added to the Aztec calendar ("intercalated") to keep it synchronized with the solar year (Graulich 2002; Šprajc 2000b). This remains an unresolved question.

5. Although it is unlikely that the annual calendar was used to schedule farming activities, there is evidence that the 260-day ritual calendar (Boone 2007) was used for these purposes. Durán (1971: 396–398), for example, says that farmers consulted an "old sorcerer" who determined the auspicious dates for planting, harvesting, and other activities by consulting the 260-day calendar. The friar criticizes this practice for its use of "superstitions, sorcery, and idolatry" (397) and notes that the dates selected sometimes conflicted with efficient farming methods. The use of astrological knowledge to schedule farming activities is common among peasants in situations of environmental uncertainty, particularly when the onset of unpredictable seasonal rains or frosts can greatly impact agricultural success (Bowen 1992). But the astrological use of the 260-day calendar has little or nothing to do with the astronomical observation of the horizon or with the orientations of temples.

6. I am using the term "ideology" in the sense of ideas and beliefs used deliberately to promote and legitimize the interest of a ruler or a dominant social class (Eagleton 1991: 28–30). Hicks (1996) distinguishes Aztec ideology—statements about power and control that promote the interests of the king and nobility—from cosmovision (religious concepts of the gods myths and cosmology without strong political or social class associations). See also Brumfiel (1998, 2001), Flannery and Marcus (1993), and Steane (2001).

7. Pohl (2003a) discusses these processes of provincial emulation in some detail.

Chapter 6. Life in Aztec Cities

1. Most of the data in table 6.1 (source "a") are from Smith et al. (1994); for the Basin of Mexico the data originally come from Hodge (1984). Estimates marked "c" are compiled from survey reports (Blanton 1972; Parsons 1971; Parsons et al. 1982; Parsons, Kintigh, and Gregg 1983) using altepetl boundaries reconstructed by Hodge (1997). This table includes cities listed in table 2.1, plus others with demographic data but no architectural remains. The urban populations are extrapolated from early colonial census data, projected back to 1519 to account for decline from early epidemics (Whitmore 1992). The figures for site area are from archaeological surveys (Sanders, Parsons, and Santley 1979), and the population densities are calculated from the two figures. For cities marked with "b" in the table, the area data were measured from archaeological maps and the populations calculated by using a standard density figure of 50 people per hectare. The populations of the second largest sites are compiled from source "c." Because of the uneven distribution of sizes, the median is a better measure of the overall trends than is the mean (the mean population for altepetl capitals is 7,325, with a standard deviation of 5,940; the mean area is 163, with a standard deviation of 125). These methods are discussed at greater length in Smith et al. (1994) and Smith (2005a).

2. In a larger sample of Aztec cities with population estimates (many lacking area measurements), cities in the Basin of Mexico appear to have been larger than cities in Morelos (Smith et al. 1994: 9).

3. The urban population densities of Aztec altepetl capitals were considerably lower than those of ancient cities in the Near East (Adams 1981), where residences were packed much more closely together. They were nevertheless relatively high in comparison with other cities in Mesoamerica.

4. Cowgill (2003) uses Antonio Gramsci's concept of hegemony to help explain why commoners identified so strongly with monumental architecture in ancient cities. Hegemony refers to "a whole range of practical strategies by which a dominant power elicits consent to its rule from those it subjugates. To win hegemony, in Gramsci's view, is to establish moral, political, and intellectual leadership in social life by diffusing one's own 'world view' throughout the fabric of society as a whole, thus equating one's own interests with the interests of society at large" (Eagleton 1991: 116). Collective action theory, explored in chapter 8, is also helpful for understanding commoner allegiance to rulers (Fargher and Blanton 2007).

5. The following discussion is based on Smith 1997, 2002, 2003a, 2003c; and Smith, Heath-Smith, and Monteil 1999.

6. The most complete early textual descriptions of the veintena ceremonies are found in Sahagún (1950–82: bk. 2; 1997) and Durán (1971), and the most complete analysis is that of Graulich (1999). Detailed descriptions and analyses of individual ceremonies in English include Graulich (1989, 1992), Broda (1970), and Brotherston (2005). Berdan (2007) discusses the material culture of these ceremonies. The most extensive native pictorial representations are in the *Codex Borbonicus* (Anders et al. 1991) and the *Primeros Memoriales* of Sahagún (1993). Although the major descriptions pertain to Tenochtitlan, two types of information suggest that the veintena ceremonies took place in all Aztec cities. First, Nicholson's (2002) review of pictorial representations of the ceremonies shows that they are included in a wide variety of codices originating in a number of central Mexican cities in addition to Tenochtitlan. Second, local descriptions of ancient rituals in the *Relaciones Geográficas* from many different towns include ceremonies from the veintena cycle; these data are reviewed by Graulich (1999).

7. Archaeologists and historians have recently recognized the importance of processions in the civic ritual of ancient societies (Ashley 2001; Moore 2005: chap. 4). Although the veintena ceremonies involved numerous examples of processions, insights from comparative studies of processions have yet to be applied to this body of material.

Chapter 8. Cities, City-States, and Aztec Urbanism

1. Speculation is an important part of the research process. In this section I present a speculative model that has two objectives. First, it may help readers to visualize some of the social dynamics that stimulated the growth and forms of Aztec cities. Second, it might encourage researchers to investigate these social dynamics by gathering new data and by developing new methods and concepts. In chapter 5, I criticized speculative interpretations of the cosmological significance of ancient cities in Mesoamerica and elsewhere. The main problem with those works is not that they employ speculation but that they present highly speculative accounts (based on little or no evidence) as if they

were strongly supported conclusions. I discuss some of the difficulties with this kind of scholarship in Smith (2005b).

2. My model deliberately ignores a crucial sector of political dynamics and exchange that could be profitably analyzed using the concepts of collective action theory: the ways in which altepetl kings and nobles interacted with the emperor and officials of empires, particularly the Triple Alliance. This topic has received considerable attention in the literature (e.g., Berdan et al. 1996; Carrasco 1999; Smith 1986), and although it is very relevant to the urban dynamics of Tenochtitlan (Brumfiel 1998), it is less important for understanding altepetl capitals.

3. Although the market for the fancier objects of ancient Maya culture is much larger and more active than the market for Aztec antiquities, it is clear that the illegal sale of Aztec objects is extensive. Examples from my personal experience will illustrate the two ends of the antiquities trade. During fieldwork at Calixtlahuaca I became aware that Mexicans and foreigners had been buying looted ceramic vessels from local residents for more than a century (some of these objects are now in foreign museums, but most are probably in private collections). I was approached several times with offers to buy pots from people who had no idea (or else did not care) that they were contributing to the destruction of the site. Needless to say, public education activities, directed in part at limiting such looting, were a prominent part of our project at the site. On another occasion I was invited to give a lecture at the opening of a small exhibit of Aztec art (at a museum in the United States) that included many privately owned ceramic vessels that had been purchased in the (illegal) antiquities market. I declined to participate on the grounds that my cooperation would legitimize the looted objects and perhaps contribute to an increase their commercial value. This in turn could stimulate further looting of Aztec sites to feed the market.

Bibliography

Abungu, George H. O.
1998 City States of the East African Coast and Their Maritime Contacts. In *Transformations in Africa: Essays on Africa's Later Past,* edited by Graham Connah, pp. 204–18. Leicester University Press, London.

Acosta, Jorge R.
1965 Tenayuca: Exploraciones de 1963. *Anales del Museo Nacional de Antropología e Historia, serie 6* 17: 117–26.
1974 La pirámide de El Corral de Tula, Hgo. In *Proyecto Tula (primera parte),* edited by Eduardo Matos Moctezuma, pp. 27–49. Colección Científica, vol. 15. Instituto Nacional de Antropología e Historia, Mexico City.

Acuña, René
1984–88 *Relaciones geográficas del siglo XVI.* 10 vols. Universidad Nacional Autónoma de México, Mexico City.

Adams, Robert McC.
1981 *Heartland of Cities: Surveys of Ancient Settlement and Land Use on the Central Floodplain of the Euphrates.* University of Chicago Press, Chicago.

Alcántara Gallegos, Alejandro
2004 Los barrios de Tenochtitlan: Topografía, organización interna y tipología de sus predios. In *Historia de la vida cotidiana en México, I: Mesoamérica y los ámbitos indígenas de la Nueva España,* edited by Pablo Escalante Gonzalbo, pp. 167–98. El Colegio de México and Fondo de Cultura Económica, Mexico City.

Alcocer, Ignacio
1935 *Apuntes sobre el antiguo México-Tenochtitlan.* Publicación, vol. 14. Instituto Panamericana de Geografía e Historia, Mexico City.

Alcock, Susan E.
2002 *Archaeologies of the Greek Past: Landscape, Monuments, and Memories.* Cambridge University Press, New York.

Allen, Robert
1997 Agriculture and the Origins of the State in Ancient Egypt. *Explorations in Economic History* 34: 134–54.

Alva Ixtlilxochitl, Fernando de
1975–77 *Obras históricas.* 2 vols. Translated by Edmundo O'Gorman. Universidad Nacional Autónoma de México, Mexico City.

Anders, Ferdinand, Maarten Jansen, and Gabina Aurora Pérez Jiménez
1994 *Códice Féjerváry-Mayer: El libro de Tezcatlipoca, señor de tiempo.* Codices Mexicanos, vol. 7. Akademische Druck- und Verlagsanstalt and Fondo de Cultura Económica, Graz and Mexico City.

Anders, Ferdinand, Maarten Jansen, and Luis Reyes García

1993 *Códice Borgia: Los templos del cielo y de la oscuridad: oráculos y liturgia.* Códices Mexicanos, vol. 5. Sociedad Estatal Quinto Centenario, Akademische Druck- und Verlagsanstalt, and Fondo de Cultura Económica, Madrid, Graz, and Mexico City.

Anders, Ferdinand, Maarten Jansen, Luis Reyes García, and Gabina Aurora Pérez Jiménez

1991 *Códice Borbónico: El libro del cihuacóatl, homenaje para el año del fuego nuevo.* Códices Mexicanos, vol. 3. Sociedad Estatal Quinto Centenario, Akademische Druck- und Verlagsanstalt, and Fondo de Cultura Económica, Madrid, Graz, and Mexico City.

Anderson, Eugene N., Aurora Dzib Zihum de Cen, Felix Medina Tzuc, and Pastor Valdez Chale

2005 *Political Ecology in a Yucatec Maya Community.* University of Arizona Press, Tucson.

Andrews, George F.

1975 *Maya Cities: Placemaking and Urbanization.* University of Oklahoma Press, Norman.

1995–99 *Pyramids and Palaces, Monsters and Masks: The Golden Age of Maya Architecture: The Collected Works of George F. Andrews.* 3 vols. Labyrinthos, Lancaster, Calif.

Angulo Villaseñor, Jorge

1976 Teopanzolco y Cuauhnahuac, Morelos. In *Los señoríos e estados militaristas,* edited by Román Piña Chán, pp. 183–208. Instituto Nacional de Antropología e Historia, Mexico City.

1979 *Una visión del Museo Cuauhnahuac en el Palacio de Cortés: Recopilación histórico-arqueológico del proceso de cambio en el estado de Morelos.* Instituto Nacional de Antropología e Historia, Mexico City.

1984 Identificación de algunas representaciones escultóricas de Coatetelco. In *Investigaciones recientes en el área maya, XVII Mesa Redonda, Sociedad Mexicana de Antropología,* vol. 4, pp. 205–17. Sociedad Mexicana de Antropología, Mexico City.

Anonymous

1935 *Tenayuca: Estudio arqueológico de la pirámide de este lugar, hecho por el Departamento de Monumentos de la Secretaría de Educación Pública.* Talleres Gráficos del Museo Nacional de Antropología, Historia y Etnografía, Mexico City.

Arana Álvarez, Raúl M.

1984 El juego de pelota en Coatetelco, Morelos. In *Investigaciones recientes en el área maya, XVII Mesa Redonda, Sociedad Mexicana de Antropología,* vol. 4, pp. 191–204. Sociedad Mexicana de Antropología, Mexico City.

Arana Álvarez, Raúl M., and Carmen Chacón

2006 Simbología y Conservación del Monumento Arqueológico Templo del Fuego Nuevo. Paper presented at the 2006 Annual Meeting, Society for American Archaeology, San Juan, Puerto Rico.

Arancón García, Ricardo

1992 La plaza: Generadora del espacio urbano mesoamericano. *Cuadernos de Arquitectura Mesoamericana* 16: 29–39.

Ashley, Kathleen
2001 Introduction: The Moving Subjects of Processional Performance. In *Moving Sub-jects: Processional Performance in the Middle Ages and Renaissance*, edited by Kathleen Ashley and Wim Hüsken, pp. 7–34. Rodopi, Amsterdam.

Ashmore, Wendy
1991 Site-Planning Principles and Concepts of Directionality Among the Ancient Maya. *Latin American Antiquity* 2: 199–226.

Ashmore, Wendy, and Jeremy A. Sabloff
2002 Spatial Orders in Maya Civic Plans. *Latin American Antiquity* 13: 201–15.

Aveni, Anthony F.
2001 *Skywatchers: A Revised and Updated Version of Skywatchers of Ancient Mexico*. University of Texas Press, Austin.
2003 Archaeoastronomy in the Ancient Americas. *Journal of Archaeological Research* 11: 149–91.

Aveni, Anthony F., and Edward E. Calnek
1999 Astronomical Considerations in the Aztec Expression of History: Eclipse Data. *Ancient Mesoamerica* 10: 87–98.

Aveni, Anthony F., Edward E. Calnek, and Horst Hartung
1988 Myth, Environment and the Orientation of the Templo Mayor of Tenochtitlan. *American Antiquity* 53: 287–309.

Ávila López, Raúl
2006 *Mexicaltzingo: Arqueología de un reino culhua-mexica*. 2 vols. Instituto Nacional de Antropología e Historia, Mexico City.

Ávila López, Raúl, and Ludwig Beutelspacher
1989 *Investigaciones arqueológicas en Mexicaltzingo, D.F.* Cuaderno de Trabajo, vol. 7. Subdirección de Salvamento Arqueológico, Instituto Nacional de Antropología e Historia, Mexico City.

Baer, Gerhard (editor)
1996 *Ancient Mexican Ceramics from the Lukas Vischer Collection, Ethnographic Museum Basel*. Corpus Americanensium Antiquatatum, Union Académique Internationale. Friedrich Reinhardt Publishers, Basel.

Balkansky, Andrew K., Verónica Pérez Rodríguez, and Stephen A. Kowalewski
2004 Monte Negro and the Urban Revolution in Oaxaca, Mexico. *Latin American Antiquity* 15: 33–60.

Baquedano, Elizabeth
1988 Iconographic Symbols in Aztec Elite Sculptures. In *Recent Studies in Pre-Columbian Archaeology, Part 1*, edited by Nicholas J. Saunders and Olivier de Montmollin, pp. 191–204. BAR International Series, vol. 421. British Archaeological Reports, Oxford.

Batres, Leopoldo
1904 *Mis exploraciones en Huexotla, Texcoco y Montículo de "El Gavilán."* J. I. Guerro, Mexico City.
1979 Exploraciones arqueológicas en la Calle de las Escalerillas. In *Trabajos arqueológicos en el centro de la Ciudad de México*, edited by Eduardo Matos Moctezuma, pp. 111–70. Instituto Nacional de Antropología e Historia, Mexico City.

Bell, Catherine M.
1997 *Ritual: Perspectives and Dimensions.* Oxford University Press, New York.

Berdan, Frances F.
1985 Markets in the Economy of Aztec Mexico. In *Markets and Marketing*, edited by Stuart Plattner, pp. 339–67. University Press of America, Lanham, Md.

1987 The Economics of Aztec Luxury Trade and Tribute. In *The Aztec Templo Mayor*, edited by Elizabeth H. Boone, pp. 161–84. Dumbarton Oaks, Washington, D.C.

1988 Principles of Regional and Long-Distance Trade in the Aztec Empire. In *Smoke and Mist: Mesoamerican Studies in Memory of Thelma D. Sullivan*, edited by J. Kathryn Josserand and Karen Dakin, pp. 639–56. BAR International Series, vol. 402, pt. 1. British Archaeological Reports, Oxford.

2007 Material Dimensions of Aztec Religion and Ritual. In *Mesoamerican Ritual Economy: Archaeological and Ethnological Perspectives*, edited by E. Christian Wells, and Karla L. Davis-Salazar, pp. 245–300. University Press of Colorado, Boulder.

Berdan, Frances F., and Patricia R. Anawalt (editors)
1992 *The Codex Mendoza.* 4 vols. University of California Press, Berkeley and Los Angeles.

Berdan, Frances F., Richard E. Blanton, Elizabeth H. Boone, Mary G. Hodge, Michael E. Smith, and Emily Umberger
1996 *Aztec Imperial Strategies.* Dumbarton Oaks, Washington, D.C.

Berman, Merrick Lex
2005 Boundaries or Networks in Historical GIS: Concepts of Measuring Space and Administrative Geography in Chinese History. *Historical Geography* 33: 118–33.

Berry, Brian J. L.
1967 *Geography of Market Centers and Retail Distribution.* Prentice-Hall, Englewood Cliffs, N.J.

Betz, Virginia
2002 The City as Invention: An Environmental Psychological Approach to the Origins of Urban Life. Ph.D. diss., Department of Anthropology, Arizona State University.

Blanton, Richard E.
1972 *Prehistoric Settlement Patterns of the Ixtapalapa Region, Mexico.* Occasional Papers in Anthropology, vol. 6. Department of Anthropology, Pennsylvania State University, University Park.

1989 Continuity and Change in Public Architecture: Periods I Through V of the Valley of Oaxaca, Mexico. In *Monte Alban's Hinterland, Part II: Prehispanic Settlement Patterns in Tlacolula, Etla, and Ocotlan, the Valley of Oaxaca, Mexico*, edited by Stephen A. Kowalewski, Gary M. Feinman, Laura Finsten, Richard E. Blanton, and Linda M. Nicholas, pp. 409–47. Memoirs, vol. 23. Museum of Anthropology, University of Michigan, Ann Arbor.

1994 *Houses and Households: A Comparative Study.* Plenum, New York.

Bloch, Marc
1961 *Feudal Society.* 2 vols. University of Chicago Press, Chicago.

Boone, Elizabeth H. (editor)

1987 *The Aztec Templo Mayor*. Dumbarton Oaks, Washington, D.C.

1994 Aztec Pictorial Histories: Records Without Words. In *Writing Without Words: Alternative Literacies in Mesoamerica and the Andes*, edited by Elizabeth Hill Boone and Walter D. Mignolo, pp. 50–76. Duke University Press, Durham, N.C.

2000a Bringing Polity to Place: Aztec and Mixtec Foundation Rituals. In *Códices y documentos sobre México: tercer simposio international*, edited by Constanza Vega Sosa, pp. 547–73. Instituto Nacional de Antropología e Historia, Mexico City.

2000b *Stories in Red and Black: Pictorial Histories of the Aztecs and Mixtecs*. University of Texas Press, Austin.

2007 *Cycles of Time and Meaning in the Mexican Books of Fate*. University of Texas Press, Austin.

Booth, David

1998 Corvée. In *Macmillan Encyclopedia of World Slavery*, edited by Paul Finkelman and Joseph C. Miller, vol. 2, pp. 464–66. Macmillan, New York.

Boserup, Ester

1965 *The Conditions of Agricultural Growth: The Economics of Agrarian Change Under Population Pressure*. Aldine, Chicago.

Bowen, John R.

1992 Centralizing Agricultural Time: A Case from South Sulawesi. In *The Politics of Time*, edited by Henry J. Rutz, pp. 171–94. AES Monograph Series, vol. 4. American Anthropological Association, Washington, D.C.

Braudel, Fernand

1981 *The Structures of Everyday Life*. Translated by Sian Reynolds. Civilization and Capitalism, 15th–18th Century, vol. 1. Harper and Row, New York.

Bribiesca Castrejón, José Luis

1958 El agua potable en la república Mexicana: Los abastecimientos en la época prehispánica. *Ingeniera Hidraúlica en México* 12(2): 69–82.

Broda, Johanna

1970 Tlacaxipeualiztli: A Reconstruction of an Aztec Calendar Festival from 16th Century Sources. *Revista Española de Antropología Americana* 5: 197–273.

1976 Los estamentos en el ceremonial mexica. In *Estratifiación social en la Mesoamérica Prehispánica*, edited by Pedro Carrasco and Johanna Broda, pp. 37–66. Instituto Nacional de Antropolgía e Historia, Mexico City.

1993 Astronomical Knowledge, Calendrics, and Sacred Geography in Ancient Mesoamerica. In *Astronomies and Cultures*, edited by Clive Ruggles and Nicholas J. Saunders, pp. 253–95. University Press of Colorado, Boulder.

Broda, Johanna, David Carrasco, and Eduardo Matos Moctezuma

1987 *The Great Temple of Tenochtitlan: Center and Periphery in the Aztec World*. University of California Press, Berkeley and Los Angeles.

Brotherston, Gordon

2005 *Feather Crown: The Eighteen Feasts of the Mexica Year*. Research Publication, vol. 154. British Museum Press, London.

Brown, Percy

1965 *Indian Architecture.* 5th ed. 2 vols. D. B. Tarapolevala Sons, Bombay.

Brüggemann, Jürgen Kurt

1987 Acozac. *Arqueología* 1: 133–80.

Brumfiel, Elizabeth M.

1980 Specialization, Market Exchange, and the Aztec State: A View from Huexotla. *Current Anthropology* 21: 459–78.

1998 Huitzilopochtli's Conquest: Aztec Ideology in the Archaeological Record. *Cambridge Archaeological Journal* 8: 3–14.

2001 Aztec Hearts and Minds: Religion and the State in the Aztec Empire. In *Empires: Perspectives from Archaeology and History*, edited by Susan Alcock, Terence D'Altroy, Kathleen Morrison, and Carla Sinopoli, pp. 283–310. Cambridge University Press, New York.

2005 *La producción local y el poder en el Xaltocan Posclásico/Production and Power at Postclassic Xaltocan.* Arqueología de México. Instituto Nacional de Antropología e Historia and University of Pittsburgh, Mexico City and Pittsburgh.

Burkhart, Louise M.

1997 Mexica Women on the Home Front: Housework and Religion in Aztec Mexico. In *Indian Women of Early Mexico*, edited by Susan Schroeder, Stephanie Wood, and Robert Haskett, pp. 25–54. University of Oklahoma Press, Norman.

Calnek, Edward E.

1974 Conjunto urbana y modelo residencial en Tenochtitlan. In *Ensayos sobre el desarrollo urbano de México*, edited by Woodrow Borah, pp. 11–65. Secretaría de Educación Pública, Mexico City.

1976 The Internal Structure of Tenochtitlan. In *The Valley of Mexico: Studies of Pre-Hispanic Ecology and Society*, edited by Eric R. Wolf, pp. 287–302. University of New Mexico Press, Albuquerque.

1988 The Calmecac and Telpochcalli in Pre-Conquest Tenochtitlan. In *The Work of Bernardino de Sahagún: Pioneer Ethnographer of Sixteenth-Century Aztec Mexico*, edited by Jorge Klor de Alva, H. B. Nicholson, and Eloise Quiñones Keber, pp. 169–77. Institute for Mesoamerican Studies, Albany, N.Y.

2003 Tenochtitlan-Tlatelolco: The Natural History of a City / Tenochtitlan-Tlatelolco: La Historia Natural de una Ciudad. In *El urbanismo en mesoamérica / Urbanism in Mesoamerica*, edited by William T. Sanders, Alba Guadalupe Mastache, and Robert H. Cobean, pp. 149–202. Proyecto Urbanismo en Mesoamérica / The Mesoamerican Urbanism Project, vol. 1. Pennsylvania State University and Instituto Nacional de Antropología e Historia, University Park and Mexico City.

Carneiro, Robert L.

1961 Slash-and-Burn Cultivation Among the Kuikuru and Its Implications for Cultural Development in the Amazon Basin. In *The Evolution of Horticultural Systems in Native South America: Causes and Consequences, A Symposium*, edited by Johannes Wilbert, pp. 47–67. Antropológica, Supplement, vol. 2. Sociedad de Ciencias Naturales La Salle, Caracas.

Carrasco, Davíd
1991 The Sacrifice of Tezcatlipoca: To Change Place. In *To Change Place: Aztec Ceremo-nial Landscapes*, edited by Davíd Carrasco, pp. 31–57. University Press of Colorado, Boulder.
1999a City as Symbol in Aztec Thought: Some Clues from the Codex Mendoza. In *City of Sacrifice: The Aztec Empire and the Role of Violence in Civilization*, pp. 15–48. Beacon Press, Boston.
1999b *City of Sacrifice: The Aztec Empire and the Role of Violence in Civilization*. Beacon Press, Boston.
Carrasco, Pedro
1984 The Extent of the Tepanec Empire. In *The Native Sources and the History of the Valley of Mexico*, edited by Jacqueline de Durand-Forest, pp. 73–93. British Archaeological Reports, International Series, vol. S204. Archaeopress, Oxford.
1999 *The Tenochca Empire of Ancient Mexico: The Triple Alliance of Tenochtitlan, Tetzcoco, and Tlacopan*. University of Oklahoma Press, Norman.
Carta de Azcapotzalco
2000 Carta de don Hernando de Molina, de don Baltazar Hernández y de los alcaldes y regidores de Azcapotzalco al rey Felipe II, en latín, Azcapotzalco, 10 de febrero de 1561. In *La nobleza indígena del central de México después de la conquista*, edited by Emma Pérez-Rocha and Rafael Tena, pp. 213–25. Instituto Nacional de Antropología e Historia, Mexico City.
Caso, Alfonso
1940 El entierro del siglo. *Revista Mexicana de Estudios Antropológicos* 4: 65–76.
Castañeda de la Paz, María
2002 De Aztlan a Tenochtitlan: Historia de una peregrinación. *Latin American Indian Literatures Journal* 18: 163–212.
Ceballos Novelo, Roque J.
1928 Tepoztlan, Teopanzolco y Xochicalco. In *Estado actual de los principales edificios arqueológicos de México: Contribución de México al XXIII Congreso de Americanistas*, edited by Dirección de Arqueología, pp. 99–116. Talleres Gráficos de la Nación, Mexico City.
Chance, John K.
1996 The Barrios of Colonial Tecali: Patronage, Kinship, and Territorial Relations in a Central Mexican Community. *Ethnology* 35: 107–39.
Charlton, Thomas H.
1970 Contemporary Settlement Patterns: The Cerro Gordo, North Slope and Upper Valley Areas. In *The Natural Environment, Contemporary Occupation and 16th Century Population of the Valley: The Teotihuacan Valley Project Final Report*, vol. 1, pp. 181–252. Occasional Papers in Anthropology, vol. 3. Pennsylvania State University, Department of Anthropology, University Park.
Charlton, Thomas H., Deborah L. Nichols, and Cynthia Otis Charlton
1991 Aztec Craft Production and Specialization: Archaeological Evidence from the City-State of Otumba, Mexico. *World Archaeology* 23: 98–114.

2000 Otumba and Its Neighbors: Ex Oriente Lux. *Ancient Mesoamerica* 11: 247–66.

Chase, Arlen F., and Diane Z. Chase

1995 External Impetus, Internal Synthesis, and Standardization: E Group Assemblages and the Crystallization of Classic Maya Society in the Southern Lowlands. In *The Emergence of Lowland Maya Civilization: The Transition from the Pre-Classic to the Early Classic*, edited by Nikolai Grube, pp. 87–101. Acta Mesoamericana, vol. 8. Verlag Anton Saurwein, Markt Schwaben.

Chase, Diane Z., Arlen F. Chase, and William A. Haviland

1990 The Classic Maya City: Reconsidering the "Mesoamerican Urban Tradition." *American Anthropologist* 92: 499–506.

Chimalpahin Cuauhtlehuanitzin, Domingo Francisco de San Antón Muñón

1997 *Codex Chimalpahin: Society and Politics in Mexico Tenochtitlan, Tlatelolco, Texcoco, Culhuacan, and Other Nahua Altepetl in Central Mexico: The Nahuatl and Spanish Annals and Accounts Collected and Recorded by don Domingo de San Antón Muñón Chimalpahin Quauhtlehuanitzin.* 2 vols. Edited by Arthur J. O. Anderson, Susan Schroeder, and Wayne Ruwet. University of Oklahoma Press, Norman.

Ciudad Ruiz, Andrés, and María Josefa Iglesias Ponce de León (editors)

2006 *Fundación, refundación y relocalización de las ciudades Maya.* Sociedad Española de Estudios Mayas, Madrid.

Ciudad Ruiz, Andrés, María Josefa Iglesias Ponce de León, and María del Carmen Martínez Martínez (editors)

2001 *Reconstruyendo la ciudad maya: el urbanismo en las sociedades antiguas.* Sociedad Española de Estudios Mayas, Madrid.

Clark, John E.

2004 Mesoamerica Goes Public: Early Ceremonial Centers, Leaders, and Communities. In *Mesoamerican Archaeology: Theory and Practice*, edited by Julia A. Hendon and Rosemary Joyce, pp. 43–72. Blackwell, Oxford.

Clark, John E., and Richard D. Hansen

2001 The Architecture of Early Kingship: Comparative Perspectives on the Origins of the Maya Royal Court. In *Royal Courts of the Ancient Maya, Volume 2: Data and Case Studies*, edited by Takeshi Inomata and Stephen Houston, pp. 1–45. Westview Press, Boulder, Colo.

Clendinnen, Inga

1991 *Aztecs: An Interpretation.* Cambridge University Press, New York.

Cobean, Robert H.

1990 *La cerámica de Tula, Hidalgo.* Instituto Nacional de Antropología e Historia, Mexico City.

Codex Mendoza

1992 *The Codex Mendoza*, edited by Frances F. Berdan and Patricia R. Anawalt. 4 vols. University of California Press, Berkeley and Los Angeles.

Codex Telleriano-Remensis

1995 *Codex Telleriano-Remensis: Ritual, Divination, and History in a Pictorial Aztec Manuscript.* Edited by Eloise Quiñones Keber. University of Texas Press, Austin.

Códice Ixtlilxochitl
1996 *Códice Ixtlilxochitl: Apuntaciones y pinturas de un historiador.* Akademische Druck- u. Verlagsanstalt and Fondo de Cultura Económica, Graz and Mexico City.

Contreras Sánchez, Eduardo
1976 La zona arqueológica de Acozac, México (Temporada 1973–1974). *Boletín del Instituto Nacional de Antropología e Historia* 16: 10–26.

Cowgill, George L.
1997 State and Society at Teotihuacan, Mexico. *Annual Review of Anthropology* 26: 129–61.

2003 Teotihuacan: Cosmic Glories and Mundane Needs. In *The Social Construction of Ancient Cities*, edited by Monica L. Smith, pp. 37–55. Smithsonian Institution Press, Washington, D.C.

Cowgill, George L., Jeffrey H. Altshul, and Rebecca S. Sload
1984 Spatial Analysis of Teotihuacan, a Mesoamerican Metropolis. In *Intrasite Spatial Analysis in Archaeology*, edited by Harold J. Hietala, pp. 154–95. Cambridge University Press, New York.

Cresson, Frank M., Jr.
1938 Maya and Mexican Sweat Houses. *American Anthropologist* 40: 88–104.

Crouch, Dora P., Daniel J. Garr, and Axel I. Mundingo
1982 *Spanish City Planning in North America.* MIT Press, Cambridge, Mass.

Cullen, Gordon
1971 *The Concise Townscape.* Architectural Press, London.

Davies, Nigel
1973 *The Aztecs: A History.* University of Oklahoma, Norman.

1980 *The Toltec Heritage: From the Fall of Tula to the Rise of Tenochtitlan.* University of Oklahoma Press, Norman.

1987 *The Aztec Empire: The Toltec Resurgence.* University of Oklahoma Press, Norman.

DeMarrais, Elizabeth, Luis Jaime Castillo, and Timothy Earle
1996 Ideology, Materialization, and Power Strategies. *Current Anthropology* 37: 15–31.

de Vega Nova, Hortensia
1996 Proyecto de investigación arqueológico en Yautepec, Morelos. In *Memoria, III Congreso Interno del Centro INAH Morelos, Acapantzingo, Cuernavaca, 1994*, pp. 149–68. Instituto Nacional de Antropología e Historia, Centro INAH Morelos, Cuernavaca, Morelos.

de Vega Nova, Hortensia, and Pablo Mayer Guala
1991 Proyecto Yautepec. *Boletín del Consejo de Arqueología* 1991: 79–84.

Díaz del Castillo, Bernal
1963 *The Conquest of New Spain.* Translated by J. M. Cohen. Penguin, New York.

Dibble, Charles E. (editor)
1980 *Códice Xolotl.* Universidad Nacional Autónoma de México, Instituto de Investigaciones Históricas, Mexico City.

1981 *Codex en Cruz.* 2 vols. University of Utah Press, Salt Lake City.

Diel, Lori Boornazian
2005 From Aztec to Spanish: Shifting Alliances in the Tira de Tepechpan. *Latin American Indian Literatures Journal* 21: 165–91.

Domar, Evsey D.
1970 The Causes of Slavery or Serfdom: A Hypothesis. *Journal of Economic History* 30: 18–32.

Donkin, R. A.
1979 *Agricultural Terracing in the Aboriginal New World.* Viking Fund Publications in Anthropology, vol. 56. University of Arizona Press, Tucson.

Douglas, Eduardo de J.
2003 Figures of Speech: Pictorial History in the Quinatzin Map of About 1542. *Art Bulletin* 85: 281–310.

Doxiadis, Constantinos A.
1972 *Architectural Space in Ancient Greece.* Translated by Jaqueline Tyrwhitt. MIT Press, Cambridge, Mass.

Drennan, Robert D.
1988 Household Location and Compact Versus Dispersed Settlement in Prehispanic Mesoamerica. In *Household and Community in the Mesoamerican Past,* edited by Richard R. Wilk and Wendy Ashmore, pp. 273–93. University of New Mexico Press, Albuquerque.

Dumarçay, Jacques, and Pascal Royère
2001 *Cambodian Architecture, Eighth to Thirteenth Centuries.* Handbook of Oriental Studies, Section Three, South-East Asia, vol. 12. Brill, Leiden.

Dupaix, Guillermo
1834 *Antiquités Mexicaines: Relation des trois expeditions du Capitaine Dupaix, ordonnées en 1805, 1806, et 1807, pour la recherche les antiquités du pays, notamment celles de Mitla et de Palenque.* 2 vols. Jules Didot l'ainé, Paris.

Durán, Fray Diego
1971 *Book of the Gods and Rites and the Ancient Calendar.* Translated by Fernando Horcasitas and Doris Heyden. University of Oklahoma Press, Norman.
1994 *The History of the Indies of New Spain.* Translated by Doris Heyden. University of Oklahoma Press, Norman.

Dyson-Hudson, Rada, and Eric Alden Smith
1978 Human Territoriality: An Ecological Reassessment. *American Anthropologist* 80: 21–41.

Eagleton, Terry
1991 *Ideology: An Introduction.* Verso, New York.

Earle, Timothy
1997 *How Chiefs Come to Power: The Political Economy in Prehistory.* Stanford University Press, Stanford, Calif.

Edelman, Murray
1964 *The Symbolic Uses of Politics.* University of Illinois Press, Urbana.

Eliade, Mircea
1959 *Cosmos and History: The Myth of the Eternal Return.* Translated by Willard R. Trask. Harper and Row, New York.

Elson, Christina M.
1999 An Aztec Palace at Chiconautla, Mexico. *Latin American Antiquity* 10: 151–67.
Elson, Christina M., and Michael E. Smith
2001 Archaeological Deposits from the Aztec New Fire Ceremony. *Ancient Mesoamerica* 12: 157–74.
Evans, Susan T.
1985 The Cerro Gordo Site: A Rural Settlement of the Aztec Period in the Basin of Mexico. *Journal of Field Archaeology* 12: 1–18.
1988 *Excavations at Cihuatecpan, an Aztec Village in the Teotihuacan Valley.* Vanderbilt University Publications in Anthropology, vol. 36. Department of Anthropology, Vanderbilt University, Nashville.
1990 The Productivity of Maguey Terrace Agriculture in Central Mexico During the Aztec Period. *Latin American Antiquity* 1: 117–32.
1991 Architecture and Authority in an Aztec Village: Form and Function of the Tecpan. In *Land and Politics in the Valley of Mexico: A Two Thousand Year Perspective,* edited by Herbert R. Harvey, pp. 63–92. University of New Mexico Press, Albuquerque.
2000 Aztec Noble Courts: Men, Women, and Children of the Palace. In *Royal Courts of the Ancient Maya, Volume 1: Theories, Themes, and Comparisons,* edited by Takeshi Inomata and Stephen Houston, pp. 237–73. Westview Press, Boulder, Colo.
2001a Research at Cihuatecpan (T.A. 81) in 1984: A Summary. In *The Teotihuacan Valley Project, Final Report, Vol. 5: The Aztec Period Occupation of the Valley. Part 2: Excavations at T.A. 40 and Related Projects,* edited by William T. Sanders and Susan T. Evans, pp. 789–834. Occasional Papers in Anthropology, vol. 26. Department of Anthropology, Pennsylvania State University, University Park.
2001b Aztec-Period Political Organization in the Teotihuacan Valley: Otumba as a City-State. *Ancient Mesoamerica* 12: 89–100.
2004 Aztec Palaces and Other Elite Residential Architecture. In *Palaces of the Ancient New World,* edited by Susan T. Evans and Joanne Pillsbury, pp. 7–58. Dumbarton Oaks, Washington, D.C.
Fargher, Lane F., and Richard E. Blanton
2007 Revenue, Voice, and Public Goods in three Pre-Modern States. *Comparative Studies in Society and History* 49:848–82.
Favro, Diane C.
1996 *The Urban Image of Augustan Rome.* Cambridge University Press, New York.
Fentress, James, and Chrius Wickham
1992 *Social Memory.* Blackwell, Oxford.
Ferguson, Yale H., and Richard W. Mansbach
1996 *Polities: Authority, Identities, and Change.* University of South Carolina Press, Columbia.
Flannery, Kent V., and Joyce Marcus
1993 Cognitive Archaeology. *Cambridge Archaeological Journal* 3: 260–70.
Florescano, Enrique, and Alejandra Moreno Toscano
1966 *Bibliografía del maíz en México.* Biblioteca de la Facultad de Filosofía, Letras y Ciencias, vol. 20. Universidad Veracruzana, Xalapa.

Fox, John W., Garrett W. Cook, Arlen F. Chase, and Diane Z. Chase
1996 The Maya State: Centralized or Segmentary? CA Forum on Theory in Anthropology. *Current Anthropology* 37: 795–830.

Fox, Richard G.
1977 *Urban Anthropology: Cities in their Cultural Settings.* Prentice-Hall, Englewood Cliffs, N.J.

Furst, Jill Leslie McKeever
1992 Aztec New Fire Ritual: A World Renewal Rite. *Journal of Latin American Lore* 18: 29–36.

Galarza, Joaquín
1990 *Amatl, amoxtli, el papel, el libro: Los codices mesoamericanos.* Editorial Tava, Mexico City.

Gamio, Manuel
1909–13 Restos de la cultura tepaneca. *Anales del Museo Nacional de Arqueología, Historia y Etnología* 1: 235–53.

García Chávez, Raúl
2004 *El Conde, Estado de México: Mini-guia.* Instituto Nacional de Antropología e Historia, Mexico City.

García García, María Teresa
1987 *Huexotla: Un sitio del Acolhuacan.* Colección Científica, vol. 165. Instituto Nacional de Antropología e Historia, Mexico City.

García Payón, José
1947 Los monumentos arqueológicos de Malinalco. *Revista Mexicana de Estudios Antropológicas* 8(1): 5–63.
1979 *La zona arqueológica de Tecaxic-Calixtlahuaca y los matlatzincas: Etnología y arqueología (textos de la segunda parte),* edited by Wanda Tommasi de Magrelli and Leonardo Manrique Castañeda. Biblioteca Enciclopédica del Estado de México, vol. 30. Estado de México, Toluca.
1981 *La zona arqueológica de Tecaxic-Calixtlahuaca y los matlatzincas: Etnología y arqueología (tablas, planos e ilustraciones de la segunda parte),* edited by Leonardo Manrique Castañeda. Biblioteca Enciclopédica del Estado de México, vol. 31. Estado de México, Toluca.

García-Zambrano, Angel J.
1994 Early Colonial Evidence of Pre-Columbian Rituals of Foundation. In *Seventh Palenque Round Table, 1989,* edited by Merle G. Robertson and Virginia M. Fields, pp. 219–29. Pre-Columbian Art Research Institute, San Francisco.

Garraty, Christopher P.
2007 Intercambio de mercado y consolidación en el corazón del Imperio Azteca. *Revista Española de Antropología Americana* 37:139-164.

Garza Tarazona de González, Silvia
1978 *Códices genealógicos: Representaciones arquitectónicas.* Instituto Nacional de Antropología e Historia, Mexico City.

Gates, Charles
2003 *Ancient Cities: The Archaeology of Urban Life in the Ancient Near East and Egypt, Greece, and Rome.* Routledge, New York.

Geertz, Clifford

1980 *Negara: The Theatre State in Nineteenth Century Bali*. Princeton University Press, Princeton, N.J.

Gendrop, Paul

1970 *Arte prehispánico en Mesoamérica*. Editorial Trillas, Mexico City.

Gerhard, Peter

1993 *A Guide to the Historical Geography of New Spain*. Rev. ed. University of Oklahoma Press, Norman.

Gibson, Charles

1964 *The Aztecs Under Spanish Rule: A History of the Indians of the Valley of Mexico, 1519–1810*. Stanford University Press, Stanford, Calif.

Gillespie, Susan D.

1989 *The Aztec Kings: The Construction of Rulership in Mexica History*. University of Arizona Press, Tucson.

1991 Ballgames and Boundaries. In *The Mesoamerican Ballgame*, edited by Vernon L. Scarborough and David R. Wilcox, pp. 317–45. University of Arizona Press, Tucson.

González Miranda, Luis Alsonso, and María Elena Salas Cuesta

2001 Evidencias de sacrificio humano en Teotihuacan. *Arqueología* 26: 35–48.

González Rul, Francisco

1996 *Tlatelolco a través de los tiempos 50 años después (1944–1994). Tomo 2: Etnohistoria*. Colección Científica, vol. 327. Instituto Nacional de Antropología e Historia, Mexico City.

1998 *Urbanismo y arquitectura en Tlatelolco*. Serie Arqueología, Colección Científica, vol. 346. Instituto Nacional de Antropología e Historia, Mexico City.

Goodsell, Charles T.

1988 *The Social Meaning of Civic Space: Studying Political Authority Through Architecture*. University Press of Kansas, Lawrence.

Grant, Ulysses S.

1999 *Personal Memoirs of U. S. Grant*. Penguin Classics. Penguin Books, New York.

Graulich, Michel

1989 Miccailhuitl: The Aztec Festivals of the Deceased. *Numen* 36(1): 43–71.

1992 Aztec Festivals of the Rain Gods. *Indiana (Berlin)* 12: 21–54.

1998 Sacrificial Stones of the Aztecs. In *The Symbolism in the Plastic and Pictorial Representations of Ancient Mexico*, edited by Jacqueline de Durand-Forest and Marc Eisinger, pp. 185–201. BAS, vol. 21. Bonner Amerikanistische Studien, Bonn.

1999 *Fiestas de los pueblos indígenas: Ritos aztecas, las fiestas de las veintanas*. Instituto Nacional Indigenista, Mexico City.

2002 Problema de ajustes de año Calendárico mesoamericano del año trópico. *Estudios de Cultura Náhuatl* 33: 45–56.

Grosby, Steven

1995 Territoriality: The Transcendal, Primordial Feature of Modern Societies. *Nations and Nationalism* 1: 143–62.

Grove, David C., and Rosemary A. Joyce (editors)

1999 *Social Patterns in Pre-Classic Mesoamerica: A Symposium at Dumbarton Oaks, 9 and 10 October 1993*. Dumbarton Oaks, Washington, D.C.

Grube, Nikolai

2000 The City-States of the Maya. In *A Comparative Study of Thirty City-State Cultures*, edited by Mogens Herman Hansen, pp. 547–66. Royal Danish Academy of Sciences and Letters, Copenhagen.

Guilliem Arroyo, Salvador

1999 *Ofrendas a Ehecatl-Quetzalcoatl en México-Tlatelolco: proyecto Tlatelolco, 1987–1996*. Colección Científica, vol. 400. Instituto Nacional de Antropología e Historia, Mexico City.

Hansen, Mogens Herman (editor)

1997 *The Polis as an Urban Centre and as a Political Community*. Acts of the Copenhagen Polis Centre, vol. 4. Royal Danish Academy of Sciences and Letters, Copenhagen.

2000a *A Comparative Study of Thirty City-State Cultures*. Royal Danish Academy of Sciences and Letters, Copenhagen.

2000b Introduction: The Concepts of City-State and City-State Culture. In *A Comparative Study of Thirty City-State Cultures*, edited by Mogens Herman Hansen, pp. 11–34. Royal Danish Academy of Sciences and Letters, Copenhagen.

Hare, Timothy S., and Michael E. Smith

1996 A New Postclassic Chronology for Yautepec, Morelos. *Ancient Mesoamerica* 7: 281–97.

Harris, Marvin

1968 *The Rise of Anthropological Theory: A History of Theories of Culture*. Thomas Y. Crowell, New York.

Harvey, Herbert R., and Barbara J. Williams

1980 Aztec Arithmetic: Positional Notation and Area Calculation. *Science* 210: 499–505.

1986 Decipherment and Some Implications of Aztec Numerical Glyphs. In *Native American Mathematics*, edited by Michael P. Closs, pp. 237–60. University of Texas Press, Austin.

Hassig, Ross

1981 The Famine of One Rabbit: Ecological Causes and Social Consequences of a Pre-Columbian Calamity. *Journal of Anthropological Research* 37: 172–82.

2001 *Time, History and Belief in Aztec and Colonial Mexico*. University of Texas Press, Austin.

Healan, Dan M.

1989 *Tula of the Toltecs: Excavations and Survey*. University of Iowa Press, Iowa City.

Henige, David P.

1982 *Oral Historiography*. Longman, New York.

Hernández Rivero, José

2004 *Ideología y práctica militar mexica: El cuauhcalli de Malinalco*. 2nd ed. Private Publication, Mexico City.

Hervik, Peter
1998 The Mysterious Maya of the National Geographic. *Journal of Latin American Anthropology* 4(1): 166–97.
Heyden, Doris
1972 What Is the Significance of the Mexica Pyramid? In *40th International Congress of Americanists (Rome and Genoa, 1972)*, vol. 1, pp. 109–15. Rome.
1989 *The Eagle, the Cactus, the Rock: The Roots of Mexico-Tenochtitlan's Foundation Myth and Symbol.* British Archaeological Reports, International Series, vol. S484. Archaeopress, Oxford.
Hicks, Frederic
1984 Rotational Labor and Urban Development in Prehispanic Tetzcoco. In *Explorations in Ethnohistory: Indians of Central Mexico in the Sixteenth Century*, edited by Herbert R. Harvey and Hanns J. Prem, pp. 147–74. University of New Mexico Press, Albuquerque.
1986 Prehispanic Background of Colonial Political and Economic Organization in Central Mexico. In *Ethnohistory*, edited by Ronald Spores, pp. 35–54. Supplement to the Handbook of Middle American Indians, vol. 4. University of Texas Press, Austin.
1996 Class and State in Aztec Official Ideology. In *Ideology and the Formation of Early States*, edited by Henri J. M. Claessen and Jarich G. Oosten, pp. 256–77. E. J. Brill, Leiden.
Hillier, Bill, and Julienne Hanson
1984 *The Social Logic of Space.* Cambridge University Press, New York.
Hingley, Richard
2005 *Globalizing Roman Culture: Unity, Diversity and Empire.* Routledge, New York.
Hirschman, Albert O.
1978 Exit, Voice and the State. *World Politics* 31: 90–107.
Hirth, Kenneth G. (editor)
2000 *Archaeological Research at Xochicalco.* 2 vols. University of Utah Press, Salt Lake City.
2003 The Altepetl and Urban Structure in Prehispanic Mesoamerica. In *El urbanismo en mesoamérica / Urbanism in Mesoamerica*, edited by William T. Sanders, Alba Guadalupe Mastache, and Robert H. Cobean, pp. 57–84. Proyecto Urbanismo dn Mesoamérica / The Mesoamerican Urbanism Project, vol. 1. Pennsylvania State University and Instituto Nacional de Antropología e Historia, University Park and Mexico City.
Hodder, Ian, and Scott R. Hutson
2003 *Reading the Past.* 3rd ed. Cambridge University Press, Cambridge.
Hodge, Mary G.
1984 *Aztec City-States.* Memoirs, vol. 18. Museum of Anthropology, University of Michigan, Ann Arbor.
1994 Polities Composing the Aztec Empire's Core. In *Economies and Polities in the Aztec Realm*, edited by Mary G. Hodge and Michael E. Smith, pp. 43–71. Institute for Mesoamerican Studies, Albany, N.Y.
1997 When Is a City-State? Archaeological Measures of Aztec City-States and Aztec

City-State Systems. In *The Archaeology of City-States: Cross-Cultural Approaches*, edited by Deborah L. Nichols and Thomas H. Charlton, pp. 209–28. Smithsonian Institution Press, Washington, D.C.

Hoekstra, Rik

1990 A Different Way of Thinking: Contrasting Spanish and Indian Social and Economic Views in Central Mexico (1550–1600). In *The Indian Community of Colonial Mexico: Fifteen Essays on Land Tenure, Corporate Organizations, Ideology, and Village Politics*, edited by Arij Ouweneel and Simon Miller, pp. 60–86. Centro de Estudios y Documentación Latinamericanos, Amsterdam.

Hopkins, Mary R.

1987 Network Analysis of the Plans of Some Teotihuacán Apartment Compounds. *Environment and Planning B: Planning and Design* 14: 387–406.

Houston, Stephen D.

1996 Symbolic Sweatbaths of the Maya: Architectural Meaning in the Cross Group at Palenque, Mexico. *Latin American Antiquity* 7: 132–51.

2006 Impersonation, Dance, and the Problem of Spectacle. In *Archaeology of Performance: Theaters of Power, Community, and Politics*, edited by Takeshi Inomata and Lawrence S. Coben, pp. 135–55. Altamira, Walnut Creek, Calif.

Inomata, Takeshi

2001 The Classic Maya Palace as a Political Theater. In *Reconstruyendo la ciudad maya: El urbanismo en las sociedades antiguas*, edited by Andrés Ciudad Ruiz, María Josefa Iglesias Ponce de León, and María del Carmen Martínez Martínez, pp. 341–62. Sociedad Española de Estudios Mayas, Madrid.

2006 Politics and Theatricality in Maya Society. In *Archaeology of Performance: Theaters of Power, Community, and Politics*, edited by Takeshi Inomata and Lawrence S. Coben, pp. 187–222. Altamira, Walnut Creek, Calif.

Inomata, Takeshi, and Lawrence S. Coben (editors)

2006 *Archaeology of Performance: Theaters of Power, Community, and Politics*. Altamira, Walnut Creek, Calif.

Inomata, Takeshi, and Stephen D. Houston (editors)

2000 *Royal Courts of the Ancient Maya. Volume 1, Theories, Themes, and Comparisons.* Westview Press, Boulder, Colo.

2001 *Royal Courts of the Ancient Maya. Volume 2, Case Studies.* Westview Press, Boulder, Colo.

Jefferson, Mark

1931 The Distribution of the World's City Folks: A Study in Comparative Civilization. *Geographical Review* 21: 446–65.

Jones, Christopher

1991 Cyles of Growth at Tikal. In *Classic Maya Political History: Hieroglyphic and Archaeological Evidence*, edited by T. Patrick Culbert, pp. 102–27. Cambridge University Press, New York.

Joyce, Rosemary A.

2000 High Culture, Mesoamerican Civilization, and the Classic Maya Tradition. In

Order, Legitimacy, and Wealth in Ancient States, edited by Janet Richards and Mary van Buren, pp. 64–76. Cambridge University Press, New York.

Kaufman, Terrence
2001 The History of the Nawa Language Group from the Earliest Times to the Sixteenth Century: Some Initial Results. University of Pittsburgh. Paper available online at *http://www.albany.edu/anthro/maldp/Nawa.pdf. Accessed February 1, 2005.*

Keith, Kathryn
2003 The Spatial Patterns of Everyday Life in Old Babylonian Neighborhoods. In *The Social Construction of Ancient Cities,* edited by Monica L. Smith, pp. 56–80. Smithsonian Institution Press, Washington, D.C.

Kellogg, Susan
1993 The Social Organization of Households Among the Tenochca Mexica Before and After the Conquest. In *Prehispanic Domestic Units in Western Mesoamerica: Studies of the Household, Compound, and Residence,* edited by Robert S. Santley and Kenneth G. Hirth, pp. 207–24. CRC Press, Boca Raton, Fla.
1995 *Law and the Transformation of Aztec Culture, 1500–1700.* University of Oklahoma Press, Norman.

Kelly, Joyce
2001 *An Archaeological Guide to Central and Southern Mexico.* University of Oklahoma Press, Norman.

Kemp, Barry J.
2000 Bricks and Metaphor. In Viewpoint: Were Cities Built as Images? *Cambridge Archaeological Journal* 10: 335–46.

Kertzer, David I.
1988 *Ritual, Politics, and Power.* Yale University Press, New Haven, Conn.

Khaldûn, Ibn
1958 *The Muqaddimah: An Introduction to History.* 3 vols. Translated by Franz Rosenthal. Bollingen Foundation, New York.

Kirchhoff, Paul, Lina Odena Güemes, and Luis Reyes García (editors)
1976 *Historia Tolteca-Chichimeca.* Instituto Nacional de Antropología e Historia, Mexico City.

Klaus, Susanne
1999 *Anales de Tlatelolco: Los manuscritos 22 y 22bis de la Bibliotèque de France.* Fuentes Mesoamericanas, vol. 2. Verlag Anton Saurwein, Markt Schwaben.

Klein, Cecelia F.
2000 The Devil and the Skirt: An Iconographic Inquiry into the Pre-Hispanic Nature of the Tzitzimime. *Ancient Mesoamerica* 11: 1–26.

Klein, Cecelia F., Eulogio Guzmán, Elisa C. Mandell, and Maya Stanfield-Mazzi
2002 The Role of Shamanism in Mesoamerican Art: A Reassessment. *Current Anthropology* 43: 383–420.

Kovar, Anton
1970 The Physical and Biological Environment of the Basin of Mexico. In *The Teotihuacan Valley Project, Final Report,* edited by William T. Sanders, Anton Kovar, Thomas H. Charlton, and Richard A. Diehl, pp. 13–68. Occasional Papers in An-

thropology, vol. 3. Department of Anthropology, Pennsylvania State University, University Park.

Krapf-Askari, Eva

1969 *Yoruba Towns and Cities: An Enquiry into the Nature of Urban Social Phenomena.* Oxford University Press, London.

Kuper, Hilda

1972 The Language of Sites in the Politics of Space. *American Anthropologist* 74: 411–25.

Kurtz, Donald V.

2001 *Political Anthropology: Paradigms and Power.* Westview Press, Boulder, Colo.

Lawrence, Denise L., and Setha M. Low

1990 The Built Environment and Spatial Form. *Annual Review of Anthropology* 19: 453–505.

Leeds, Anthony

1980 Towns and Villages in Society: Hierarchies of Order and Cause. In *Cities in a Larger Context,* edited by T. Collins, pp. 6–33. University of Georgia Press, Athens.

Leong, Sau Heng

1990 Collecting Centres, Feeder Points and Entrepôts in the Malay Peninsula, 1000 B.C.–A.D. 1400. In *The Southeast Asian Port and Polity: Rise and Demise,* edited by J. Kathirithamby-Wells and John Villiers, pp. 17–38. Singapore University Press, Singapore.

Lesbre, Patrick

1998 Teocalli de Tezcoco. *Trace* 34: 15–21.

Levi, Margaret

1981 The Predatory Theory of Rule. *Politics and Society* 10: 431–66.

Lewis, Oscar

1952 Urbanization Without Breakdown: A Case Study. *Scientific Monthly* 75: 31–41.

Ley, David

2000 Townscape. In *The Dictionary of Human Geography,* edited by R. J. Johnston, Derek Gregory, Geraldine Pratt, and Michael Watts, pp. 843–844. 4th ed. Blackwell, Oxford.

Lilley, Keith D.

2002 *Urban Life in the Middle Ages, 1000–1450.* Palgrave, New York.

2005 Urban Landscapes and Their Design: Creating Town from Country in the Middle Ages. In *Town and Country in the Middle Ages: Contrasts, Contacts and Intercommunications, 1100–1500,* edited by Christopher Dyer and Kate Giles, pp. 229–49. Society for Medieval Archaeology Monograph, vol. 22. Maney, London.

Lind, Michael D.

n.d. The Great City Square: Government in Ancient Cholula. Unpublished manuscript (2001).

Lockhart, James

1992 *The Nahuas After the Conquest: A Social and Cultural History of the Indians of Central Mexico, Sixteenth Through Eighteenth Centuries.* Stanford University Press, Stanford, Calif.

López Austin, Alfredo
1994 *Tamoanchan y Tlalocan.* Fondo de Cultura Económica, Mexico City.
López Austin, Alfredo, and Leonardo López Luján
2001 El chacmool mexica. *Caravelle: Cahiers du Monde Hispanique et Luso-Bresilien* 76–77: 59–84.
López González, Valentín
1966 *Cuernavaca: Visión retrospectiva de una ciudad.* Imprenta "Tlahuica," Cuernavaca.
López Luján, Leonardo
1994 *The Offerings of the Templo Mayor of Tenochtitlan.* Translated by Bernard R. Ortiz de Montellano, and Thelma Ortiz de Montellano. University Press of Colorado, Boulder.
2005 *The Offerings of the Templo Mayor of Tenochtitlan.* Rev. ed. Translated by Bernard R. Ortiz de Montellano and Thelma Ortiz de Montellano. University of New Mexico Press, Albuquerque.
2006 *La Casa de las Águilas: un ejemplo de arquitectura religiosa de Tenochtitlan.* Fonda de Cultura Económica, Conaculta, and Instituto Nacional de Antropología e Historia, Mexico City.
López Luján, Leonardo, Hector Neff, and Saburo Sugiyama
2000 The 9-Xi Vase: A Classic Thin Orange Vessel Found at Tenochtitlan. In *Mesoamerica's Classic Heritage: From Teotihuacan to the Aztecs,* edited by Davíd Carrasco, Lindsay Jones, and Scott Sessions, pp. 219–49. University Press of Colorado, Boulder.
López Luján, Leonardo, Jaime Torres, and Aurora Montúfar
2004 Los materiales constructivos del Templo Mayor de Tenochtitlan. *Estudios de Cultura Náhuatl* 34: 137–66.
López Luján, Leonardo, and Javier Urcid
2002 El chacmool de Míxquic y el sacrificio humano. *Estudios de Cultura Náhuatl* 33: 25–43.
Lorenzo Monterrubio, Antonio
2001 Códice de Nicolás Flores. In *Códices del Estado de Hidalgo / State of Hidalgo Codices,* edited by Laura Elena Sotelo Santos, Víctor Manuel Ballesteros García, and Evaristo Luvián Torres, pp. 70–75. Universidad Autónoma del Estado de Hidalgo, Pachuca.
Lynch, Kevin
1981 *A Theory of Good City Form.* MIT Press, Cambridge, Mass.
MacDonald, William L.
1986 *Architecture of the Roman Empire, Volume 2: An Urban Appraisal.* Yale University Press, New Haven, Conn.
Malville, John McKim, and Lalit M. Gurjal (editors)
2000 *Ancient Cities, Sacred Skies: Cosmic Geometries and City Planning in Ancient India.* Indira Gandhi National Centre for the Arts, New Delhi.
Mann, Michael
1986 *The Sources of Social Power, Volume 1: A History of Power from the Beginning to A.D. 1760.* Cambridge University Press, New York.

Mannikka, Eleanor

1996 *Angkor Wat: Time, Space, and Kingship*. University of Hawaii Press, Honolulu.

Marcus, Joyce

1983 On the Nature of the Mesoamerican City. In *Prehistoric Settlement Patterns: Essays in Honor of Gordon R. Willey*, edited by Evon Z. Vogt and Richard M. Leventhal, pp. 195–242. University of New Mexico Press, Albuquerque.

Marquina, Ignacio

1935 Estudio arquitectónico. In *Tenayuca: Estudio arqueológico de la pirámide de este lugar, hecho por el Departamento de Monumentos de la Secretaría de Educación Pública*, pp. 77–102. Talleres Gráficos del Museo Nacional de Antropología, Historia y Etnografía, Mexico City.

1951 *Arquitectura prehispánica*. Instituto Nacional de Antropología e Historia, Mexico City.

1960 *El templo mayor de México*. Instituto Nacional de Antropología e Historia, Mexico City.

1964 *Arquitectura prehispánica*. 2nd ed. Instituto Nacional de Antropología e Historia, Mexico City.

Martin, Simon, and Nikolai Grube

2000 *Chronicle of the Maya Kings and Queens: Deciphering the Dynasties of the Ancient Maya*. Thames and Hudson, New York.

Martínez Vargas, Enrique

1993 Trascendental hallazgo en Zultepec. *Arqueología Mexicana* 4: 62–64.

2003 Zultepec-Tecoaque: Sacrificios de espanoles y sus aliados durante la conquista. *Arqueología Mexicana* 63: 52–57.

Martínez Vargas, Enrique, and Ana María Jarquín Pacheco

1998 *Materiales arqueológicas del noroeste de Tlaxcala*. Instituto Nacional de Antropología e Historia, Mexico City.

Mason, Roger D.

1980a Community Pattern of a Tlahuica Regional Center: Coatlan Veijo, Río Chalma Valley, Morelos. In *Rutas de Intercambio en Mesoamérica y Norte de México: XVI Meso Redonda (Saltillo, 1979)*, vol. 2, pp. 251–60. Sociedad Mexicana de Antropología, Mexico City.

1980b Economic and Social Organization of an Aztec Provincial Center: Archaeological Research at Coatlan Viejo, Morelos, Mexico. Ph.D. diss., Department of Anthropology, University of Texas.

Mastache, Alba Guadalupe, Robert H. Cobean, and Dan M. Healan

2002 *Ancient Tollan: Tula and the Toltec Heartland*. University Press of Colorado, Boulder.

Matos Moctezuma, Eduardo

1967 Restos de un basamento prehispánico en Mexicaltzingo, D. F. *Boletín del I.N.A.H.* 30: 32–36.

1979 *Trabajos arqueológicos en el centro de la ciudad de México*. Instituto Nacional de Antropología e Historia, Mexico City.

1988 *The Great Temple of the Aztecs*. Thames and Hudson, New York.

1999 Malinalco prehispánico. In *Estudios mexicas*, edited by Eduardo Matos Moctezuma, vol. 1 (2), pp. 199–218. El Colegio Nacional, Mexico City.

2001 The Ballcourt in Tenochtitlan. In *The Sport of Life and Death: The Mesoamerican Ballgame*, edited by E. Michael Whittington, pp. 88–95. Thames and Hudson, New York.

2002 Sahagún and the Ceremonial Precinct of Tenochtitlan: Ritual and Place. In *Representing Aztec Ritual: Performance, Text, and Image in the Work of Sahagún*, edited by Eloise Quiñones Keber, pp. 43–62. University Press of Colorado, Boulder.

2003 Buildings in the Sacred Precinct of Tenochtitlan. In *El urbanismo en mesoamérica / Urbanism in Mesoamerica*, edited by William T. Sanders, Alba Guadalupe Mastache, and Robert H. Cobean, pp. 119–40. Proyecto Urbanismo dn Mesoamérica/ Mesoamerican Urbanism Project, vol. 1. Pennsylvania State University and Instituto Nacional de Antropología e Historia, University Park and Mexico City.

McCafferty, Geoffrey G.

1996 Reinterpreting the Great Pyramid of Cholula. *Ancient Mesoamerica* 7: 1–18.

McCafferty, Sharisse D., and Geoffrey G. McCafferty

1991 Spinning and Weaving as Female Gender Identity in Post-Classic Central Mexico. In *Textile Traditions of Mesoamerica and the Andes: An Anthology*, edited by M. Schevill, Janet C. Berlo, and E. Dwyer, pp. 19–46. Garland, New York.

Medellín Zeñil, Alfonso

1952 *Exploraciones de Quauhtochco*. Gobierno del Estado de Veracruz, Jalapa.

Milbrath, Susan

1999 *Star Gods of the Maya: Astronomy in Art, Folklore, and Calendars*. Linda Schele Series in Maya and Pre-Columbian Studies. University of Texas Press, Austin.

Miller, Virginia E.

1999 The Skull Rack in Mesoamerica. In *Mesoamerican Architecture as a Cultural Symbol*, edited by Jeff Karl Kowalski, pp. 340–60. Oxford University Press, New York.

Minc, Leah D.

2006 Monitoring Regional Market Systems in Prehistory: Models, Methods, and Metrics. *Journal of Anthropological Archaeology* 25: 82–116.

Modelski, George

2003 *World Cities: -3000 to 2000*. Faros 2000, Washington, D.C.

Molina, Fray Alonso de

1970 *Vocabulario en lengua castellana y mexicana, y mexicana y castellana*. Porrúa, Mexico City.

Moore, Jerry D.

1996 *Architecture and Power in the Ancient Andes: The Archaeology of Public Buildings*. Cambridge University Press, New York.

2005 *Cultural Landscapes in the Ancient Andes: Archaeologies Of Place*. University Press of Florida, Gainesville.

Morrison, Kathleen D.

1997 Commerce and Culture in South Asia: Perspectives from Archaeology and History. *Annual Review of Anthropology* 26: 87–108.

Motolinía, Fray Toribio de

1979 *Historia de los indios de la Nueva España*. Sepan Cuantos. Editorial Porrúa, Mexico City.

Motolinía, Fray Toribio de Benavente

1971 *Memoriales, o libro de las cosas de la Nueva España y de los naturales de ella*. Edited by Edmundo O'Gorman. Universidad Nacional Autónoma de México, Mexico City.

Moya Rubio, Victor José

1982 *La vivienda indígena de México y del mundo*. Universidad Nacional Autónoma de México, Mexico City.

Muir, Edward

1997 *Ritual in Early Modern Europe*. Cambridge University Press, New York.

Mundy, Barbara E.

1996 *The Mapping of New Spain: Indigenous Cartography and the Maps of the Relaciones Geograficas*. University of Chicago Press, Chicago.

Netting, Robert McC.

1993 *Smallholders, Householders: Farm Families and the Ecology of Intensive, Sustainable Agriculture*. Stanford University Press, Stanford, Calif.

Nichols, Deborah L.

2004 The Rural and Urban Landscapes of the Aztec State. In *Mesoamerican Archaeology: Theory and Practice*, edited by Julia A. Hendon and Rosemary Joyce, pp. 265–95. Blackwell, Oxford.

Nichols, Deborah L., Elizabeth M. Brumfiel, Hector Neff, Mary Hodge, Thomas H. Charlton, and Michael D. Glascock

2002 Neutrons, Markets, Cities, and Empires: A 1000-Year Perspective on Ceramic Production and Distribution in the Postclassic Basin of Mexico. *Journal of Anthropological Archaeology* 21: 25–82.

Nichols, Deborah L., Mary Jane McLaughlin, and Maura Benton

2000 Production Intensification and Regional Specialization: Maguey Fibers and Textiles in the Aztec City-State of Otumba. *Ancient Mesoamerica* 11: 267–92.

Nicholson, H. B.

1971a Pre-Hispanic Central Mexican Historiography. In *Investigaciones contemporáneas sobre la historia de México*, pp. 38–81. El Colegio de México and University of Texas Press, Mexico City and Austin.

1971b Religion in Pre-Hispanic Central Mexico. In *Archaeology of Northern Mesoamerica, Part 1*, edited by Gordon F. Ekholm and Ignacio Bernal, pp. 395–446. Handbook of Middle American Indians, vol. 10. University of Texas Press, Austin.

1990 Late Pre-Hispanic Central Mexican ("Aztec") Sacred Architecture: The "Pyramid Temple." In *Circumpacifica: Festschrift für Thomas S. Barthel*, edited by Bruno Illius and Matthias Laubscher, vol. 1, pp. 303–24. Peter Lang, Frankfurt.

1991 The Octli Cult in Late Pre-Hispanic Central Mexico. In *To Change Place: Aztec Ceremonial Landscapes*, edited by David Carrasco, pp. 158–87. University Press of Colorado, Boulder.

2002 Representing the *Veintena* Ceremonies in the *Primeros Memoriales*. In *Repre-*

senting Aztec Ritual: Performance, Text, and Image in the Work of Sahagún, edited by Eloise Quiñones Keber, pp. 63–106. University Press of Colorado, Boulder.

2003a The Annual "Royal Ceremony" on Mt. Tlaloc: Mountain Fertility Ritualism in the Late Pre-Hispanic Basin of Mexico. In *Mesas and Cosmologies in Mesoamerica*, edited by Douglas Sharon, pp. 33–49. Papers, vol. 42. San Diego Museum of Man, San Diego.

2003b Sahagún's Itemization of the Structure of the Templo Mayor Precinct of Mexico-Tenochtitlan: "Legend" of a Lost Diagram. In *Sahagún at 500: Essays on the Quincentenary of the Birth of Fr. Bernardino de Sahagún*, edited by John F. Schwaller, pp. 255–64. Academy of American Franciscan History, Berkeley, Calif.

2005 A Tale of Two Ballcourts: Laguna de Moctezuma, Sierra de Tamaulipas (Tm r 304), and Ixtapaluca Viejo (Acozac), Basin of Mexico. In *Archaeology Without Limits: Papers in Honor of Clement W. Meighan*, edited by Brian D. Dillon and Matthew A. Boxt, pp. 309–24. Labyrinthos, Lancaster, Calif.

Nicholson, H. B., and Eloise Quiñones Keber

1991 Ballcourt Images in Central Mexican Native Traditional Pictorial Manuscripts. In *The Mesoamerican Ballgame: Papers Presented at the International Colloquium, "The Mesoamerican Ballgame, 2000 BC-AD 2000,"* edited by Gerard W. van Bussell, Paul L. F. van Dongen, and Ted J. J. Leyenaar, pp. 119–33. Rijksmuseum voor Volkenkunde, Leiden.

Noguera, Eduardo

1927 Los altares del sacrificio de Tizatlán, Tlaxcala. In *Ruinas de Tizatlán*, edited by Agustín García Vega, pp. 23–62. Publicaciones, vol. 15. Secretaría de Educación Pública, Mexico City.

1937 *El altar de los cráneos esculpidos de Cholula*. Talleres Gráficos de la Nación, Mexico City.

1972 Arqueología de la región tetzcocana. *Artes de México* 151: 75–96.

Noguez, Xavier (editor)

1978 *Tira de Tepechpan: Códice colonial procedente del Valle de México*. 2 vols. Biblioteca Enciclopédica del Estado de México. Estado de México, Mexico City.

2006 El templo monolítico de Malinalco, Estado de México. *Arqueología Mexicana* 78: 68–73.

Norris, Susan

2002 Political Economy of the Aztec Empire: A Regional Analysis of Obsidian Craft Production in the Provinces of Huaxtepec and Cuauhnahuac, Mexico. Ph.D. diss., Department of Anthropology, Harvard University.

North, Douglass C.

1981 *Structure and Change in Economic History*. Norton, New York.

Novic, Juliana

2006 *The Calli of Tenochtitlan: Early Colonial Houses and Their Implications for Archaeology*. Master's thesis, Department of Anthropology, State University of New York, Albany.

Nowotny, Karl Anton

2005 *Tlacuilolli: Style and Content of the Mexican Pictorial Manuscripts with a Cata-*

log of the Borgia Group. Translated by George A Everett Jr. and Edward B. Sisson. University of Oklahoma Press, Norman.

Offner, Jerome A.

1983 *Law and Politics in Aztec Texcoco.* Cambridge University Press, New York.

Ohnersorgen, Michael A.

2006 Aztec Provincial Administration at Cuetlaxtlan, Veracruz. *Journal of Anthropological Archaeology* 25: 1–32.

Ojo, G. J. Afolabi

1966 *Yoruba Palaces: A Study of Afins of Yorubaland.* University of London Press, London.

Olivier, Guilhem

1995 Les paquets sacrés ou la mémoire cachée des indiens du Mexique central (XV–XVI siècles). *Journal de la Société des Américanistes* 81: 105–41.

2003 *Mockeries and Metamorphoses of an Aztec God: Tezcatlipoca, "Lord of the Smoking Mirror."* University Press of Colorado, Boulder.

Olko, Justyna

2001 Mesoamerican Ballgame and Associated Ritual Behaviors: A Reappraisal and New Insights. *Ethnologia Polona* 22: 45–66.

2005 *Turquoise Diadems and Staffs of Office: Elite Costume and Insignia of Power in Aztec and Early Colonial Mexico.* Polish Society for Latin American Studies, Warsaw.

Olmeda Vera, Bertina

2002 *Los templos rojos del recinto sagrado de Tenochtitlan.* Colección Científica, vol. 439. Instituto Nacional de Antropología e Historia, Mexico City.

Olson, Jan M.

2007 A Socio-Economic Interpretation of Figurine Assemblages from Late Postclassic Morelos, Mexico. In *Commoner Ritual, Commoner Ideology: Evidence from Households Across Mesoamerica,* edited by Nancy Gonlin and Jon C. Lohse, pp. 251–79. University Press of Colorado, Boulder.

Olson, Mancur

1965 *The Logic of Collective Action: Public Goods and the Theory of Groups.* Harvard University Press, Cambridge.

2000 *Power and Prosperity: Outgrowing Communist and Capitalist Dictatorships.* Basic Books, New York.

Ortiz de Montellano, Bernard R.

1990 *Aztec Medicine, Health, and Nutrition.* Rutgers University Press, New Brunswick, N.J.

Otis Charlton, Cynthia L.

1993 Obsidian as Jewelry: Lapidary Production in Aztec Otumba, Mexico. *Ancient Mesoamerica* 4: 231–43.

1994 Plebians and Patricians: Contrasting Patterns of Production and Distribution in the Aztec Figurine and Lapidary Industries. In *Economies and Polities in the Aztec Realm,* edited by Mary G. Hodge and Michael E. Smith, pp. 195–219. Institute for Mesoamerican Studies, Albany.

Oudijk, Michel R.

2002 La toma de posesión: Un tema mesoamericano para la legitimación del poder. *Relaciones (El Colegio de Michoacán)* 23(91): 96–131.

Pareyon Moreno, Eduardo

1972 Las pirámides de doble escalera. In *Religión en Mesoamérica: XII Mesa Redonda, Sociedad Mexicana de Antropología*, edited by Jaime Litvak King and Noemí Castillo Tejero, pp. 117–26. Sociedad Mexicana de Antropología, Mexico City.

Parish, Steven M.

2005 Mind and Experience in a Hindu City. *Ethos* 33: 480–86.

Parry, William J.

2001 Production and Exchange of Obsidian Tools in Late Aztec City-States. *Ancient Mesoamerica* 12: 101–12.

Parsons, Jeffrey R.

1971 *Prehistoric Settlement Patterns in the Texcoco Region, Mexico.* Memoirs, vol. 3. Museum of Anthropology, University of Michigan, Ann Arbor.

1976 The Role of Chinampa Agriculture in the Food Supply of Aztec Tenochtitlan. In *Cultural Change and Continuity: Essays in Honor of James B. Griffin*, edited by Charles Cleland, pp. 233–57. Academic Press, New York.

1996 Tequesquite and Ahuauhtle: Rethinking the Prehispanic Productivity of Lake Texcoco-Xaltocan-Zumpango. In *Arqueología Mesoamericana: Homenaje a William T. Sanders*, edited by Alba Guadalupe Mastache, Jeffrey R. Parsons, Robert S. Santley, and Mari Carmen Serra Puche, vol. 1, pp. 439–59. Instituto Nacional de Antropología e Historia, Mexico City.

Parsons, Jeffrey R., Elizabeth M. Brumfiel, Mary H. Parsons, Virginia H. Popper, and Mary Taft

1982 *Late Prehispanic Chinampa Agriculture on Lake Chalco-Xochimilco: Preliminary Report.* Report submitted to the Instituto Nacional de Antropología e Historia, Ann Arbor.

Parsons, Jeffrey R., Keith W. Kintigh, and Susan A. Gregg

1983 *Archaeological Settlement Pattern Data from the Chalco, Xochimilco, Ixtapalapa, Texcoco, and Zumpango Regions, Mexico.* Technical Reports, vol. 14. Museum of Anthropology, University of Michigan, Ann Arbor.

Pasztory, Esther

1997 *Teotihuacan: An Experiment in Living.* University of Oklahoma Press, Norman.

Pauketat, Timothy R.

2000 The Tragedy of the Commoners. In *Agency in Archaeology*, edited by Marcia-Anne Dobres and John E. Robb, pp. 113–29. Routledge, London.

Pérez Negrete, Miguel

2002 El Templo del Fuego Nuevo del Huixachtécatl: Un espacio ritual en el Cerro de la Estrella. In *Huizachtepetl: geografía sagrada de Iztapalapa*, edited by Ismael Arturo Montero García, pp. 87–113. Delegación Iztapalapa, Mexico City.

Pijoan, Carmen María, Alejandro Pastrana, and Consuelo Maquivar

1989 El tzompantli de Tlatelolco: Una evidencia de sacrificio humano. In *Estudios de antropología biológica*, edited by Carlos Serrano and M. Salas, pp. 561–83. Universidad Nacional Autónoma de México, Mexico City.

Plutarch

1936 *De Fortuna Romanorum*. Harvard University Press, Cambridge. Available online at   *http://penelope.uchicago.edu/Thayer/E/Roman/Texts/Plutarch/Moralia/Fortuna_Romanorum.html*. Accessed December 1, 2004.

Pohl, John M. D.

1994 *The Politics of Symbolism in the Mixtec Codices*. Vanderbilt University Publications in Anthropology, vol. 46. Department of Anthropology, Vanderbilt University, Nashville.

2003a Creation Stories, Hero Cults and Alliance Building: Confederacies of Central and Southern Mexico. In *The Postclassic Mesoamerican World*, edited by Michael E. Smith and Frances F. Berdan, pp. 61–66. University of Utah Press, Salt Lake City.

2003b Royal Marriage and Confederacy Building Among the Eastern Nahuas, Mixtecs, and Zapotecs. In *The Postclassic Mesoamerican World*, edited by Michael E. Smith and Frances F. Berdan, pp. 243–48. University of Utah Press, Salt Lake City.

Pollock, Harry E. D.

1936 *Round Structures of Aboriginal Middle America*. Publications, vol. 471. Carnegie Institution of Washington, Washington, D.C.

Pomar, Juan Bautista

1986 Relación de la ciudad y provincia de Texcoco. In *Relaciones Geográficas del Siglo XVI*, edited by René Acuña, vol. 8, pp. 23–113. Universidad Nacional Autónoma de México, Mexico City.

Preucel, Robert W., and Lynn Meskell (editors)

2004 *Blackwell Companion to Social Archaeology*. Blackwell, Oxford.

Pugh, Timothy W.

2001 Flood Reptiles, Serpent Temples, and the Quadripartite Universe: The Imago Mundi of Late Postclassic Mayapan. *Ancient Mesoamerica* 12: 247–58.

Quiñones Keber, Eloise

1995 *Codex Telleriano-Remensis: Ritual, Divination, and History in a Pictorial Aztec Manuscript*. University of Texas Press, Austin.

Rapoport, Amos

1988 Levels of Meaning in the Built Environment. In *Cross-Cultural Perspectives in Non Verbal Communication*, edited by Fernando Poyatos, pp. 317–36. C. J. Hogrefe, Toronto.

1990a *The Meaning of the Built Environment: A Nonverbal Communication Approach*. Rev. ed. University of Arizona Press, Tucson.

1990b Systems of Activities and Systems of Settings. In *Domestic Architecture and the Use of Space: An Interdisciplinary Cross-Cultural Study*, edited by Susan Kent, pp. 9–20. Cambridge University Press, New York.

Redfield, Robert

1941 *The Folk Culture of Yucatan*. University of Chicago Press, Chicago.

Reese-Taylor, Kathryn, and Rex Koontz
2001 The Cultural Poetics of Power and Space in Ancient Mesoamerica. In *Landscape and Power in Ancient Mesoamerica*, edited by Rex Koontz, Kathryn Reese-Taylor, and Annabeth Headrick, pp. 1–27. Westview Press, Boulder, Colo.

Renfrew, Colin
1984 *Approaches to Social Archaeology*. Harvard University Press, Cambridge.

Reyes García, Luis
1977 *Cuauhtinchan del siglo XII al XVI: Formación y desarollo histórico de un señorío prehispánico*. Franz Steiner Verlag GMBH, Wiesbaden.

Reygadas Vértiz, José
1928 Santa Cecilia. In *Estado actual de los principales edificios arqueológicos de México: Contribución de México al XXIII Congreso de Americanistas*, edited by Dirección de Arqueología, pp. 93–100. Talleres Gráficos de la Nación, Mexico City.

Ringle, William M., and George J. Bey, III
2001 Post-Classic and Terminal Classic Courts in the Northern Maya Lowlands. In *Royal Courts of the Ancient Maya, Volume 2: Data and Case Studies*, edited by Takeshi Inomata and Stephen D. Houston, pp. 266–307. Westview Press, Boulder, Colo.

Ringle, William M., Tomás Gallareta Negrón, and George J. Bey, III
1998 The Return of Quetzalcoatl: Evidence for the Spread of a World Religion During the Epiclassic Period. *Ancient Mesoamerica* 9: 183–232.

Robelo, Cecilio Agustín, Manuel de Olaguíbel, and Antonio Peñafiel
1966 *Nombres geográficas indígenas del Estado de México: Estudio crítico etimológico*. Enciclopedia Bibliográfico del Estado de México, vol. 6. Estado de México, Toluca.

Robertson, Donald
1959 *Mexican Manuscript Painting of the Early Colonial Period: The Metropolitan Schools*. Yale University Press, New Haven, Conn.
1974 The Treatment of Architecture in the Florentine Codex of Sahagún. In *Sixteenth-Century Mexico: The World of Sahagún*, edited by Munro S. Edmonson, pp. 151–64. University of New Mexico Press, Albuquerque.

Rojas, José Luis de
1986 *México Tenochtitlan: Economía e sociedad en el siglo XVI*. Fondo de Cultura Económica, Mexico City.
2001 El abastecimiento de Tenochtitlan: Un modelo probablemente poco modélico. In *Reconstruyendo la ciudad maya: El urbanismo en las sociedades antiguas*, edited by Andrés Ciudad Ruiz, María Josefa Iglesias Ponce de León, and María del Carmen Martínez Martínez, pp. 491–502. Sociedad Española de Estudios Mayas, Madrid.
2006 El almacenamiento en el imperio mexica: Una necesidad evidente en busca de evidencia. In *Arqueología del almacenamiento, desde el Norte de México hasta el Altiplano central*, edited by Severine Bortot. CEMCA, Mexico City.

Roseberry, William
1988 Political Economy. *Annual Review of Anthropology* 17: 161–85.

Rykwert, Joseph

1988 *The Idea of a Town: The Anthropology of Urban Form in Rome, Italy, and the Ancient world*. MIT Press, Cambridge, Mass.

Sack, Robert D.

1986 *Human Territoriality: Its Theory and History*. Cambridge University Press, New York.

Sahagún, Fray Bernardino de

1950–82 *Florentine Codex, General History of the Things of New Spain*. 12 books. Translated and Edited by Arthur J.O. Anderson and Charles E. Dibble. School of American Research and the University of Utah Press, Santa Fe and Salt Lake City.

1993 *Primeros Memoriales*. Facsimile ed. Edited by Ferdinand Anders. University of Oklahoma Press, Norman.

1997 *Primeros Memoriales: Paleography of Nahuatl Text and English Translation*. Translated by Thelma D. Sullivan. University of Oklahoma Press, Norman.

Sanders, William T., and Susan T. Evans (editors)

2001 *The Teotihuacan Valley Project, Final Report, Vol. 5: The Aztec Period Occupation of the Valley. Part 3: Syntheses and General Bibliography*. Occasional Papers in Anthropology, vol. 27. Department of Anthropology, Pennsylvania State University, University Park.

Sanders, William T., Alba Guadalupe Mastache, and Robert H. Cobean (editors)

2003 *El urbanismo en mesoamérica / Urbanism in Mesoamerica*. Proyecto Urbanismo en Mesoamérica / Mesoamerican Urbanism Project, vol. 1. Pennsylvania State University and Instituto Nacional de Antropología e Historia, University Park and Mexico City.

Sanders, William T., Jeffrey R. Parsons, and Robert S. Santley

1979 *The Basin of Mexico: Ecological Processes in the Evolution of a Civilization*. Academic Press, New York.

Sanders, William T., and Barbara J. Price

1968 *Mesoamerica: The Evolution of a Civilization*. Random House, New York.

Sanders, William T., and Robert S. Santley

1983 A Tale of Three Cities: Energetics and Urbanization in Pre-Hispanic Central Mexico. In *Prehistoric Settlement Patterns: Essays in Honor of Gordon R . Willey*, edited by Evon Z. Vogt and Richard Leventhal, pp. 243–91. University of New Mexico Press, Albuquerque.

Sanders, William T., and David Webster

1988 The Mesoamerican Urban Tradition. *American Anthropologist* 90: 521–46.

Santamarina, Carlos

2005 Memoria y olvido, ostracismo y propaganda: El Imperio Tepaneca en fuentes e historiografía. *Revista Española de Antropología Americana* 35: 117–31.

2006 *El sistema de dominación azteca: El imperio tepaneca*. Fundación Universitaria Española, Madrid.

Scarborough, Vernon L., and David R. Wilcox (editors)

1991 *The Mesoamerican Ballgame*. University of Arizona Press, Tucson.

Schele, Linda, and David Freidel
1990 *A Forest of Kings: The Untold Story of the Ancient Maya*. William Morrow, New York.
Schroeder, Susan
1991 *Chimalpahin and the Kingdoms of Chalco*. University of Arizona Press, Tucson.
Scott, James C.
1998 *Seeing Like a State: How Certain Schemes to Improve the Human Condition Have Failed*. Yale University Press, New Haven, Conn.
Séjourné, Laurette
1983 *El pensamiento náhuatl cifrado por los calendarios*. Siglo Veintiuno, Mexico City.
Seler, Eduard
1927 *Einige Kapitel aus dem Geschichtswerke des Fray Bernardino de Sahagún aus den Aztekischen übersetzt*. Edited by Caecilie Seler-Sachs. Strecker und Schroeder, Stuttgart.
1993 The Wall Sculptures in the Temple of the Pulque God at Tepoztlan. In *Collected Works in Mesoamerican Linguistics and Archaeology*, vol. 4, pp. 266–80. Labyrinthos, Culver City, Calif.
1998 The Ruins of Chichen Itza in Yucatan. In *Collected Works in Mesoamerican Linguistics and Archaeoalogy*, vol. 6, pp. 41–165. Labyrinthos, Culver City, Calif.
Sellen, Adam T.
2003 Estrategias de orientación en el valle de Tenancingo. In *Cartografía de tradición hispanoindígena: Mapas de mercedes de tierra, siglos XVI y XVII*, edited by Mercedes Montes de Oca Vega, Dominique Raby, Salvador Reyes Equiguas, and Adam T. Sellen, vol. 1, pp. 185–96. Universidad Nacional Autónoma de México and Archivo General de la Nación, Mexico City.
Sisson, Edward B., and T. Gerald Lilly
1994 A Codex-style Mural from Tehuacan Viejo, Puebla, Mexico. *Ancient Mesoamerica* 5: 33–44.
Sjoberg, Gideon
1960 *The Preindustrial City: Past and Present*. Free Press, New York.
Skinner, G. William (editor)
1977 *The City in Late Imperial China*. Stanford University Press, Stanford, Calif.
Smith, A. Ledyard
1955 *Archaeological Reconnaissance in Central Guatemala*. Publications, vol. 608. Carnegie Institution of Washington, Washington, D.C.
Smith, Adam T.
2000 Rendering the Political Aesthetic: Political Legitimacy in Urartian Representations of the Built Environment. *Journal of Anthropological Archaeology* 19: 131–63.
2003 *The Political Landscape: Constellations of Authority in Early Complex Polities*. University of California Press, Berkeley and Los Angeles.
Smith, Michael E.
1979 The Aztec Marketing System and Settlement Pattern in the Valley of Mexico: A Central Place Analysis. *American Antiquity* 44: 110–25.
1984 The Aztlan Migrations of the Nahuatl Chronicles: Myth or History? *Ethnohistory* 31: 153–86.

1986 The Role of Social Stratification in the Aztec Empire: A View from the Provinces. *American Anthropologist* 88: 70–91.

1989 Cities, Towns, and Urbanism: Comment on Sanders and Webster. *American Anthropologist* 91: 454–61.

1992 *Archaeological Research at Aztec-Period Rural Sites in Morelos, Mexico. Volume 1, Excavations and Architecture/Investigaciones Arqueológicas en Sitios Rurales de la Época Azteca en Morelos, Tomo 1, Excavaciones y Arquitectura.* University of Pittsburgh Memoirs in Latin American Archaeology, vol. 4. University of Pittsburgh, Pittsburgh.

1993 Houses and the Settlement Hierarchy in Late Postclassic Morelos: A Comparison of Archaeology and Ethnohistory. In *Prehispanic Domestic Units in Western Mesoamerica: Studies of the Household, Compound, and Residence,* edited by Robert S. Santley and Kenneth G. Hirth, pp. 191–206. CRC Press, Boca Raton, Fla.

1994 Social Complexity in the Aztec Countryside. In *Archaeological Views from the Countryside: Village Communities in Early Complex Societies,* edited by Glenn Schwartz and Steven Falconer, pp. 143–59. Smithsonian Institution Press, Washington, D.C.

1997 Life in the Provinces of the Aztec Empire. *Scientific American* 277(3): 56–63.

2000 Aztec City-States. In *A Comparative Study of Thirty City-State Cultures,* edited by Mogens Herman Hansen, pp. 581–95. Royal Danish Academy of Sciences and Letters, Copenhagen.

2001 Urbanization. In *The Oxford Encyclopedia of Mesoamerican Cultures: The Civilizations of Mexico and Central America,* edited by Davíd Carrasco, vol. 3, pp. 290–94. Oxford University Press, New York.

2002 Domestic Ritual at Aztec Provincial Sites in Morelos. In *Domestic Ritual in Ancient Mesoamerica,* edited by Patricia Plunket, pp. 93–114. Monograph, vol. 46. Cotsen Institute of Archaeology, University of California, Los Angeles.

2003a *The Aztecs.* 2nd ed. Blackwell Publishers, Oxford.

2003b Can We Read Cosmology in Ancient Maya City Plans? Comment on Ashmore and Sabloff. *Latin American Antiquity* 14: 221–28.

2003c Economic Change in Morelos Households. In *The Postclassic Mesoamerican World,* edited by Michael E. Smith and Frances F. Berdan, pp. 249–58. University of Utah Press, Salt Lake City.

2003d Key Commodities. In *The Postclassic Mesoamerican World,* edited by Michael E. Smith and Frances F. Berdan, pp. 117–25. University of Utah Press, Salt Lake City.

2003e A Quarter-Century of Aztec Studies. *Mexicon* 25: 1–10.

2004 The Archaeology of Ancient State Economies. *Annual Review of Anthropology* 33: 73–102.

2005a City Size in Late Postclassic Mesoamerica. *Journal of Urban History* 31: 403–34.

2005b Did the Maya Build Architectural Cosmograms? *Latin American Antiquity* 16: 217–24.

2006 *Reconocimiento superficial del Valle de Yautepec, Morelos: Informe final.* Report submitted to the Instituto Nacional de Antropología e Historia.

2007a Form and Meaning in the Earliest Cities: A New Approach to Ancient Urban Planning. *Journal of Planning History* 6(1): 3–47.

2007b Tula and Chichén Itzá: Are We Asking the Right Questions? In *Twin Tollans: Chichén Itzá, Tula, and the Epiclassic–Early Postclassic Mesoamerican World*, edited by Cynthia Kristan-Graham and Jeff Karl Kowalski, pp. 579–617. Dumbarton Oaks, Washington, D.C.

2008 *Tlahuica Ceramics: The Aztec-Period Ceramics of Morelos, Mexico*. IMS Monographs, vol. 15. Institute for Mesoamerican Studies, Albany.

n.d.a Excavations at Postclassic Houses in the Aztec City of Yautepec / *Excavaciones de casas postclásicas en la zona urbana Azteca de Yautepec, Morelos*. University of Pittsburg Memoirs in Latin American Archaeology (in press). University of Pittsburgh, Pittsburgh.

n.d.b El almacenamiento en la economía Azteca: Una perspectiva comparativa. In *Arqueología del almacenamiento, desde el Norte de México hasta el Altiplano central*, edited by Severine Bortot (in press). CEMCA, Mexico City.

n.d.c Graneros y almacenamiento de maíz en Morelos Postclásico. In *Arqueología del almacenamiento, desde el Norte de México hasta el Altiplano central*, edited by Severine Bortot (in press). CEMCA, Mexico City.

n.d.d The Archaeology of Aztec City-State Capitals: Four Views of Aztec Urbanism/ La arqueología de las capitales de las ciudades-estado azteca. In *El urbanismo en mesoamérica/Urbanism in Mesoamerica*, edited by William T. Sanders and Robert H. Cobean (in press). Proyecto Urbanismo en Mesoamérica/Mesoamerican Urbanism Project, vol. 2. Pennsylvania State University and Instituto Nacional de Antropología e Historia, University Park and Mexico City.

Smith, Michael E., and Frances F. Berdan (editors)

2003 *The Postclassic Mesoamerican World*. University of Utah Press, Salt Lake City.

Smith, Michael E., Adrian Burke, Timothy S. Hare, and Michael D. Glascock

2007 Sources of Imported Obsidian at Postclassic Sites in the Yautepec Valley, Morelos: A Characterization Study Using XRF and INAA. *Latin American Antiquity* 18: .

Smith, Michael E., and John F. Doershuk

1991 Late Postclassic Chronology in Western Morelos, Mexico. *Latin American Antiquity* 2: 291–310.

Smith, Michael E., Cynthia Heath-Smith, Ronald Kohler, Joan Odess, Sharon Spanogle, and Timothy Sullivan

1994 The Size of the Aztec City of Yautepec: Urban Survey in Central Mexico. *Ancient Mesoamerica* 5: 1–11.

Smith, Michael E., Cynthia Heath-Smith, and Lisa Montiel

1999 Excavations of Aztec Urban Houses at Yautepec, Mexico. *Latin American Antiquity* 10: 133–50.

Smith, Michael E., and Kenneth G. Hirth

1988 The Development of Prehispanic Cotton-Spinning Technology in Western Morelos, Mexico. *Journal of Field Archaeology* 15: 349–58.

Smith, Michael E., Juliana Novic, Peter C. Kroefges, and Angela Huster

2007 A New Map of the Aztec-Period City of Calixtlahuaca in Central Mexico. *Antiq-*

uity (Project Gallery) 81. Available online at http://www/antiquity.ac.uc/ProjGall/ smith1/index.html. Accessed January 10, 2007.

Smith, Michael E., Jennifer Wharton, and Melissa McCarron
2003 Las ofrendas de Calixtlahuaca. Expresión Antropológica 19: 35–53.

Smith, Monica L.
2005 Networks, Territories and the Cartography of Ancient States. Annals of the Association of American Geographers 95: 832–849.

Solís Olguín, Felipe R.
1981 Escultura del Castillo de Teayo, Veracruz, México: Catálogo. Cuadernos de Historia del Arte, vol. 16. Universidad Nacional Autónoma de México, Instituto de Investigaciones Estéticas, Mexico City.

Soustelle, Jacques
1970 The Four Suns: Recollections and Reflections of an Ethnologist in Mexico. Grossman Publishers, New York.
1993 La familia otomí-pame del México central. Translated by Nilda Mercado Baigorria. 1937. Reprint, Fondo de Cultura Económica, Mexico City.

Šprajc, Ivan
2000a Astronomical Alignments at the Templo Mayor of Tenochtitlan, Mexico. Archaeoastronomy (Journal for the History of Astronomy, Vol. 31, Archaeoastronomy Supplement) 25: S11–S40.
2000b Problema de ajustes del año calendárico mesoamericano al año trópico. Anales de Antropología 34: 133–60.
2001 Orientaciones astronómicas en la arquitectura prehispánica del centro de México. Colección Científica, vol. 427. Instituto Nacional de Antropología e Historia, Mexico City.
2004 The South-of-East Skew of Mesoamerican Architectural Orientations: Astronomy and Directional Symbolism. In Etno y Arqueo-Astronomía en las Américas, edited by Maxime Boccas, Johanna Broda, and Gonzalo Pereira, pp. 161–76. Congreso Internacional Americanista, Santiago de Chile.

Stanton, Travis W., and David A. Freidel
2005 Placing the Centre, Centring the Place: The Influence of Formative Sacbeob in Classic Site Design at Yaxuná, Yucatán. Cambridge Archaeological Journal 15: 225–49.

Stark, Barbara L.
1999 Formal Architectural Complexes in South-Central Veracruz, Mexico: A Capital Zone? Journal of Field Archaeology 26: 197–226.

Stark, Barbara L., and Alanna Ossa
2005 Los asentamientos urbanos de jardines-huertos en la planicie costera de Veracruz. Anales de Antropología 39(1): 39–50.

Steane, John M.
2001 The Archaeology of Power: England and Northern Europe, AD 800–1600. Tempus, Gloucestershire.

Steinhardt, Nancy S.
1990 Chinese Imperial City Planning. University of Hawaii Press, Honolulu.

Stone, Glenn Davis
2001 Agricultural Change Theory. In *International Encyclopedia of the Social and Behavioral Sciences*, edited by Neil J. Smelser and P. Baltes, vol. 1, pp. 329–33. Pergamon, Oxford.

Storey, Glenn (editor)
2006 *Urbanism in the Preindustrial World: Cross-Cultural Approaches*. University of Alabama Press, Tuscaloosa.

Sullivan, Thelma D.
1971 The Finding and Founding of Mexico Tenochtitlan, from the Crónica Mexicayotl by Fernando Alvarado Tezozomoc. *Tlalocan* 6: 312–26.

Taladoire, Eric
1981 *Les terrains de jeu de balle (Mésoamérique et sud-ouest des Etats-Unis)*. Etudes Mesoamericaines, vol. 4. Mission archéologique et ethnologique française au Mexique, Mexico City.
2001 The Architectural Background of the Pre-Hispanic Ballgame: An Evolutionary Perspective. In *The Sport of Life and Death: The Mesoamerican Ballgame*, edited by E. Michael Whittington, pp. 96–115. Thames and Hudson, New York.

Terraciano, Kevin
2001 *The Mixtecs of Colonial Oaxaca: Ñudzahui History, Sixteenth Through Eighteenth Centuries*. Stanford University Press, Stanford, Calif.

Thompson, J. Eric S.
1934 Skybearers, Colors and Directions in Maya and Mexican Religion. In *Contributions to American Anthropology and History, No. 10*. Publications, vol. 436. Carnegie Institution of Washington, Washington, D.C.
1941 The Missing Illiustrations of the Pomar Relation. *Carnegie Institution of Washington, Notes on Middle American Archaeology and Ethnology* 1(4): 15–21.

Tira de la Peregrinación
1944 *Tira de la peregrinación mexicana*. Libreria Anticuaria G. M. Echaniz, Mexico City.

Titiev, Mischa.
1938 Dates of Planting at the Hopi Indian Pueblo of Oraibi. *Museum of Northern Arizona, Museum Notes* 11: 39–42.

Torquemada, Fray Juan de
1975–83 *Monarquía indiana*. 7 vols. Edited by Miguel León-Portilla. Universidad Nacional Autónoma de México, Mexico City.

Townsend, Richard F.
1982 Malinalco and the Lords of Tenochtitlan. In *The Art and Iconography of Late Post-Classic Central Mexico*, edited by Elizabeth H. Boone, pp. 111–40. Dumbarton Oaks, Washington, D.C.
1992 The Renewal of Nature at the Temple of Tlaloc. In *The Ancient Americas: Art from Sacred Landscapes*, edited by Richard F. Townsend, pp. 170–85. Art Institute of Chicago, Chicago.

Trexler, Richard C.
1980 *Public Life in Renaissance Florence*. Academic Press, New York.

Trigger, Bruce G.

1972 Determinants of Urban Growth in Pre-Industrial Societies. In *Man, Settlement, and Urbanism*, edited by Peter J. Ucko, Ruth Tringham, and G. W. Dimbleby, pp. 579–99. Schenkman, Cambridge.

1990 Monumental Architecture: A Thermodynamic Explanation of Behavior. *World Archaeology* 22: 119–132.

2003 *Understanding Early Civilizations: A Comparative Study.* Cambridge University Press, New York.

Umberger, Emily

1987 Antiques, Revivals, and References to the Past in Aztec Art. *RES: Anthropology and Aesthetics* 13: 62–105.

1996 Appendix 3: Material Remains in the Central Provinces. In *Aztec Imperial Strategies*, by Frances F. Berdan, Richard E. Blanton, Elizabeth H. Boone, Mary G. Hodge, Michael E. Smith, and Emily Umberger, pp. 247–64. Dumbarton Oaks, Washington, D.C.

1998 New Blood from an Old Stone. *Estudios de Cultura Náhuatl* 28: 241–56.

2007 Historia del arte e Imperio Azteca: la evidencia de las esculturas. Revista Española de Antropología Americana 37:165-202..

Umberger, Emily, and Cecilia Klein

1993 Aztec Art and Imperial Expansion. In *Latin American Horizons*, edited by Don S. Rice, pp. 295–336. Dumbarton Oaks, Washington, D.C.

Vega Sosa, Constanza (editor)

1979 *El recinto sagrado de Mexico-Tenochtitlan: Excavaciones 1968–69 y 1975–76.* Instituto Nacional de Antropología e Historia, Mexico City.

Wake, Eleanor

2002 Codex Tlaxcala: New Insights and New Questions. *Estudios de Cultura Náhuatl* 33: 91–140.

Webster, David, and William T. Sanders

2001 La antigua ciudad mesoamericana: teoría y concepto. In *Reconstruyendo la ciudad maya: El urbanismo en las sociedades antiguas*, edited by Andrés Ciudad Ruiz, María Josefa Iglesias Ponce de León, and María del Carmen Martínez Martínez, pp. 43–64. Sociedad Española de Estudios Mayas, Madrid.

Weigand, Phil C., and Acelia García de Weigand

1996 La arquitectura prehispánica y la secuencia cultural en la cuenca de Chapala, Jalisco: Observaciones preliminares. In *Las cuencas del occidente de México: Época prehispánica*, edited by Eduardo Williams and Phil C. Weigand, pp. 293–323. Colección Memorias. El Colegio de Michoacán, Zamora, Mexico.

Wheatley, Paul

1971 *The Pivot of the Four Quarters: A Preliminary Enquiry into the Origins and the Character of the Ancient Chinese City.* Aldine, Chicago.

Whitehand, J. W. R.

2001 British Urban Morphology: The Conzenian Tradition. *Urban Morphology* 5: 103–09.

Whitmore, Thomas M.

1992 *Disease and Death in Early Colonial Mexico: Simulating Amerindian Depopulation.* Westview Press, Boulder, Colo.

Whitmore, Thomas M., and Barbara J. Williams

1998 Famine Vulnerability in the Contact-Era Basin of Mexico: A Simulation. *Ancient Mesoamerica* 9: 83–98.

Wicke, Charles, and Fernando Horcasitas

1957 Archaeological Investigations on Monte Tlaloc, Mexico. *Mesoamerican Notes* 5: 83–96.

Wirth, Louis

1938 Urbanism as a Way of Life. *American Journal of Sociology* 44: 1–24.

Wood, Stephanie

1998a Gender and Town Guardianship in Mesoamerica: Directions for Future Rersearch. *Journal de la Société des Américanistes* 84(2): 243–76.

1998b The Social vs. Legal Context of Náhuatl Títulos. In *Native Traditions in the Postconquest World*, edited by Elizabeth Hill Boone and Tom Cummins, pp. 201–31. Dumbarton Oaks, Washington, D.C.

Wrigley, E. A.

1990 Brake or Accelerator? Urban Growth and Population Growth Before the Industrial Revolution. In *Urbanization in History: A Process of Dynamic Interactions*, edited by Ad van de Woude, Akira Hayami, and Jan de Vries, pp. 101–12. Clarendon Press, Oxford.

Zanker, Paul

1998 *Pompeii: Public and Private Life.* Translated by Deborah Lucas Schneider. Harvard University Press, Cambridge.

Zorita, Alonso de

1963 *Life and Labor in Ancient Mexico: The Brief and Summary Relation of the Lords of New Spain.* Translated by Benjamin Keen. Rutgers University Press, New Brunswick, N.J.

Index

Michael E. Smith is professor of anthropology at Arizona State University. He has directed excavations at several Aztec sites in central Mexico and has published numerous books and articles, including *The Aztecs* (2003). He also writes on the comparative analysis of ancient cities and empires around the world.